# Industrial Policies for Technological Upgrading in Western Balkan Countries

Fadil Sahiti

# Industrial Policies for Technological Upgrading in Western Balkan Countries

## Economic Growth and Development

palgrave
macmillan

Fadil Sahiti
Gërmia Campus
RIT Kosovo
Prishtina, Kosovo

ISBN 978-3-031-51428-9 ISBN 978-3-031-51429-6 (eBook)
https://doi.org/10.1007/978-3-031-51429-6



This Palgrave Macmillan imprint is published by the registered company Springer Nature Switzerland AG.
The registered company address is: Gewerbestrasse 11, 6330 Cham, Switzerland

Paper in this product is recyclable.

*I dedicate this book to those who fell for the freedom of my country!*

# Acknowledgements

My special thanks go to Professor S. Radosevic. The advice and suggestions of an expert in this field have been both invaluable and encouraging. I will be eternally grateful for his professional and personal relationship with me.

I am very grateful to many other friends and colleagues for their support and reassurance during the book writing process. All have taken an active interest in my research and offered thoughtful comments and guidance.

Finally, particular gratitude goes to my family—my wife, my son and daughter-in-law, my beautiful daughters and my very beloved grandsons and granddaughters who, when I was perhaps feeling less than optimistic about the project, lifted my spirits and gave me the enthusiasm to complete the book.

# Contents

# Abbreviations

| | |
|---|---|
| BEEPS | Business Environment and Enterprise Performance Survey |
| CAD | Comparative Advantage Defying |
| CFA | Confirmatory Factor Analysis |
| DNS | Developmental Network State |
| EBRD | European Bank for Reconstruction and Development |
| EU | European Union |
| FDI | Foreign Direct Investment |
| GDP | Gross Domestic Product |
| GII | Global Innovation Index |
| GNP | Gross National Product |
| GVC | Global Value Chain |
| IFC | International Finance Corporation |
| IMAD | Institute of Macroeconomic Analysis and Development |
| KFW | Kreditanstalt für Wiederaufbau |
| KIESA | Kosovo Investment and Enterprise Support Agency |
| KMO | Kaiser-Meyer-Olkin |
| MNC | Multinational Corporation |
| NASRI | National Agency for Scientific Research and Innovation |
| NTB | Non-tariff Barriers |
| OECD | Organisation for Economic Cooperation and Development |
| PCA | Principal Confirmatory Analysis |
| PRO | Public Research Organization |
| SBA | Small Business Administration |
| SBIC | Small Business Investment Company |
| SBIR/STTR | Small Business Innovation Research and Technology Transfer |
| SIP | Slovenian Industrial Policy |
| SME | Small and Medium-sized Enterprise |

| | |
|---|---|
| SOEs | State-Owned Enterprises |
| TFP | Total Factor Production |
| TIDZ | Technological Industrial Development Zones |
| USDA | US Department of Agriculture |
| WB | Western Balkans |
| WEF | World Economic Forum |

# List of Figures

# List of Tables

CHAPTER 1

# Introduction

## 1.1 Aims and Objectives

> Industrial policy is back in fashion, and rightly so...Appropriately designed government policies can lead to better outcomes. While this is true even for developed countries, it is perhaps particularly true for developing countries, and this is so even if developing countries have less developed governmental institutions. Limitations on the capacity of government should affect the choice of instruments for carrying out industrial policies, but not whether they should undertake industrial policies. (Stiglitz, 2017, p. 23)

Since the publication of Adam Smith's book, *The Wealth of Nations* in the late eighteenth century, how to achieve sustainable economic growth has been a persistent topic in economic debate (North, 2005). Smith believed in the mechanism of the 'invisible hand' (free market forces) which resulted in a state of equilibrium between demand and supply. He argued, also, that in free market conditions, the economy functions because everyone works in his/her own interest. The invisible hand metaphor was adopted by the neoclassicists, whose theories dominated economic thinking for several decades. Neoclassicists believe that market forces are the primary mechanism determining prices and, in turn, that prices allocate resources from less productive to more productive economic agents. Market distortions can occur, but order is naturally restored by internal market forces.



F. Sahiti, *Industrial Policies for Technological Upgrading in Western Balkan Countries*, https://doi.org/10.1007/978-3-031-51429-6_1

Based on neoclassical fundamental principles, the Washington Consensus promoted policy packages with minimal government intervention and encouraged privatization, trade and financial liberalization, Foreign Direct Investment (FDI) by Multinational Corporations (MNCs) and strong property rights (Williamson, 1990). The idea was that economic growth could be achieved through imitation of the practices and institutions in advanced economies (Lee, 2019). Following a series of failures and poor performance, the renowned scholar, Dani Rodrik (2006), declared the Washington consensus dead and called for an alternative, supported by other well-known scholars including Nobel laureate Joseph Stiglitz and former vice-president of the World Bank, Justin Lin.

In contemporary discourse on the factors of economic growth, another 'consensus' is emerging, that is, the idea that the market, as a single mechanism, cannot provide economic efficiency in terms of a desirable distribution of income, distribution of resources among sectors, etc. Rather, it is the state, through the implementation of industrial policies, that should address market failure.

Debate among economists is less about whether governments should intervene by introducing industrial policy packages and more about how to design policies to suit specific economic environments and, especially, how they should be implemented (Juhász et al., 2023). The emphasis on industrial policies is being driven, also, by the emergence of more complex and important (compared to the past) economic issues, including problems related to Global Value Chains (GVCs), intense global market competition, international trade tensions, productivity slowdowns, digital transformation, climate change and a range of shocks such as the 2008 financial crisis and the COVID-19 pandemic (Criscuolo et al., 2022). These and other events underline the urgency of state intervention in the economy and the formulation, in particular, of large-scale and comprehensive recovery plans. Governments around the world are responding by formulating new industrial strategies. Examples are the European Union (EU) New Industrial Strategy, published in 2020 and updated in 2021, the 2019 European Green Deal, the 2020 EU Next Generation Fund, the 2021 American Rescue Plan Act and the Korean New Deal (2020) among others.

The book has three main objectives. First, to investigate the industrial policies being implemented in three Western Balkans (WB) economies—Albania, North Macedonia and Kosovo. We compare these three economies to Slovenia—our reference country.

Second, to explore the potential of a new approach to industrial policy that focuses on supporting the national innovation system through technology upgrading and greater use of technology, which are considered vital foundations for sustainable development in the three WB economies. These three countries belong to the group of middle-income countries, a grouping that determines the nature of their innovative and industrial activities and has implications for their industrial policies. Their economic and technological transformation is especially urgent in the context of their aspirations to become full EU members, which will have implications for their competitiveness. The book argues that well-designed industrial policy packages, appropriate to the individual country's socio-economic circumstances and conditions, would produce successful outcomes. Current evidence suggests that the design and proper implementation of industrial policy packages have had major impacts on economic industrialization in many previously underdeveloped countries such as Malaysia, South Korea and Taiwan. Their economic transformation demonstrates that well-designed industrial policies can produce positive results, even in contexts where government institutions are less well developed. Stiglitz (2017) pointed out that eventual limitations related to government capacity might influence the mechanisms used to implement industrial policies but should not decide whether or not countries should adopt industrial policies. Several middle-income economies (e.g., countries in Asia and Latin America) consider industrial policy to be the solution to the 'middle-income trap' (see Felipe et al., 2014) and, in some African countries, industrial policy is contributing to efforts to mitigate the effects of poverty (Noman & Stiglitz, 2015; Kanbur et al., 2019).

The empirical evidence shows that since the great social and economic changes that occurred in the 1990s, industrial production in the WB economies has been on a downward path. Any growth seems to be driven primarily by the availability of the factors of production or by resources (inputs). The World Economic Forum's (WEF) Global Competitiveness Reports describe these economies as factor- and efficiency-oriented economies and define high-income economies as innovation-driven. Manufacturing organizations in factor-oriented and efficiency-oriented economies produce undifferentiated products that are sold mainly in the local and regional markets. Their production process is based on foreign technologies that have been tested and proven elsewhere. The entire focus of the firms in these economies is either on how to increase production capacity or how to increase the capabilities to produce to match international efficiency and quality standards, rather than on how to innovate. The result is that the economic structures, productivity levels and technology and industrial improvements in these countries lag behind the developed economies.

To facilitate the technological and industrial upgrading in the WB economies, this book proposes new policy thinking and policy practices. The new approach to building industrial policies proposed in this book is based on the social and economic specificities of the countries being considered. It proposes alternatives based on the positive and negative experience of the structural reforms and 'old' industrial policies implemented in these and other economies. The empirical findings from these countries are benchmarked against the economy of Slovenia.

It is hoped that this book will offer readers a different perspective on industrial policies and their design, a perspective based on the specific capacities and novel policies of the economies that are the subject of this book. The analysis uses a 'technology upgrading' lens, what Gereffi (1999, pp. 51–24) describes as a 'shift to higher value-added products and production stages through increasing specialization'. Along with R&D and innovation, this definition includes manufacturing capabilities and aspects of structural change and the knowledge interactions with the global economy (see Radosevic & Yoruk, 2018).

The third aim of this book is to explore and measure the technological capabilities of WB manufacturing firms. We use cross-section data, which we investigate and interpret longitudinally. We are interested in the dynamics of firm growth and how it is conditioned by the interplay between internal and external factors specific to lower income economies. The data for our analysis were collected in Kosovo from a sample of 101 manufacturing firms. We conducted in-depth and semi-structured interviews and administered a survey, which was responded to by managers in 101 manufacturing firms and was aimed at gathering as much data as possible on firm skills. We are interested in the differentiation among firms, in terms of resources or inputs related to physical equipment, finance and human capital, and the factors related to production (management) capabilities and organizational capabilities such as networks, technology and R&D capacity. We conducted three case studies of three Kosovan manufacturing firms: two in the beverage sector and one in the confectionery sector.

This book will contribute to the existing academic and policy literatures on economic growth. Although several empirical studies have investigated industrial policies and their role in manufacturing sector growth, most focus on developed economies. In this book, we try to shed more light on the effects of industrial policies on manufacturing firm growth in less developed countries. We also propose a new analytical framework to examine policies focused on technological improvements in developing economic contexts. We test our framework, which combines different theories, to try to understand the factors that determine technology capabilities and firm growth. We believe that the book will provide a better understanding of economic growth and technology upgrading in developing economies.

## 1.2 Setting the Context for the Book

As discussed above, the book investigates industrial policy packages and their role in shaping the manufacturing sectors in the three WB economies of Albania, North Macedonia and Kosovo. Whenever relevant and subject to data availability, the findings for the three selected WB economies are compared to the economy of Slovenia. Our choice of WB countries was based on several criteria, including similar history (North Macedonia and Kosovo were socialist states in the former Yugoslavia), similar economic structure and geographic proximity. These three economies continue to display similarities in their economic and social development (migration issues), incomplete economic transition from a controlled economy, aspirations to become full members of the EU, etc. The selection of Slovenia as our reference economy introduces a different perspective and is a source of learning in relation to the types of industrial policies that lead to manufacturing sector growth.

By industrial policies we mean government efforts to shape the economy, through the promotion of the whole manufacturing sector or particular sub-sectors and specific manufacturing firms. The means to achieve these goals can include R&D subsidies, tax and tariff incentives related to the purchase of technology, infrastructure developments, protective regulation, etc.

Theoretically, the manufacturing sector is fundamental to national economic development (Stiglitz et al., 2014). The importance of this sector is based on the greater tendency of manufacturing firms to invest more in R&D, introduce new products to the market and achieve productivity growth. Also, manufacturing products account for a large proportion of tradable goods (75% of EU exports) and make an important contribution to the national external balance (see Stöllinger et al., 2013; Baily & Bosworth, 2014; Szirmai & Verspagen, 2015 and Stöllinger, 2016).

The empirical data suggest that manufacturing sector growth had a significant impact on economic growth in the East Asian economies of

South Korea, Taiwan and Vietnam.[1] Its impact on economic growth is evident, also, in some former socialist economies that, now, are EU members. The evidence suggests that most recent members of the EU have recorded an increase in their manufacturing value added, for example, Lithuania, Poland, Hungary, Romania, Slovenia and the Czech Republic (OECD, 2023).

The WB countries and WB enterprises are service-oriented and include numerous Small and Medium-sized Enterprises (SMEs), concentrated in the wholesale, transport, accommodation and food sectors (see Table 1.1). Manufacturing sector enterprises account for close to 13% of all enterprises in the WB region, the highest percentage (24.7%) being in North Macedonia.

The WB economies are characterized by rapid structural change and a strong process of deindustrialization. The production sectors in these economies have suffered dramatic decline. For example, in North Macedonia, the production sector contribution to Gross Domestic Product (GDP) was 28% in 1992 and over the course of a decade dropped to 8%. The expansion of other economic sectors—and services, in

**Table 1.1** Firm distribution by sectors across three WB economies and Slovenia 2021

| | *ALB* | *MKD* | *KOS* | *SVN* |
|---|---|---|---|---|
| Agriculture, forestry and fishing | | 3.84 | 1.81 | |
| Mining and quarrying | 0.7 | 0.51 | 0.4 | 0.58 |
| Manufacturing | 7.0 | 24.73 | 12.8 | 13.3 |
| Utilities | 0.7 | 2.28 | 0.3 | 0.3 |
| Construction | 4.8 | 9.13 | 8.4 | 13.4 |
| Wholesale and retail trade | 38.3 | 29.43 | 38.6 | 17.1 |
| Transportation and storage | 8.4 | 8.53 | 3.5 | 5.7 |
| Accommodation and restaurants | 15.6 | 7.7 | 9.6 | 8.4 |
| Information and communication | 2.63 | 4.72 | 3.5 | 7 |
| Other services | 21.87 | 9.13 | 21.09 | 34.22 |

Source: Statistical offices of the three WB economies and Eurostat for Slovenia

[1]According to a British Chamber of Commerce Vietnam report (2022), the contribution of manufacturing to GDP in 2021 was 25.1%, compared to 13.7% in 2015; https://britchamvn.com/wp-content/uploads/2022/03/52856e70-f9c3-4566-83a2-d7e4c6ab8fd7.pdf.

particular—has been at the expense of the manufacturing sector. In almost all EU member countries, there has been a reallocation of resources and employment from agriculture and manufacturing to the service sector; in the WB countries this process was particularly rapid and has reduced the contribution of manufacturing to levels incompatible with their relatively low levels of economic development (Damiani & Uvalic, 2018).

Table 1.2 shows no significant changes since 2012 and suggests that the WB countries have failed to find an export-led economic growth strategy to reduce their trade deficit. The WB economies continue to be dependent on imports of goods, which significantly affects their trade balance. The difficulties related to reducing the trade deficit by increasing exports are evident in the preferences of foreign investors. During 2001 to 2008, in particular, most foreign investment went to the most profitable non-tradable services sectors, such as retail trade, telecommunications, banking and real estate. The result is that neither direct nor indirect investment has had an effect on the restructuring and modernization of many traditional industrial sectors (Estrin & Uvalic, 2014). Despite slightly increased foreign investment in manufacturing, in most cases, it has not had a significant impact on added value, employment or exports in the WB economies (Estrin & Uvalic, 2016).

The poor performance of the manufacturing sector in developing countries is a source of concern among academics and practitioners that this decline will spread to other sectors. Pisano and Shih (2012) warn of possible backlash that would negatively affect other value chain activities, including those related to innovation and technology. Over the long term, decreased manufacturing capacity in developing countries, such as Albania, North Macedonia and Kosovo, could affect the competitiveness of these economies in their regional and international markets.

**Table 1.2** Manufacturing value added (% of GDP)

| *Year* | *2012* | *2013* | *2014* | *2015* | *2016* | *2017* | *2018* | *2019* | *2020* | *2021* | *2022* |
|---|---|---|---|---|---|---|---|---|---|---|---|
| Albania | 5 | 5 | 5 | 6 | 6 | 6 | 6 | 6 | 6 | 7 | 7 |
| N. Macedonia | 10 | 10 | 11 | 12 | 12 | 13 | 13 | 13 | 13 | 13 | 13 |
| Kosovo | 13 | 14 | 13 | 13 | 13 | 13 | 13 | 13 | 13 | 13 | 14 |
| Slovenia | 19 | 19 | 20 | 20 | 20 | 21 | 20 | 21 | 21 | 21 | 19 |

Source: World Development Indicators Database

Appropriate industrial policies could be used to develop the manufacturing sector (Stiglitz, 2017). Experience shows that well-designed and well-implemented industrial policy packages could achieve the transformation from an agriculture-dominated economy to a modern industrial economy. Examples include countries in Western Europe, North America and East Asia. The transformation in these countries is due to policies that have helped individual firms resolve coordination and externality problems (Lin, 2017), with the result that these countries are continuing to design and implement policies to promote manufacturing. However, the situation is different in the WB and other developing countries. Justin Lin (2017, p. 4) shows that, despite continuous efforts, many developing country governments have failed to design and implement policies that help businesses.

After World War II, many former socialist countries tried to build similar capital-intensive industries to those in the advanced economies (Lin, 2017). The Kosovan economy relied mainly on heavy industry and mineral resources (Sahiti, 2019). Its development was based on adoption of a CAD or Comparative Advantage Defying strategy that relied on the dominant structuralist economic thinking during the 1950s and 1960s. The CAD strategy was aimed at encouraging firms to ignore the advantages arising from existing comparative economics in their entry/choice of industry/technology (Lin, 2017). The governments that implemented the CAD strategy continued to protect those economic enterprises considered of crucial importance for national economic development. Temporary measures implemented included allowing market monopolies, provision of preferential loans, currency overvaluation and controlled prices for certain raw materials. The ultimate goal was to reduce the cost of investment and increase the operational efficiency of firms.

However, these measures have been unsuccessful and, in some cases, have even had negative effects, in the form of large shortages of funds, negative foreign exchange and significant shortages of raw materials. The former socialist countries do have some internationally competitive industries, but adoption of the CAD strategy has had a negative effect on the distribution of economic resources, work incentives, income distribution, etc. (Lin, 2017).

However, industrial policy packages are implemented by most world governments. In North Macedonia, these policies have increased manufacturing sector added value by up to 3% since 2012 (see Table 1.2). In some cases, implementation of industrial policies has reduced the gap with the developed industrialized countries and some countries have achieved developed status as a result of these policies. For example, in the 1950s, Japan moved from a low-income economy to a high-income economy, based on around 10% annual growth, driven mainly by the transformation of agriculture and the creation of industrial sectors related to agriculture. These developments also occurred in other Asian countries.

Stiglitz et al. (2014) contend that the manufacturing sector is a driver of economic development but requires appropriate policies. This raises questions about how much governments should intervene to strengthen specific sectors, technologies and economic activities. We need also to examine current industrial policies in the three WB economies and how they differ from those implemented in Slovenia. We try to explain why the new industrial policy approach, based on technology improvements, proposed in this book, might be appropriate and productive for the WB economies.

## 1.3 The Conceptual Foundations of the Book

This book draws on several literature streams, including work on catch-up, technology upgrading and innovation. The catch-up literature argues that there are several ways that developing economies (latecomers) can achieve catch-up (in terms of per capita income) with developed economies. The catch-up effect refers to the advantages open to latecomer countries able to achieve higher rates of economic growth based on employment of professionals and machinery that embody advanced knowledge (Veblen, 1915). However, whether developing countries can achieve the economic level of developed economies is debatable. Neoclassicists believe that it requires a free market context. They consider knowledge to be a public good, meaning that everyone has access to the same body of knowledge. Based on real cases (including the most typical case of nineteenth-century Germany), institutional economists (see, e.g., Gerschenkron, 1962, 1963) point out that catching-up is possible. Other researchers (see Perez & Soete, 1988) have suggested that latecomers have advantages with respect to radical technological change, which can provide windows of opportunity. However, the evidence suggests that achieving catch-up is rare and applies to only a few cases such as Germany, Japan and some East Asian countries. In reality, the gap between the developing and developed economies has continued to widen and, especially, since the 1980s (Gill & Kharas, 2015). A World Bank (2012) study that makes reference to the middle-income trap suggests that since 1960, only 12 out of 101 middle-income economies have achieved high-income status—9 of which were originally upper middle-income economies.

An important and persistent question is whether it is possible for developing countries to reach the level of development of the developed countries. A study by Keun Lee (2019) suggests that it is possible for emerging economies to catch-up through openness to free trade, development of what they call social capabilities, development of capabilities to absorb new technology and creation of a business environment that attracts foreign capital and allows these countries to become active players in the global market. In order to enter GVC, countries can adopt a range of strategies that depend on their stage of development. Lee et al. (2018) describe this as an in-out-in approach. They suggest that in early-stage development the catch-up process appears more rapid and the focus on participating in GVCs decreases to allow more emphasis on the building of internal technological capabilities. The focus then switches to the development of innovation capabilities and production of higher value-added goods (Lee et al., 2018). Meanwhile, latecomer participation in the GVC process may increase the technology upgrading through technology transfer and learning, although participation in GVCs does not necessarily increase or enhance technological capabilities since developing country firms are obliged to conform to MNC strategies. MNCs dominate GVCs, which makes it difficult for developing country firms to advance from the so-called own design manufacturing level. However, it is important for developing countries and developing economy firms to design strategies that facilitate their participation in GVCs and to increase their technological capabilities (Hansen & Ockwell, 2014).

Latecomers catch-up is a difficult, complex and uncertain process, but Lee and Malerba (2017) show that it is not impossible if supported by a well-designed leapfrogging strategy. Technological capabilities upgrading requires more than increased production capacity or adoption of foreign technology. Lee (2016) points to the difficulties related to the transition from design to implementation capabilities, for example. Implementation capabilities tend to be embedded in firms and countries and reinforced by routines. Their accumulation requires institutional support, which, if lacking, leads to latecomer economies succumbing to the middle-income trap.

Is the key to successful development, technology upgrading? The empirical evidence and stylized facts on technology upgrading emphasize that the focus should be on improving technological capabilities. However, their accumulation is not straightforward. Individual countries need to adapt their industrial policies to their economic and social conditions.

Technological capabilities are at the heart of our analysis. The literature on economic growth suggests that long-run development is driven primarily by innovation (Nelson & Winter, 1982). This relationship has been explored using different theoretical and conceptual frameworks, from evolutionary economics to technology accumulation, capability theory and the resource-based view (see, e.g., Nelson & Winter, 1982; Lall, 1992; Cimoli et al., 2009; Hall & Rosenberg, 2010, etc.). The empirical findings in the literature have improved our understanding of the patterns of technology upgrading across firms, sectors and economies (Kamien & Schwartz, 1982; Freeman & Soete, 1997; Fagerberg et al., 2005; Tassey, 2007; Malerba & Vonortas, 2009; Cohen, 2010; Gallouj & Djellal, 2010; Link & Vonortas, 2013; Malerba & McKelvey, 2019) and suggest that technology upgrading is what distinguishes economies that are able to solve the problem of growth slowdown in middle-income economies and escape the middle-income trap (see, e.g., Lee, 2013; Paus, 2017). By shifting resources to more productive sectors and/or by importing technology from advanced economies, low-income countries can achieve middle-income status. However, since technology improvements and growth are often non-linear processes with significant time lags, and because MIC often are unable to deepen and diversify their industrial structure and technological knowledge, their transition to high-income economies is difficult (Lee, 2016; Vivarelli, 2016).

Technological capabilities are a crucial component of innovation, which, by deepening and diversifying industrial activities, facilitates economic growth (see Abramovitz, 1986; Kim & Nelson. 2000; Fagerberg et al., 2007). The link between the innovation process, growth and technological capabilities means that, in the absence of technological capabilities, economic growth is impossible. The notion of technology upgrading is related to the process of increasing technological capabilities at the firm, sector and country levels. The early technology upgrading literature refers to the characteristics of technology capabilities at different stages of development. For example, Hobday (1995) considers that technological improvement follows the stages of own equipment manufacturing, own design manufacturing and own brand manufacturing. Kim (1997) also suggests three stages related to technology upgrading—adoption, assimilation and innovation. Lee (2005, 2013) tries to link these stages to different types of learning. He suggests that learning goes from operational skills, to process technology, to design technology and, finally, to new product development technology. Others investigate technology upgrading in the context of learning and international technology transfer, through FDI, exporting, technology licensing, imports of capital goods and personnel exchanges (Lee et al., 2021). These factors increase absorptive capacity which is vital for successful technology improvements (Cohen & Levinthal, 1990; Amsden, 2001).

What is meant by technological capability? Technological capability refers to the ability of business enterprises to use technology and technical knowledge to create goods and services with added value. It implies an ability to absorb and assimilate existing knowledge and create new technologies, including those related to production, investment and innovation (Westphal et al., 1985; Katz, 1987; Kim, 1997). A large part of these capabilities is idiosyncratic, difficult to create and, in particular, difficult to replicate and transfer across firms. Technology competencies include those skills implied in discussions related to the resource-based theory of the firm (Barney, 1991). They include dynamic capabilities, which allow the capture and realization of new opportunities and exploitation of the returns from investment in innovation activities (Teece, 1998).

Technological capabilities are a major firm resource and are composed of production capabilities, investment capabilities and innovation capabilities (Dahlman et al., 1987; Kim, 1997). In business firms, these capabilities are determined by their human capital, technology and managerial competencies and practice levels (Bell & Pavitt, 1995; Leonard-Barton, 1995; Teece, 2012; Bloom et al., 2019). Production capability characterizes economies whose development is based on the capabilities to manufacture products with a certain level of technology, at world-class levels of efficiency or productivity. In this case, growth is driven not by innovation, but by excellent operational efficiency (Bell & Pavitt, 1995). What is required is the ability to purchase the technology, which is operationalized by a workforce with good technical skills, supported by blue-collar workers. Product and process engineering to improve existing products and processes involves more complex skills and requires engineering expertise. Process and product engineering is a part of manufacturing capability and involves incremental innovation, that is, improvements to existing products and processes.

Some studies (see, e.g., Amsden & Tschang, 2003; Radosevic & Yoruk, 2016a, 2016b, 2018) point out that technological capability is not necessarily related to R&D capabilities and is linked more closely to product development capabilities enabling advanced developments and production prototyping, whereas the exploratory development phase is related to the development of a prototype in a specific system. Manufacturing capability, process and product engineering and advanced development are more feasible for firms operating in industries and countries behind the technology frontier, while exploratory and innovative development is a feature of design manufacturers and is more feasible for industries and countries operating at the technology frontier (Radosevic & Yoruk, 2018).

The role of R&D differs with the level of development of the economy. In middle-income economies it centres on imitation; in high-income countries, the focus is on competitiveness. In emerging economies, it drives innovation and is involved in absorption and exploitation of foreign knowledge. Reinstaller and Unterlass (2011) use micro-data from a Community Innovation Survey of 17 EU countries and show that the determinants of successful product innovation by European firms differ across countries depending on their distance from the technology frontier. The farther from the frontier, the greater the importance of technology transfer compared to R&D; the closer to the frontier, the more important are cooperation with universities, in-house research, highly skilled personnel and intellectual property rights.

The idea of capability upgrading can be applied at the country level also (see, e.g., Lall, 1992). At this level, it refers to the technological capabilities of all the actors, including business firms. The literature discusses the role of social capabilities in terms of societal technological capabilities (Fagerberg et al., 2007; Cimoli & Porcile, 2011; Castellacci & Natera, 2013). The idea of technology upgrading is distinct from the notion of national innovation system, which refers to institutional characteristics and their influence on firms' technological capabilities (Freeman, 1987; Lundvall, 1992; Nelson, 1993).

Those mainly responsible for technology upgrading are business organizations, but the accumulation of technological capabilities must be supported by specific policies and an appropriate institutional infrastructure. The transition from technology adoption (catch-up) to technology creation (post-catch-up) depends largely on policies and the institutional infrastructure supporting innovation activity (Choung et al., 2014). The policy and physical infrastructures are essential factors in the technology upgrading trajectory. A weak policy infrastructure will have a negative effect on firms' competitive ability. Subsequent chapters show that production capacities in the WB economies have declined since the 1990s.

These countries' manufacturing firms are producing commoditized and largely undifferentiated goods, using imported equipment, and traded in domestic and regional markets. These firms need to focus on how to increase the quality and efficiency of their production processes and produce goods that meet international quality standards. In general, productivity and technological upgrading levels are lagging behind those in the advanced economies. To achieve economic and technological transformation will require a new industrial policy approach, adapted to these countries' economic and political developments, to enhance the technological capabilities in these economies. The new policy approach draws on the positive and negative experiences of structural reform and old industrial policy. The new policy conceptualization aims to acquaint the reader with a new approach to the design and implementation of industrial policy, an approach that takes into account the innovative and political capacities of the economies for which the policies are designed. The new approach centres on technology upgrading and a shift to higher value-added production and higher value goods through increased specialization. This will require R&D and innovation capabilities, production capabilities, structural change and interactions with external knowledge.

## 1.4 The Structure of the Book

Chapter 2 provides a brief overview of the three WB economies and Slovenia. It discusses their economic composition, economic productivity and innovation system performance and examines business indicators, such as firm demographics, contribution of economic sectors to GDP, etc. It includes a section devoted to the manufacturing sector and its dynamics. Chapter 2 aims to capture the similarities and differences among the four economies.

Chapter 3 is a review of the industrial policy literature. It discusses academic debate on the role of industrial policy in promoting economic growth and analyses the practical and theoretical arguments related to state intervention in the economy. Chapter 3 also examines three arguments related to the importance of industrial policy for the manufacturing sector: the interdependence between the manufacturing and other economic sectors, accumulation of production skills and the risk and uncertainty experienced by manufacturing firms in business operations. We discuss the part played by finance in successful industrial policies.

Chapter 4 examines the industrial policies implemented in the three WB countries. We contrast the industrial policies designed and implemented in Albania, North Macedonia and Kosovo with those implemented in Slovenia, whose industry measures are considered the 'learning benchmark' for other WB economies. Chapter 4 concludes by identifying emerging trends, common themes and industrial policy practices.

Chapter 5 describes the analytical framework used to explore technology upgrading in the WB economies. It discusses the statistical indicators used to frame discussion of industrial and innovation policy issues in the WB subregion. The data are drawn on to propose a new industrial policy approach based on technology upgrading.

Chapter 6 investigates a new way to promote manufacturing firm growth through implementation of a new industrial policy approach to encourage intensive technology upgrading to support sustainable economic growth in Albania, North Macedonia and Kosovo. The middle-income status of these countries determines the nature of their business activities and their inclusion in this group has substantial implications for their industrial policies. Membership of the EU will require their economic and technological transformation. In this chapter, our new industrial policy includes measures to enable accumulation of the technological capabilities required for technology upgrading.

In Chap. 7, we investigate the technological capabilities of 101 manufacturing firms operating in Kosovo. Using a conceptual lens, we examine the continuous and reciprocal interactions between resources (inputs), managerial and production capabilities and dynamic organizational capabilities. Technological capabilities are split into distinct, but also partially overlapping static and dynamic organizational capabilities. Static capabilities are closely related to production capabilities. They are static in the sense that they are related to the generation of production knowledge and management practices with potential for the achievement of world-class productivity. On the other hand, strategic innovation and technology enhancement requires the creation of dynamic organizational capabilities. R&D capabilities, technological capabilities, networking and dynamic capabilities are all dynamic organizational capabilities. Change-generating capabilities, such as R&D, technological and networking capabilities, are important and can lead to high levels of firm growth. However, successful firms are distinguished by dynamic capabilities, that is, the abilities to develop change-generating routines in all dimensions of the firm's capabilities.

Chapter 8 summarizes the results of our research and discusses the findings for industrial policies and the impact of technological capabilities on manufacturing firm and manufacturing sector growth. It includes a discussion, some implications for policy and managers, and outlines the contributions made by this book to the economic growth and industrial policy literatures. It also discusses some limitations of our research and suggests directions for future research.

## References

Abramovitz, M. (1986). Catching up, forging ahead, and falling behind. *The Journal of Economic History, 46*(2), 385–406.

Amsden, A. (2001). *The rise of 'the rest': Challenges to the west from late-industrializing economies.* Oxford University Press.

Amsden, A. H., & Tschang, F. (2003). A new approach to assessing the technological complexity of different categories of R&D (with examples from Singapore). *Research Policy, Elsevier, 32*(4), 553–572.

Baily, M. N., & Bosworth, B. P. (2014). US manufacturing: Understanding its past and its potential future. *Journal of Economic Perspectives, 28*(1), 3–26.

Barney, J. B. (1991). Firm resources and sustained competitive advantage. *Journal of Management, 17*, 99–120.

Bell, M., & Pavitt, K. (1995). The development of technological capabilities. In I. U. Haque (Ed.), *Trade, technology and international competitiveness* (pp. 69–100). Economic Development Institute of the World Bank.

Bloom, N., Brynjolfsson, E., Foster, F., Jarmin, J., Patnaik, M., Saporta-Eksten, I., & Van Reenen, J. (2019). What drives differences in management practices? *American Economic Review, 109*(5), 1648–1683.

Castellacci, F., & Natera, J. M. (2013). The dynamics of national innovation systems: A panel cointegration analysis of the coevolution between innovative capability and absorptive capacity. *Research Policy, 42*(3), 579–594.

Choung, J. Y., Hwang, H. R., & Song, W. (2014). Transitions of innovation activities in latecomer countries: An exploratory case study of South Korea. *World Development, 54*(2), 156–167.

Cimoli, M., Dosi, G., & Stiglitz, J. E. (2009). The political economy of capabilities accumulation: The past and future of policies of industrial development. In M. Cimoli, G. Dosi, & J. E. Stiglitz (Eds.), *Industrial policy and development: The political economy of capabilities accumulation* (pp. 1–16). Oxford University Press.

Cimoli, M., & Porcile, G. (2011). Global growth and international cooperation: A Structuralist perspective. *Cambridge Journal of Economics, 35*, 383–400.

Cohen, W. M. (2010). Fifty years of empirical studies of innovative activity and performance. In B. H. Hall & N. Rosenberg (Eds.), *Handbook of the economics of innovation, volumes I and II* (pp. 129–213). Elsevier.

Cohen, W. M., & Levinthal, D. A. (1990). Absorptive capacity: A new perspective on learning and innovation. *Administrative Science Quarterly, 35*(1), 128–152.

Criscuolo, C., Gonnei, N., Kitazawai, K., & Lalanneiet, G. (2022). Are industrial policy instruments effective?: A review of the evidence in OECD countries, OECD Science, Technology and Industry Policy Papers, No. 128, OECD Publishing, Paris, https://doi.org/10.1787/57b3dae2-en.

Dahlman, C. J., Ross-Larson, B., & Westphal, L. E. (1987). Managing technological development: Lessons from the newly industrializing countries. *World Development, 15*(6), 759–775.

Damiani, M., & Uvalic, M. (2018). Structural change in the European Union and its periphery: Current challenges for the Western Balkan economies. *Southeastern Europe, 42*(2), 145–176.

Estrin, S., & Uvalic, M. (2014). Foreign direct investment into transition economies: Are the Balkans different? *The Economics of Transition, 22*(2), 281–312.

Estrin, S., & Uvalic, M. (2016). Foreign direct Investment in the Western Balkans: What role has it played during transition? *Comparative Economic Studies, 58*, 1–29.

Fagerberg, J., Mowery, D. C., & Nelson, R. R. (2005). *The Oxford handbook of innovation*. Oxford University Press.

Fagerberg, J., Srholec, M., & Knell, M. (2007). The competitiveness of nations: Why some countries prosper while others fall behind. *World Development, 35*(10), 1595–1620.

Felipe, J., Kumar, U., & Galope, R. (2014). Middle-income transitions: Trap or myth? ADB Economics Working Paper Series, No. 421. for International Economics.

Freeman, C. (1987). *Technology policy and economic performance: Lesson from Japan*. Pinter Publisher.

Freeman, C., & Soete, L. (1997). *The economics of industrial innovation* (3rd ed.). The MIT Press.

Gallouj, F., & Djellal, F. (2010). *The handbook of innovation and services*. Edward Elgar.

Gereffi, G. (1999). International trade and industrial upgrading in the apparel commodity chain. *Journal of International Economics, 48*(1), 37–70.

Gerschenkron, A. (1962). *Economic backwardness in historical perspective*. Harvard University Press.

Gerschenkron, A. (1963). The early phases of industrialization in Russia: Afterthoughts and Counterthoughts. In W. W. Rostow (Ed.), *The economics of take-off into sustained growth. International Economic Association series*. Palgrave Macmillan.

Gill, I., & Kharas, H. (2015). The middle-income trap turns ten. Policy Research Working Paper No. 7403, 151–169.

Hall, B. H., & Rosenberg, N. (2010). *Handbook of the economics of innovation, volumes I and II*. Elsevier.

Hansen, U. E., & Ockwell, D. (2014). Learning and technological capability building in emerging economies: The case of the biomass power equipment industry in Malaysia. *Technovation, 34*(10), 617–630.

Hobday, M. (1995). *Innovation in East Asia*. Edward Elgar.

Juhász, R., Lane, N. J., & Rodrik, D. (2023). The new economics of industrial policy. National Bureau of Economic Research. http://www.nber.org/papers/w31538.pdf

Kamien, M. I., & Schwartz, N. L. (1982). *Market structure and innovation*. Cambridge University Press.

Kanbur, R., Noman, A., & Stiglitz, J. (2019). *Quality of growth in Africa*. Columbia University Press.

Katz, J. (Ed.). (1987). *Technology generation in Latin American manufacturing industries*. Macmillan Press Ltd.

Kim, L. (1997). *Imitation to innovation: The dynamics of Korea's technological learning*. Harvard Business School Press.

Kim, L., & Nelson, R. R. (2000). *Technology learning and innovation: Experiences of newly industrializing economies*. Cambridge University Press.

Lall, S. (1992). Technological capabilities and industrialization. *World Development, 20*(2), 165–186.

Lee, J., Lee, K., Meissner, D., Radosevic, S., & Vonortas, N. S. (2021). Technology upgrading and economic catch-up: Context, overview, and conclusions. In *The challenges of technology and economic catch-up in emerging economies*. Oxford University Press.

Lee, J. D. (2016). Middle innovation trap: Transition failure from implementation capability to concept design capability as a source of the middle-income trap. Paper for HSE international research conference on foresight and STI policy Moscow: The National Research University—Higher School of Economics (HSE).

Lee, K. (2005). Making a technological catch-up: Barriers and opportunities. *Asian Journal of Technology Innovation, 13*(2), 97–131.

Lee, K. (2013). Capability failure and industrial policy to move beyond the middle-income trap: From trade-based to technology-based specialization. In J. E. Stiglitz & J. Y. Lin (Eds.), *The industrial policy revolution! The role of government beyond ideology* (pp. 244–272). Palgrave Macmillan.

Lee, K. (2019). *In the art of economic catch-up: Barriers, detours and leapfrogging in innovation systems* (pp. 244–269). Cambridge University Press. https://doi.org/10.1017/9781108588232.009

Lee, K., & Malerba, F. (2017). Catch-up cycles and changes in industrial leadership: Windows of opportunity and responses of firms and countries in the evolution of sectoral systems. *Research Policy, 46*, 338–351.

Lee, K., Szapiro, M., & Zhuqing, M. (2018). From global value chains (GVC) to innovation systems for local value chains and knowledge creation. *The European Journal of Development Research, 30*(3), 424–441.

Leonard-Barton, D. A. (1995). *Wellsprings of knowledge: Building and sustaining the sources of innovation*. Harvard Business School Press.

Lin, J. Y. (2017). Industrial policies for avoiding the middle-income trap: Anew structural economics perspective. *Journal of Chinese Economic and Business Studies, 15*(1), 5–18. https://doi.org/10.1080/14765284.2017.1287539

Link, A. O., & Vonortas, N. S. (2013). *Handbook on the theory and practice of program evaluation*. Edward Elgar Publishers.

Lundvall, B. A. (1992). *National Systems of innovation: Towards a theory of innovation and interactive learning*. Pinter Publishers.

Malerba, F., & McKelvey, M. (2019). *Knowledge-intensive innovative entrepreneurship*. NOW Press.

Malerba, F., & Vonortas, N. S. (2009). *Innovation networks in industries*. Edward Elgar.

Nelson, R. R. (1993). *National innovation systems: A comparative analysis*. University of Illinois at Urbana-Champaign's Academy for Entrepreneurial Leadership Historical Research Reference in Entrepreneurship.

Nelson, R. R., & Winter, S. G. (1982). *The evolutionary theory of economic change*. Belknap Press.

Noman, A., & Stiglitz, J. E. (2015). Economics and policy: Some lessons from Africa's experience. In I. C. Monga & J. Y. Lin (Eds.), *The Oxford handbook of Africa and economics, vol. 2: Policies and practices*. Oxford University Press.

North, D. C. (2005). *Understanding the process of economic change*. Princeton University Press.

OECD. (2023). Industrial production (indicator). Retrieved October 06, 2023, from https://doi.org/10.1787/39121c55-en

Paus, E. (2017). *Escaping the middle-income trap: Innovate or perish. ADBI working paper 685*. Asian Development Bank Institute.

Perez, C., & Soete, L. (1988). Catching-up in technology: Entry barriers and windows of opportunity. In G. Dosi, C. Freeman, R. Nelson, G. Silverberg, & L. Soete (Eds.), *Technical change and economic theory* (pp. 458–479). Pinter Publishers.

Pisano, G. P., & Shih, W. C. (2012). *Producing prosperity: Why America needs a manufacturing renaissance*. Harvard Business Press Books.

Radosevic, S., & Yoruk, E. (2016a). Why do we need theory and metrics of technology upgrading? *Asian Journal of Technology Innovation, 24*(Sup 1), 8–32. https://doi.org/10.1080/19761597.2016.1207415

Radosevic, S., & Yoruk, E. (2016b). A new metrics of technology upgrading: The central and east European countries in a comparative perspective. In: GRINCOH working paper series, series 3 knowledge innovation, technology, paper no. 3.04.

Radosevic, S., & Yoruk, E. (2018). Technology upgrading of middle-income economies: A new approach and result. *Technological Forecasting and Social Change, 129*, 56–75.

Reinstaller, A., & Unterlass, F. (2011). Sectoral innovation modes and the state of economic development: Implications for innovation policy in the new member states. In S. Radosevic & A. Kaderabkova (Eds.), *Innovation policy in multi-tier Europe. The specific challenges of the central and Eastern European countries*. Edward Elgar.

Rodrik, D. (2006). Goodbye Washington consensus, hello Washington confusion? A review of the World Bank' s economic growth in the 1990s: Learning from a decade of reform. *Journal of Economic Literature, 44*(4), 973–987.

Sahiti, F. (2019). *The growth of firms in less developed countries: Lessons learned from Kosovo*. Palgrave Macmillan.

Stiglitz, J. E. (2017). Industrial policy, learning and development. In J. Page & F. Tarp (Eds.), *The practice of industrial policy: government-business coordination in Africa and East Asia* (WIDER studies in development economics). Oxford University Press.

Stiglitz, J. E., Lin, J. Y., & Patel, E. (2014). *The industrial policy revolution, vol. 2: Africa in the 21st Century*. Palgrave Macmillan.

Stöllinger, R. (2016). Structural change and global value chains in the EU. *Empirica, 43*(4), 801–829.

Stöllinger, R., Foster-McGregor, N., Holzner, M., Landesmann, M., Pöschl, J., & Stehrer, R. (2013). A manufacturing imperative in the EU—Europe's position in global manufacturing and the role of industrial policy, WIIW research report, 391, The Vienna Institute for International Economic Studies, October.

Szirmai, A., & Verspagen, B. (2015). Manufacturing and economic growth in developing countries, 1950–2005. *Structural Change and Economic Dynamics, 34*, 46–59.

Tassey, G. (2007). *The technology imperative*. Edward Elgar.

Teece, D. J. (1998). Capturing value from knowledge assets: The new economy, markets for know-how, and intangible assets. *California Management Review, 40*(3), 55–79.

Teece, D. J. (2012). Dynamic capabilities: Routines versus entrepreneurial action. *Journal of Management Studies, 49*(8), 1395–1401.

Veblen, T. (1915). *Imperial Germany and the industrial revolution*. Macmillan.

Vivarelli, M. (2016). The middle-income trap: A way out based on technological and structural change. *Economic Change and Restructuring, 49*(2–3), 159–193.

Westphal, L. E., Kim, L., & Dahlman, C. J. (1985). Reflections on the Republic of Korea's acquisition of technological capability. In N. Rosenberg & C. Frischtak (Eds.), *International technology transfer: Concepts, measures, and comparison*. Praeger.
Williamson, J. (1990). What Washington means by policy reform. In J. Williamson (Ed.), *Latin American adjustment: How much has happened?* Institute.
World Bank. (2012). *China 2030: Building a modern, harmonious, and creative high-income society*. World Bank.

CHAPTER 2

# Economic Profiles of Three Western Balkans Economies and Slovenia

## 2.1 Introduction

In this chapter, we examine the economic profiles of the three Western Balkan (WB) economies. We conduct a comparative analysis of our findings using Slovenia as the benchmark country. Our focus is primarily on the economic composition, economic productivity and performance of these countries' innovation systems. We identify similarities and differences among the four economies. We see that their similarities relate, for the most part, to their histories (all were former socialist economies), but also to their population size and geographic proximity. The differences among Albania, Kosovo and North Macedonia are relatively small, but the economic differences between these three countries and Slovenia are sizeable. For 50 years, Kosovo, North Macedonia and Slovenia were part of the former Yugoslavia, but, even then, there were some differences among them. For example, in 1990, per capita gross national product was, respectively, Dinars 65 and Dinars 200, compared to Dinars 24 in Kosovo. Similarly, unemployment rates in Slovenia and North Macedonia were, respectively, 5.1% and 23.0%, compared to 38.8% in Kosovo (Štiblar, 2013).

Sections 2.2, 2.3, 2.4 and 2.5 discuss the composition, productivity and innovation capabilities of the four countries. Section 2.6 examines



F. Sahiti, *Industrial Policies for Technological Upgrading in Western Balkan Countries*, https://doi.org/10.1007/978-3-031-51429-6_2

manufacturing firms' dynamics and firm turbulence from a cross-country perspective. In Sect. 2.7 we draw some conclusions from the analysis in this chapter.

## 2.2 The Albanian Economy: Composition, Productivity and Innovative Capabilities

Albania is a small and an open economy, with a population of 2.775 million and is included in the World Bank group of high middle-income economies ($US6.8 per capita). World Bank (2022) data suggest that the distribution of Gross Domestic Product (GDP) across economic sectors has not changed significantly in recent years: in 2021, the share of services in GDP was 47.7%, in which industry, including construction, represented 21.82% of GDP, agriculture 17.66% and manufacturing 6.23% of GDP. It is clear that the agricultural sector is important for the Albanian economy, although its share in GDP has shown a significant decline since 2006. INSTAT (2021) data suggest that services account for the highest share of total employment at almost 80% of the working population in 2020.

INSTAT (2021) data suggest, also, that recent economic growth has been driven by the rapid expansion of tourism, supported by the large agricultural sector and to the detriment of manufacturing output. These data show that tourism experienced rapid growth starting in the last decade. In terms of economic impact, tourism is the most influential sector, contributing 21.2% to GDP, a significantly higher share than the other WB economies where the average is 14.94% (OECD, 2022). The downward trend shown by agriculture has resulted in the agricultural sector in Albania representing less than 20% of GDP, although it accounts for around 40% of employment. In other words, the agricultural sector is the main source of income and employment for Albanian families.

It appears that the manufacturing sector continues to struggle to achieve its potential and accounts for employment mostly in urban areas and is dominated by textiles. The low level of productivity in the manufacturing sector shows no signs of reversal, although there are some indications of promising developments in the auto parts sector, based on Foreign Direct Investment (FDI), low labour costs, greater economic stability and an improved investment climate which is attracting foreign firms. Although FDI levels in Albania are comparable to those in the other WB countries (see Table 2.1), in Albania some 70% of its foreign investment consists of

**Table 2.1** Economic indicators for three WB countries and Slovenia

| | *MIC* | *SVN* | *ALB* | *MKD* | *KOS* |
|---|---|---|---|---|---|
| Size of population 2022 (thousands) | n.a. | 2108 | 2775 | 2057 | 1762 |
| GDP per capita (US$) 2022 | 6388 | 29,457 | 6803 | 6592 | 5351 |
| GDP (current US$) 2022 (millions) | n.a. | 62,117 | 18,882 | 13,563 | 9429 |
| GDP growth (annual %)—2022 | 3.5 | 5.4 | 4.8 | 2.1 | 3.5 |
| Profit tax (% of commercial profits)—2019 | 17.0 | 12.7 | 14.1 | 11.0 | 9.3 |
| Rate of unemployment—2021 | 6.4 | 4.45 | 11.5 | 15.8 | 20.4 |
| Manufacturing, value added (% of GDP) 2022 | 21 | 19 | 7 | 13 | 14 |
| Informal payments to public officials (% of firms) 2019 | 21 | 4.4 | 31.6 | 4.3 | 6.5 |
| Informal economy | n.a. | 23.8 | 31.9 | 33.4 | 40.0 |
| Personal remittances, received (% of GDP) 2022 | 1.5 | 1.1 | 9.2 | 3.4 | 17.1 |
| Foreign direct investment, net inflows (% of GDP) | 1.3 | 2.8 | 7.6 | 6.4 | 8.6 |
| Lending interest rates—2022 | n.a. | 2.48 | 6.5 | 4.6 | 6.3 |
| Number of active firms—thousands 2021 | n.a. | 150.5 | 104 | 72.9 | 45.5 |
| Number of active manufacturing firms—thousands 2021 | n.a. | 10.3 | 7.7 | 7.9 | 5.8 |

Source: World Bank, Eurostat and official statistical agencies
Note: Data on the informal economy in Albania are from World Economics
Note: Data on unemployment in Albania refer to 2019 and for N. Macedonia to 2022

energy and mining sector rents. FDI aimed at increasing manufacturing efficiency is concentrated mostly in labour-intensive sub-sectors, such as clothing and footwear and, more recently, the auto parts sector (INSTAT, 2021), but are more modest. It should be noted that the private sector's contribution to employment is showing continuous growth.

The population of business firms in Albania is dominated by Small and Medium-sized Enterprises (SMEs), which account for 99.8% of all enterprises and 81.9% of employment in Albania. These SMEs were hit hard by the COVID-19 pandemic but are showing signs of gradual recovery (European Commission, 2021). Many SMEs operate in sectors with relatively low added value, such as food and beverages, retail trade and basic manufacturing of food, textiles and clothing. Section 3.2 discusses business dynamics in more detail. World Bank (2019) data show that Albanian firms are less productive than those in other WB countries and in Europe as a whole and show, also, that their productivity has declined since 2013 in particular. Value added per worker is particularly low in manufacturing, accommodation and food services, at less than 10% of the European

Union (EU) average (World Bank, 2019). Productivity in other sectors (trade, transport, information technology) is higher, but is still at only 15% of the EU average with productivity growth in the manufacturing sector especially slow.

The low productivity of Albanian firms is due to several factors. First, Albania's large informal economy (see Table 2.1) has an effect on firm dynamics and allows inefficient firms to continue to operate in the market which is a barrier to the growth and expansion of more productive firms. The International Finance Corporation (IFC) (2022) notes that labour productivity has stagnated and is well below the average in other WB economies and Europe. Manufacturing firm productivity growth is substantially slower than other countries in the region; there is little factor reallocation from less to more productive firms and scarce upgrading of internal capabilities and replacement of less efficient incumbent firms by more efficient companies. This widespread informality is hampering the 'creative destruction' effect and allowing low-productivity firms to survive.

The low levels of productivity of Albanian firms is due also to weak (IFC, 2022) knowledge and managerial capabilities, lack of know-how to access foreign markets and lack of financial sophistication in terms of capacity to develop business plans and obtain financing (O'Brien et al., 2017). Private investment in R&D is rare in Albanian firms with only 2.4% of firms, on average, reporting investment in R&D, well below the 13.5% average in the upper-middle-income countries (Fig. 2.1).

Albania has a very poor record of R&D spending for innovation, adoption of new technologies and innovative products, patent registrations, introduction of products and services new to the market, etc. The 2021 Global Innovation Index (GII) ranked Albania 84th for overall innovation indicators, well behind Slovenia (32nd) and North Macedonia (59th). This is evidence of problems faced by the country to create a favourable innovation environment.

In 2020, public spending on scientific research was only 0.04% of GDP, a figure that is just above Kosovo which has the lowest level of public spending in this area (IFC, 2022). Albania is a participant in the European Union (EU) research and innovation project (European Commission, 2020), but the data suggest that it has registered a low level of success (7.8%, roughly half the average of 15.3% achieved by the other participating countries) (European Commission n.d.).

Data from various local and international reports (see, e.g., IFC, 2022) indicate that the business climate in Albania has shown significant

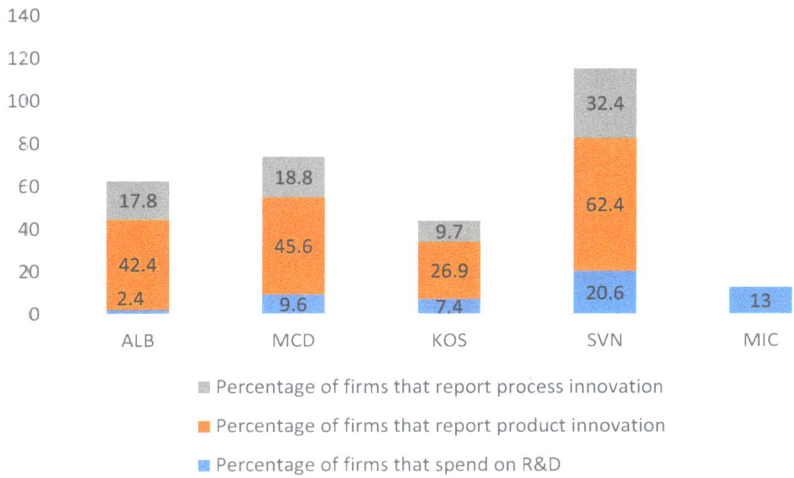


**Fig. 2.1** Firm investment in R&D and innovation performance (2019). Source: World Bank Enterprise Surveys. Note: No data for product and process innovation in middle-income countries (MIC)

improvement in relation to simpler licensing procedures, incentives for private investment, more formalization of firms, improved access to land, better dispute resolution mechanisms and better infrastructure (especially energy) and public services. However, problems persist in relation to policy implementation, regulatory efficiency, contract execution and enforcement, etc. (European Commission, 2022a). Also, in Albania's public sector, corruption is a major problem; Organisation for Economic Cooperation and Development (OECD) (2021) data show that, in 2020, more than 36% of companies had received the offer of at least one bribe—a level significantly higher than the average of 8.7% in Europe and the Central Asia region. The Transparency International (2022) Corruption Perceptions Index identifies Albania and Bosnia and Herzegovina as having the highest levels of corruption in the WB countries. The major issues identified by Albanian companies are high tax rates and access to electricity, which suggests the need for urgent improvements in these areas (OECD, 2022). Despite significant progress in Albania's physical infrastructure, OECD (2022) notes that the gaps related to road and rail networks, electricity supply and broadband Internet access are much wider than in the other WB countries.

Low levels of skill among workers is a major problem (especially in Albania) and this is related to the quality of the education system in that country. In 2013, only 6% of the firms that participated in the World Bank enterprise surveys identified lack of skilled workers as a major constraint; in 2019, this share had risen to 25% (IFC, 2022).

## 2.3 The North Macedonian Economy: Composition, Productivity and Innovative Capabilities

North Macedonia is a small and open economy and is included in the World Bank high middle-income economy category. Data for 2022 record the population of North Macedonia at around 2.057 million and per capita GDP as $US 6.59 thousand (World Bank, n.d.). Compared to the other WB economies, North Macedonia's sectors of economic activity are relatively balanced, with services accounting for 57% of GDP, industry 22.6% and agriculture 9.1% in 2020. Its industry sector is based mainly on manufacturing (13% of GDP), especially chemical products, basic iron, steel and ferroalloys, machinery and textiles. Its main sectors in terms of employment are services (55% of the workforce), industry (31%) and agriculture (14%) (MAKStat, 2021).

Similar to Albania, North Macedonia's economy is dominated by the service sector, which accounts for 54.5% of GDP and 55% of total employment (International Labor Organization, 2021). Its main sub-sectors include wholesale and retail trade, Information and Communication Technology (ICT), transport, logistics, etc. (MAKStat, 2021). Since 2003, the industry and construction sectors have experienced significant growth and their joint contribution to total employment has increased from 23% to 31.1% (ILO, 2021). The most significant growth was recorded in the manufacturing sector, whose contribution to GDP increased from 8.8% in 2009 to 13.3% in 2019 (MAKStat, 2021). On the other hand, the agriculture, forestry and fishery sectors have declined steadily and now jointly contribute only about 14% to total employment (ILO, 2021).

Domestic and international data show that, since 2013, the North Macedonian economy has experienced increased external demand, driven mainly by inflows of export-oriented production FDI, concentrated mainly in the automotive industry, which has resulted in an increase in total exports of 61% (World Bank, n.d.). Service sector exports also increased to reach 25% of total exports (MAKStat, 2021).

These data show, also, that since 2013, productivity growth has slowed. The World Bank (2020) suggests that this stems from poor productivity in all economic sectors and too slow reallocation of economic inputs from less productive to more productive firms and sectors. This weak increase in economic productivity suggests failings in how (mainly public) investments are realized and distributed. Significant amounts of public money have been invested in projects to construct monuments, which have limited potential to increase national economic productivity (IBRD/World Bank, 2018). The lack of dynamism in the domestic market (similar to the case of Kosovo) does not allow market mechanisms to reallocate capital and inputs from less to more productive sectors and firms. Due to numerous structural problems, including insufficient access to external financial resources, unfair market competition, a large informal sector, unpredictable and discretionary enforcement of regulation, high levels of corruption, etc., North Macedonia also lacks market mechanisms to redistribute economic resources (IBRD/World Bank, 2018). This has resulted in a decline in GDP growth from 3.5% during 2001–2010 to 2.6% in 2011–2019 (World Bank, 2020).

In addition to weak firm dynamics, North Macedonian firms' productivity performance is constrained by their weak capabilities. The European Innovation Scoreboard classifies North Macedonia as an emerging innovator; other rankings categorize North Macedonia as an intermediate knowledge economy, constrained mainly by lack of availability of a workforce with adequate business skills (EBRD, 2019). These poor workforce skills are the result of a poor education system (European Commission, 2022b). Education and professional training to meet private sector requirements is a major economic problem in North Macedonia. OECD (2022) shows that enrolment in vocational schools is high (see Chap. 6, Table 6.1) but does not include sufficient practical work.

Expenditure by Macedonian companies on the development of scientific research is higher than in Albania and Kosovo, but much lower than in Slovenia and the other middle-income countries. Only 9.6% of Macedonian firms invest in R&D, compared to the average of 13.5% for the high middle-income economies (Fig. 2.1).

North Macedonia is lagging behind Slovenia for R&D investment, adoption of new technologies and other innovations, patent registrations, introduction of products and services new to the market, etc. The 2021 GII ranks North Macedonia 59th for overall innovation indicators, well behind Slovenia at 32nd. This is evidence of North Macedonia's failure to create a favourable environment for innovation.

In 2020, public spending on scientific research was only 0.38% of GDP, much lower than in Slovenia (2.4%) and the group of middle-income countries 1.86% (World Bank, n.d.). North Macedonia is a participant in a (EU Horizon, 2020) project, but the data suggest that it has been the least successful of all participating countries, with an overall success rate of 9% (European Commission, n.d.).

According to the most recent European Commission (2022b) data, the business environment in North Macedonia has improved since 2012, but there continue to be several institutional and structural deficiencies. These include the time and cost related to contract enforcement, inefficient customs arrangements, unfair competition and limited alternative dispute resolution mechanisms, which have a negative impact on doing business. In addition, access to external finance is a substantial problem for firms and, especially, SMEs. Lending institutions require large collateral and a good credit history and alternative financing options are limited. The Innovation Fund has improved access to finance, but problems remain, especially in the context of private sector firms' alternatives to bank finance (OECD, 2021). Although a new bankruptcy law was published in North Macedonia, institutional and legal obstacles, such as public administration transparency and the extended time and high costs of dispute procedures, remain obstacles for business (European Commission, 2022b).

Other problems include an informal economy and corruption. The informality in the agriculture, construction, domestic services, wholesale and retail trade sectors continues to hinder the creation of a business-friendly environment. The large grey economy creates strong competition for registered businesses and erodes the potential tax revenue base for financing public programmes.

The North Macedonia statistics agency estimates that the informal economy accounts for around 20% of GDP, but other estimates suggest a significantly larger informal economy—ranging between 24% and 47% (see Table 2.1). The European Bank for Reconstruction and Development (EBRD)-World Bank Survey on the Business Environment and Enterprise Performance (BEEPS) highlights unfair market competition as one of the main barriers to doing business. Specifically, 26% of respondents consider unfair market competition as the main obstacle to business (Kresic et al., 2017). The North Macedonian economy historically has been plagued by high levels of corruption, although several international reports show that the situation has improved (see Transparency International, 2022).

## 2.4 The Kosovan Economy: Composition, Productivity and Innovative Capabilities

Kosovo is also included in the World Bank classification of upper-middle-income country; its per capita GDP is around US$5.351 and its population in 2022 was 1.76 million. Kosovo is well-known for its rich natural resource reserves, including lignite (about 12.5 billion tons) and lead, zinc, silver, nickel, cobalt, copper, chromium, magnesium, iron and bauxite (Ministry of Economic Development, 2017). Nevertheless, Kosovo is the poorest and least developed country in Europe.

Kosovo is a small open economy with limited productivity growth and is dominated by services, which account for 45.86% of GDP and 56.5% of total employment (globalEDGE, n.d.). The service sector is led by firms operating in the wholesale and retail trade, real estate, transport and storage, and financial services sectors (Kosovo Statistics Agency, 2021). In terms of other economic sectors, industry accounts for 28.2% of GDP, almost five percentage points more than North Macedonia, and for approximately 24.8% of the workforce, while manufacturing and agriculture contribute, respectively, 13.56% and 7.39% of GDP (globalEDGE, n.d.). Since 2008, the contribution of the agriculture, forestry and fisheries sector to GDP has declined from 15% to 6.9%; however, this sector continues to be a significant contributor to overall employment accounting for 5.5% of formal employment and around 35% of informal employment (Cojocaru, 2017). In the period 2015–2019, Kosovo experienced relatively significant economic growth, driven mainly by flows of remittances (over 15% of GDP) and loans from the expanding financial sector. The country's limited productive base means that its consumption-based economic growth is due mainly to imports, which, in 2019, accounted for 56.1% of GDP. This indicator, combined with Kosovo's relatively weak export base—29.1% of GDP—has resulted in substantial trade imbalances, including high trade and current account deficits, which, in 2019, reached, respectively, 43.8% and 5.6% of GDP (World Bank, 2021). Unlike other countries in the region, FDI has not been a significant driver of structural transformation in Kosovo, including in sectors with export potential.

Several national and international reports show that Kosovo's economy has been characterized by relatively poor productivity and particularly slow growth since 2018. Compared to the EU countries, labour productivity in all economic sectors is less than 25% of the EU member state average (World Bank, 2021). Due to the poor functioning of market mechanisms, reallocation of resources from less productive sectors and firms to more productive ones has decreased (European Commission, 2022c), with the failure of market mechanisms to distribute investment through the reallocation of capital and other inputs from non-productive sectors and firms to more productive sectors and firms. The low productivity of Kosovan companies stems from its poor-quality education system, unfair market competition, its business conditions, its physical infrastructure, etc. However, it has been shown (see, e.g., OECD, 2022 and EBRD, 2022) that it is due, mainly, to Kosovo's large informal economy and weak firm capabilities. Unfortunately, the informal sector is continuing to grow (see Table 2.1). Empirical research shows that informal firms are characterized by low levels of human and physical capital, difficulties related to accessing finance and a short-term focus which traps them in a vicious circle of low investment and low productivity (OECD/ILO, 2019). Without major economic changes, its firms are likely to remain uncompetitive and small.

The low level of firm capabilities is linked to poor organizational and managerial skills in Kosovan firms, which hamper participation in foreign markets and ability to develop new products and services (Sahiti, 2019). Kosovan firms equal Albanian firms for very low investment in R&D. The 2019 World Bank Survey found that, on average, only 7.4% of Kosovan firms reported R&D activities, well below the average for the WB economies, Slovenia and the remaining upper-middle-income countries (see Fig. 2.1).

Kosovo is in the initial phase of building an innovation ecosystem, indicating its poor knowledge economy development and poor implementation of innovation support policies. Policy makers are making efforts to design a framework to allow the development of innovation, but policies are fragmented, lack clear objectives and suffer from weak implementation (OECD, 2022). Financial support is limited; there are no data on current investment in R&D, but the European Commission (2022c) estimates that funding of R&D does not exceed 0.1% of GDP, significantly below the 0.7% mandated Kosovo's law. According to EBRD (2022), innovation system capabilities in Kosovo are weak and the knowledge economy is nascent. EBRD (2019) ranked Kosovo in the bottom quintile in the knowledge economy index for EBRD investment. EBRD ranks Kosovo's economy 35th out of 38 economies and particularly lagging in innovation skills and ICT infrastructure.

International organizations, such as the OECD (2022), emphasize the progress that has been made by Kosovo in improving the environment for doing business. However, the European Commission (2022c) states that, despite these improvements, the business community in Kosovo continues to face persistent problems. There are significant problems related to implementation of business contracts, unfair market competition, high levels of corruption and an informal economy which accounts for more than a third of total employment (IMF, 2022). According to Transparency International's Corruption Perception index, Kosovo has achieved improvements, with a ranking in 2021, of 87th out of 180 countries, which is 17 positions higher than in 2020 (European Commission, 2022). The cost of lending continues to be high in line with the high credit risks affecting commercial banks and the lack of alternative financing options (OECD, 2022).

The European Commission (2022c) emphasizes that Kosovo has made significant progress in improving its road, water and telecommunications infrastructure, but its rail and energy networks continue to be very poor. In order to grow, Kosovo needs stable water and energy supply systems.

## 2.5 The Slovenian Economy: Composition, Productivity and Innovation Capabilities

Slovenia is included in the World Bank group of developed countries; it has a per capita GDP of $US29,457 and its population numbers around 2.08 million. It is a small, open economy with high productivity growth. Almost two-thirds of the working population are employed in services with the remainder employed mainly in industry and construction. The service sector accounts for 75% of GDP, industry accounts for 28.28% and the agriculture contributes 1.69% of GDP (globalEDGE, n.d.). Slovenia is known for its strong manufacturing sector, which contributes 20.03% to GDP. The main manufacturing industries include ferrous metals and aluminium products, lead and zinc smelting, electronics including military electronics, trucks, etc.

In 2021, Slovenian productivity, measured as GDP per employed person, was 84% of the EU average (SURS, 2022). Its productivity has been supported by export-oriented sectors, such as manufacturing. In the period 2005–2021, the real terms highest increase in value added per hour worked was in manufacturing at 71%, which is above the EU average of 41%. Official data show that, over the long term, traditional market services recorded reasonably high productivity growth, but negative growth of ICT services (SURS, 2022). Export competitiveness has increased but is based on energy-intensive and high-emissions activities.

Slovenia is among the small group of world countries that is considered to have macroeconomic stability (World Economic Forum, 2019), which makes it a low-risk destination for potential investors. Its economy is diversified and well connected to European production chains. The Institute of Macroeconomic Analysis and Development (IMAD) (2022) shows that, in recent years, Slovenia's business environment and, especially, its bankruptcy legislation, judicial efficiency, public procurement process, bureaucracy and digital public services have improved greatly. Nevertheless, international comparisons show that other countries have advanced more and faster than Slovenia in terms of regulatory changes and reduced bureaucracy, both of which affect business competitiveness and attraction of foreign investment. The main weaknesses in Slovenia's business environment are related to its institutions (bureaucracy, regulatory framework, tax system, etc.), which remain inefficient or not business friendly (IMAD, 2022). Despite its recent growth, Slovenia has one of the lowest shares of inward FDI in GDP among EU member states (UNCTAD, 2022). Economists estimate that the incentives for foreign investors are very low compared to other EU member countries (IMD, 2022).

Although the innovation system is far better and is more advanced in Slovenia than the other WB countries, according to the European Commission (2023), Slovenia's innovation activity lags behind the EU average. According to the European Innovation Scoreboard, the Slovenian economy is a moderate innovator, with performance at 95.1% of the EU average. The data show that entrepreneurial activity (startups) and net FDI flows add positively to the innovation climate, while R&D spending and buyer sophistication add negatively. Slovenia has the highest percentage of innovators who do not innovate themselves and non-innovators with the potential to innovate. Entrepreneurship training and government procurement, which are among the drivers of research and innovation, are below the EU average. The 2022 World Intellectual Property Organization report ranks Slovenia as going from 32nd to 33rd in the GII. Its lack of market sophistication is related, mainly, to insufficient investment and creative output, due, in turn, to lack of intangible assets such as organizational capabilities, management competences, etc.

## 2.6 Business Indicators

In most contemporary world countries, the firm sector is composed, mostly, of SMEs and this includes the three WB countries and Slovenia. In these four economies, most firms have fewer than 250 workers and their focus is on the generation of economic value and providing employment. National governments recognize the value of SMEs for their countries' economic development and try to provide them with institutional support.

Figure 2.2 shows that large firms (250+ employees) represent less around 1% of all firms in the WB countries including Slovenia.

Figure 2.3 depicts number of employees by firm size and shows that over 75% of employment in Albania and Kosovo and, respectively, 73.5% and 73.9% of employment in North Macedonia and Slovenia is in SMEs.

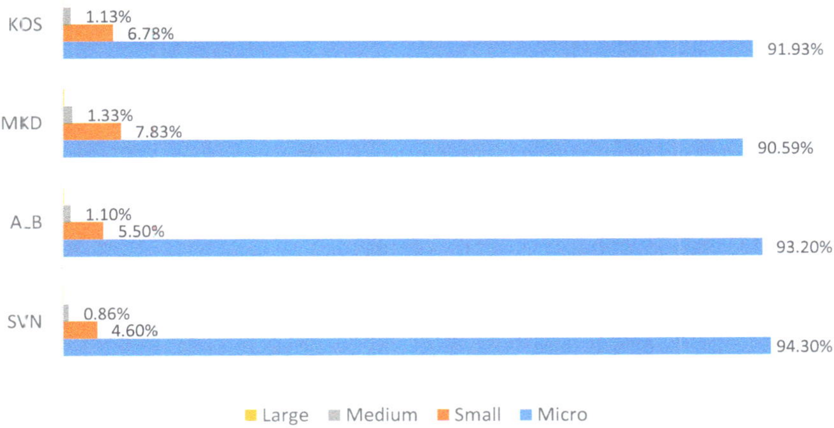


**Fig. 2.2** Firm size (2020). Source: The Kosovo, North Macedonia, Albania and Slovenia statistics agencies

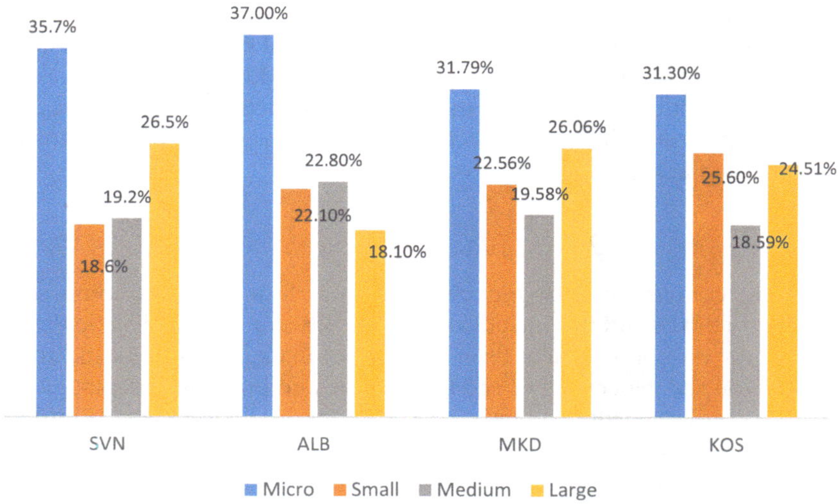


**Fig. 2.3** Firm employment (2020). Source: The Kosovo, North Macedonia, Albania statistics agencies and EUROSTAT for Slovenia

SMEs are important not only because they dominate the population of business firms and contribute the most to employment but also because of other economic indicators. Romer's (1990) empirical study demonstrates the effect of the creation and dissemination of knowledge on economic growth and the crucial role in this of SMEs. Similarly, Audretsch et al. (2007) show that SMEs are an important innovation diffusion channel and point out that SMEs are potentially more suited to current economic conditions and are more innovative due to their ability to make faster decisions, their greater flexibility, etc., compared to more bureaucratic and less flexible large firms (Audretsch et al., 2007).

The greater dynamism of smaller firms means that they put pressure on larger firms. Their ability to innovate forces large firms to improve their market offering or exit the market (Bartlesman et al., 2013). New and small firms increase the competition which has a positive effect on economic growth (Disney et al., 2003). Figure 2.4 depicts the relative contribution of SMEs to value added and shows that it is relatively lower than their share of employment. Compared to SMEs in the EU countries, which, in 2019, contributed 56.3% of total value added, SMEs in Kosovo

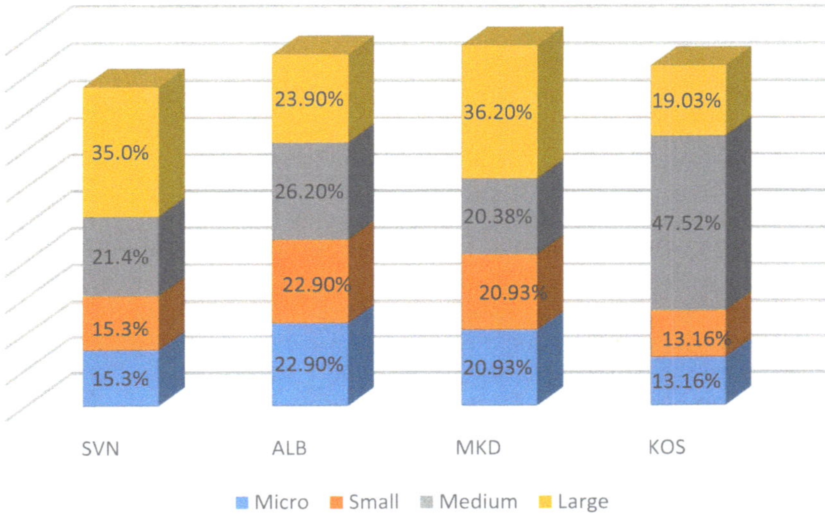


**Fig. 2.4** Gross value added by enterprise size class (2020). Source: The Kosovo, North Macedonia, Albania statistics agencies and EUROSTAT for Slovenia

and North Macedonia contributed, respectively, 81% and 64%. These data suggest that, in the middle-income countries, SMEs are the backbone of the private sector, whereas in the average EU country, large enterprises continue to produce a relatively high share of gross value added.

In sum, there are three reasons why SMEs play an important part in economic growth and social prosperity. First, in most countries, the firm population is composed of SMEs; the entrepreneurship literature suggests that large firms account for less than 2% of all firms in most countries (Storey & Greene, 2010). Our data confirm this and confirm, also, that SMEs are the dominant employers and contribute significantly to gross value added. The contribution to gross value added applies especially to our three WB economies.

## 2.7 An Overview of Manufacturing Sector Dynamics

We examine data on manufacturing firms in North Macedonia, Kosovo and Slovenia (data for Albania are not available), over the ten-year period 2011 to 2020. The data are from the respective country statistics agencies and Eurostat. The Kosovo Agency for Business Registration provides information on newly established and exiting firms during the period 2011–2020, while Kosovo Agency of Statistics data provide information on all active firms during the same period. Neither data set incudes firms resulting from restructuring, mergers or firms that went bankrupt during the period. North Macedonia and Slovenia data were obtained, respectively, from the national statistics agency and Eurostat.

The number of active manufacturing firms is substantially lower in Kosovo compared to North Macedonia and Slovenia. Kosovo Agency for Business Registration data show that the number of firms that entered the market during the period 2011 to 2020 increased compared to 2010 but was significantly smaller than in Slovenia (6085 compared to 10,543). Kosovo also experienced fewer firm exits, 2605 compared to over 10,000 for both North Macedonia and Slovenia.

The high rate of firm entry in Kosovo and North Macedonia (11.3%—see Fig. 2.5) is due to the low base of active firms in these markets and confirms the findings in other studies of developing economies, of high levels of firm entry and low levels of firm exit (Bartelsman et al., 2013).

Kosovan incumbent manufacturing firms are predominantly very small firms; 91.9% have fewer than five employees, whereas in North Macedonia and Slovenia the proportions of firms with between one and four employees are, respectively, 68.1% and 61.1% (see Table 2.2). In Kosovo, firms with fewer than five employees, five to nine employees and more than ten employees account, respectively, for 62.2%, 14.5% and 23.3% of total employment. However, in North Macedonia and Slovenia, the largest contribution to employment comes from firms employing more than ten workers. For example, in North Macedonia, 15.6% of employment is in firms with fewer than ten workers, and 84.4% of employment is in firms with more than ten workers. In the case of Slovenia, 87.7% of total employment is accounted for by firms with more than ten workers, with 6.9% and 5.4% accounted for by firms with up to four workers and five to nine workers (see Table 2.2).

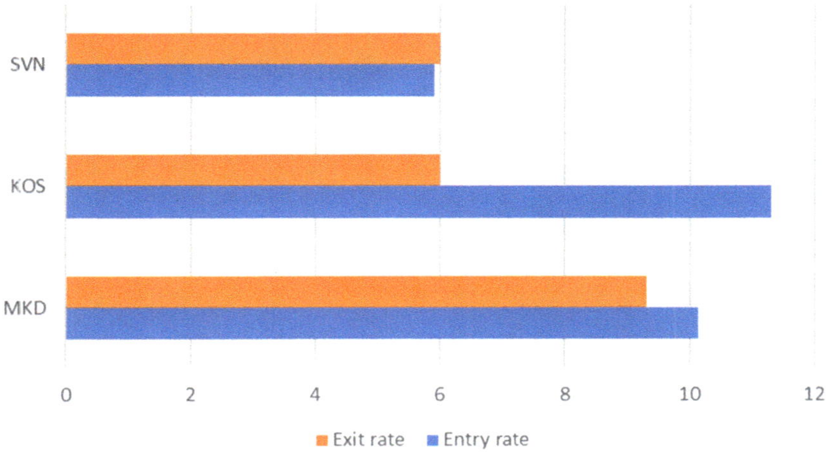


**Fig. 2.5** Firm entry and exit rates in 2020. Source: Eurostat for Slovenia and North Macedonia; Kosovo statistics agency and Kosovo Agency for Business Registration for Kosovo

**Table 2.2** Manufacturing firms by size and employee numbers in 2020

| | *SVN* | *MKD* | *KOS* |
|---|---|---|---|
| Incumbent firms: the percentage of size class in total | | | |
| 0–4 workers | 61.1 | 68.1 | 91.9 |
| 5–9 workers | 15.8 | 12.8 | 4.9 |
| 10+ workers | 23.0 | 19.1 | 3.2 |
| Firm entry: the percentage of size class in total | | | |
| 0–4 workers | 88.9 | 93.4 | 93.9 |
| 5–9 workers | 9.1 | 3.7 | 4.9 |
| 10+ workers | 1.9 | 2.8 | 1.2 |
| Employment: the percentage of size class in total | | | |
| 0–4 workers | 6.9 | 15.6 | 62.2 |
| 5–9 workers | 5.4 | | 14.5 |
| 10+ workers | 87.7 | 84.4 | 23.3 |
| Firm exit: the percentage of size class in total | | | |
| 0–4 workers | 94.8 | 98.0 | 97.5 |
| 5–9 workers | 3.5 | 1.2 | 2.3 |
| 10+ workers | 1.7 | 0.8 | 0.2 |

Source: Eurostat for Slovenia and North Macedonia and Kosovo statistics agency for Kosovo

The findings for sub-sectors are interesting. National statistics for Kosovo for 2021 show that more than 50% of total manufacturing firms in Kosovo operate in the food and beverages and tobacco, and non-metallic mineral products sectors. Food and beverages and tobacco account for 31% of all manufacturing firms and 30.8% of manufacturing employment; non-metallic mineral products accounts for 21.7% of firms and 21% of total employment. However, in Slovenia, 23.4% of active manufacturing firms are in the fabricated metal products and basic metals and fabricated metal sub-sector (23.37%).

## 2.8 Conclusions

This chapter examined economic composition, firm productivity and national innovation system performance in the three WB economies and Slovenia. As expected, the results show similarities in terms of economic structure, productivity levels and innovation performance. However, in the three WB economies, the contribution of the agricultural sector to GDP is significantly greater than in Slovenia and ranges from 7% in Kosovo to 8% in North Macedonia and 19% in Albania compared to less than 2% in Slovenia. In terms of the contribution of the manufacturing sector to GDP, this is 19% in Slovenia, but never exceeds 24% in the WB economies. In the case of firm productivity and, especially, manufacturing productivity, the low levels in the three WB economies are the result of their large informal economies, weak firm dynamics, negligible innovation performance and concentration in low value-added sub-sectors such as food, textiles, clothing and metal manufacturing. Our findings underline the importance of firm-level innovation to enable growth of more sophisticated sub-sectors.

Data from various organizations (World Bank, IFC, EBRD) show that productivity growth in the manufacturing sector is particularly slow, which is due to several factors, generally high level of informality, weak capabilities and lack of innovation capabilities. The large informal sectors in these countries affect the reallocation of resources from less productive to more productive firms. The low levels of productivity in these countries are due to weak capabilities and scarce investment in R&D and training by the firms in this region. The percentage of companies that invest in the development of capabilities is less than 10% compared to Slovenia at more than 20%.

The data highlight the poor state of the national innovation systems in the WB countries and the low level of both public and private sector spending on R&D. The link between R&D investment and innovation suggests the need for more effective investment of available resources.

## References

Audretsch, D. B., Grilo, I., & Thurik, R. (2007). Handbook of research on entrepreneurship policy. ISBN: 978-1-84542-409-1

Bartelsman, E., Haltiwanger, J., & Scarpetta, S. (2013). Cross-country differences in productivity: The role of allocation and selection. *The American Economic Review, 103*, 305–334.

Cojocaru, A. (2017). Kosovo jobs diagnostic, international bank for reconstruction and development and the world bank. http://documents1.worldbank.org/curated/en/814361497466817941/pdf/Kosovo-Jobs-Diagnostic.pdf

Disney, R., Haskel, J., & Heden, Y. (2003). Restructuring and productivity growth in UK manufacturing. *The Economic Journal, 113*(489), 666–694. http://www.jstor.org/stable/3590194

EBRD. (2019). Introducing the knowledge economy index, London. https://www.ebrd.com/news/publications/brochures/ebrd-knowledge-economy-index.html

EBRD. (2022). Kosovo country diagnostic: Private investment challenges and opportunities, London. https://www.ebrd.com/kosovo-country-diagnostic.pdf

European Commission. (2020). Directorate-General for Research and Innovation, Horizon 2020 – European Green Deal call, Publications Office of the European Union, 2020. https://data.europa.eu/doi/10.2777/200559

European Commission. (2021). Commission staff working document: Kosovo* 2021 report, European Commission, Strasbourg. https://ec.europa.eu/neighbourhood-enlargement/kosovo-report-2021_en

European Commission. (2022). 2022 economic reform programmes of Albania, Montenegro, North Macedonia, Serbia, Turkey, Bosnia and Herzegovina and Kosovo*. https://economy-finance.ec.europa.eu/system/files/2022-07/ip180_en.pdf

European Commission. (2022a). Commission staff working document, Albania 2022 report, Brussels. https://neighbourhood-enlargement.ec.europa.eu/system/files/2022-10/Albania%20Report%202022.pdf

European Commission. (2022b). North Macedonia Report 2022. https://neighbourhood-enlargement.ec.europa.eu/system/files/2022-10/North%20Macedonia%20Report%202022.pdf

European Commission. (2022c). Kosovo report 2022. https://neighbourhood-enlargement.ec.europa.eu/system/files/2022-10/Kosovo%20Report%202022.pdf

European Commission. (2023). European innovation scoreboard 2023 country profile Slovenia. Retrieved September 3, 2023, from https://ec.europa.eu/assets/rtd/eis/2023/ec_rtd_eis-country-profile-si.pdf

European Commission. (n.d.). Albania horizon 2020 country profile, Horizon 2020 country profile. https://webgate.ec.europa.eu/dashboard/extensions/CountryProfile/CountryProfile.html?Country=Albania

Eurostat. (2022). Eurostat [database]. https://ec.europa.eu/eurostat/data/database

globalEDGE. (n.d.). Global business knowledge. Retrieved September 2, 2023, from https://globaledge.msu.edu/countries/kosovo/economy

IBRD/World Bank. (2018). Seizing a brighter future for all: Former Yugoslav Republic of Macedonia: Systematic country diagnostic, World Bank Group. http://pubdocs.worldbank.org/en/606381543434479145/MKD-SCD-2018-ENG-Web.pdf

IFC. (2022). Creating markets in Albania: Country private sector diagnostic. https://www.ifc.org/content/dam/ifc/doc/mgrt/cpsd-albania.pdf

ILO. (2021). Strengthening social dialogue in North Macedonia, International Labour Organization. website. https://www.ilo.org/budapest/what-we-do/projects/WCMS_679543/lang%2D%2Den/index.htm

IMAD. (2022). *Development Report 2022.* Institute of Macroeconomic Analysis and Development. https://www.umar.gov.si/fileadmin/user_upload/razvoj_slovenije/2022/angleski/Development_Report_2022.pdf

IMD. (2022). *The IMD world competitiveness ranking [data portal].* International Monetary Fund. https://worldcompetitiveness.imd.org/rankings/wcy

IMF. (2022). Article IV consultation. Retrieved September 2, 2023, from https://www.imf.org/-/media/Files/Publications/CR/2022/English/1KOSEA2022001.ashx

INSTAT. (2021). Albania in figures. http://www.instat.gov.al/media/8988/albania-in-figures-2020.pdf

Kosovo Agency of Statistics. (2021). Statistical business register: The number of new and reregistered enterprises by sections of economic activities, 2012–2020. https://askdata.rksgov.net/PXWeb/pxweb/en/askdata/askdata__Statistical%20business%20register__Statistical%20repertoire/enterprises01.px/table/tableViewLayout1/?rxid=849047f5-19f1-46f0-81f5-019778e93dad

Kresic, A., Milatovic, J., & Sanfey, P. (2017). Firm performance and obstacles to doing business in the Western Balkans: Evidence from the BEEPS. EBRD Working Paper No. 200. https://ssrn.com/abstract=3119154 or https://doi.org/10.2139/ssrn.3119154

MAKStat. (2021). Structural business statistics. https://www.stat.gov.mk/PrethodniSoopstenijaOblast.aspx?id=111&rbrObl=39

Ministry of Economic Development. (2017). Energy strategy of the Republic of Kosovo 2017–2026, Pristina.

O'Brien, T., Nedelkoska, L., & Frasheri, E. (2017). *What is the binding constraint to growth in Albania?* Harvard Center for International Development.

OECD. (2021). *Competitiveness in south East Europe 2021: A policy outlook, competitiveness and private sector development*. OECD Publishing. https://doi.org/10.1787/dcbc2ea9-en

OECD. (2022). *SME policy index: Western Balkans and Turkey 2022: Assessing the implementation of the small business act for Europe, SME Policy Index*. OECD Publishing. https://doi.org/10.1787/b47d15f0-en

OECD/ILO. (2019). *Tackling vulnerability in the informal economy*. Development Centre Studies, ECD Publishing. https://doi.org/10.1787/939b7bcd-en

Romer, P. M. (1990). Endogenous technological change. *Journal of Political Economy, 98*(5), S71–S102. http://www.jstor.org/stable/2937632

Sahiti, F. (2019). *The growth of firms in less developed countries: Lessons learned from Kosovo*. Palgrave Macmillan.

Štiblar, F. (2013). *Economic growth and development in post Yugoslav countries*. Wilson Center, Global Europe Program.

Storey, D. J., & Greene, F. J. (2010). *Small business and entrepreneurship*. Pearson.

SURS. (2022). *SI-STAT [database]*. Statistical Office of the Republic of Slovenia. https://pxweb.stat.si/SiStat/sl

Transparency International. (2022). Corruption perceptions index 2021. https://www.transparency.org/en/cpi/2021/index/mkd

UNCTAD. (2022). *UNCTADstat [database]*. United Nations Conference on Trade and Development. https://unctadstat.unctad.org/

World Bank. (2019). Growth and jobs policy implementation support. Unlocking jobs and growth through productivity: A firm-level diagnostic of Albania.

World Bank. (2020). World development indicators, World Bank Databank website. https://databank.worldbank.org/source/world-development-indicators

World Bank. (2021). *Macro poverty outlook—Kosovo*. World Bank. https://pubdocs.worldbank.org/en/993701492011106034/mpo-ksv.pdf

World Bank. (2022). The World Bank Data. Retrieved June 12, 2023, from https://data.worldbank.org/indicator/NY.GDP.PCAP.KD

World Bank. (n.d.). Current account balance (% of GDP) - North Macedonia, World Bank Data Bank website. https://data.worldbank.org/indicator/BN.CAB.XOKA.GD.ZS?locations=MK

World Economic Forum. (2019). The global competitiveness report 2019. Retrieved September 2, 2023, from https://www3.weforum.org/docs/WEF_TheGlobalCompetitivenessReport2019.pdf?fbclid=IwAR0POZ8-xjHK1pMs

CHAPTER 3

# The Need for Industrial Policies: A Review of the Literature

## 3.1 Introduction

Promoting economic growth has been a topic of economic debate since the late eighteenth century and publication of Adam Smith's works. Most economic researchers agree that it is market forces that regulate market prices and enable the distribution of resources from less productive to more productive entities. However, it has been shown that government intervention is required to achieve overall economic transformation. Both historically and currently, the instrument typically used by governments to promote industrial and economic development is industrial policy.

In both the academic and policymaking arenas, debate on the relevance of industrial policy is ongoing. However, currently, discussion is focused less on whether or not governments should implement industrial policies and more on how they should be implemented (Juhász et al., 2023). Industrial policies have been aimed, in particular, at the manufacturing sector, whose decline (especially after the 2008 financial crisis) has increased interest in these instruments (Warwick, 2013). This greater emphasis on industrial policies has been accompanied by the emergence of more complex and more important (compared to the past) Global Value Chains (GVCs) and more intense global market competition.

Shocks, such as the COVID-19 pandemic, highlighted the need for governments to be more active in leading and managing structural change



F. Sahiti, *Industrial Policies for Technological Upgrading in Western Balkan Countries*, https://doi.org/10.1007/978-3-031-51429-6_3

in the business sector, which is suffering from international trade tensions, productivity slowdowns, digital transformation, climate change, etc. (Criscuolo et al., 2022). These and other events underline the urgency for state intervention in the economy and the formulation, in particular, of large-scale and wide-ranging recovery plans. Governments around the world have responded by formulating new industrial strategies. These efforts include the European Union's (EU) New Industrial Strategy, drafted in 2020 and updated in 2021, the 2019 European Green Deal, the 2020 Next Generation EU Fund, the US American Rescue Plan Act (2021), South Korea's Korean New Deal (2020), etc.

The 2008 financial crisis underlined the value of industrial policy and made it more visible, especially in the most influential economies such as the US and Germany (Mazzucato, 2013). However, the importance of industrial policy is understood by policy makers in all countries, including developing countries. Several middle-income economies, such as countries in Asia and Latin America, consider industrial policy to be the solution to the 'middle-income trap' (see Felipe et al., 2014 and Noman & Stiglitz, 2016). In several African countries, industrial policies are seen as contributing to efforts to alleviate the effects of poverty (Kanbur et al., 2019).

Several scholars are dubious about the relevance of industrial policies, although others, such as Justin Lin, Joseph Stiglitz and Dani Rodrik, consider that they have a very positive influence on national economic development. Lin, Stiglitz and Rodrik have made efforts to move debate from a focus on ideology and a framework of the old style (e.g., tariff protection) policies to an emphasis on productivity and growth, innovation, R&D, technology upgrading, competitiveness, the environment, etc.

Chapter 3 examines the issues related to the debate on the pros and cons of industrial policies, their historical development, rationale and problems, etc. The chapter is organized as follows. Section 3.2 reviews the historical development of industrial policy to provide a better understanding of its nature and evolution. Section 3.3 summarizes academic debate on the role of industrial policies for promoting economic growth and analyses the practical and theoretical arguments for state intervention in the economy via industrial policies. We investigate three arguments: the interdependence among economic sectors; the accumulation of productive skills; and risk and uncertainty. Section 3.4 reprises some of the basic arguments in the industrial policy literature related to why the manufacturing sector is the main focus of industrial policies. In Sect. 3.5, we discuss the importance of finance in the context of industrial policy, and in Sect. 3.6, we outline the related definitions and concepts.

## 3.2 A Short History of Industrial Policy

Industry policies emerged at the end of the eighteenth century. Great Britain was considered the pioneer of industry policy design and implementation (Gerschenkron, 1962) and was the first country in the world to impose trade tariffs on other countries using 'unequal agreements' (Chang, 2002). In the mid-nineteenth century, countries such as Germany, France and the US collaborated with Great Britain in a series of technological and industrial innovations, mainly, applicable to the heavy chemicals sector. These developments were supported by several economic and, especially, financial institutions. After the inclusion of Japan (considered one of the first industrialized countries to introduce industrial policies) in this group of countries, it became known as the 'Big Five' group (Ohno, 2013).

Starting in the mid-nineteenth century, Great Britain, Germany, France, the US and Japan, all industrialized countries, began to experiment with the implementation of industrial policies. Although these policies resembled commercial policies, they were fundamental for the protection of 'infant' industries (Chang, 2007; Reinert, 2007). Industrial policy measures were based, mainly, on the assumption that to be more competitive required the development and accumulation of production capabilities (Hirschman, 1981; Chang & Andreoni, 2020). Thus, industrial policies should be designed to support firms in their learning and accumulation of production skills. Some industrialized economies provided protection through the imposition of trade tariffs; between 1939 and 1945, the US imposed tariffs of up to 50% on manufacturing imports, which made the US one of most protected countries in the world in terms of imports (Chang, 2002).

Also, and especially towards the end of the nineteenth century, Germany began to impose tariffs to protect its nascent industries. The German government's aim was to promote specific industries while simultaneously building a coalition of interests to support Germany's industrialization (Chang, 2002). Under the leadership of Chancellor Otto von Bismarck, the German state introduced selective tariffs to support heavy industries such as iron and steel. Protection of steel production was based on the fact that steel was at the core of the new industrial paradigm and the development of the heavy machinery industries. Tariffs also enabled the allocation of rents to powerful societal interest groups and cemented a landlord-industrialist political coalition (Chang, 2002).

Japan's government was one of the first to draft well-structured industrial policies with clear objectives. The Japanese government created state-owned firms in a number of sectors—especially shipbuilding, mining, textiles and military—and began experimenting with the design of industrial policy instruments. For example, to protect its shipbuilding, mining, textiles and military industries, Japan introduced support for internal learning and accumulation of technological skills (Chang, 1994). Although most of these state-owned firms were later privatized, they continued to receive government subsidies—especially shipbuilding companies. The Japanese experience was regarded by other countries as a model for the creation of institutional mechanisms to support learning and accumulation of production skills. Japan's industrial policies then began to focus, also, on imports of productive assets and technologies (Chang, 2002), although it was not until 1911 that it introduced customs duties and these were at very low rates—maximum 5%.

Thus, until 1945, industrial policies in most countries took the form of customs tariffs. In the years after 1945, more sophisticated policies emerged, aimed at preparing the industrial system for a new industrial development paradigm and focused on industry restructuring, increasing manufacturing firm innovation capacity, encouraging applied research, and providing development funding and hybrid finance solutions such as subsidies, grants and strategic procurement. These measures became the backbone of industrial policies in early industrializing countries. It became clear that tariffs aimed at protecting new industries were no longer effective in the context of emerging market liberalization and that a multilateral approach to trade liberalization was needed. The General Agreement on Tariffs and Trade and the World Trade Organization facilitated access by early industrializers to developing country markets (Stiglitz, 1999).

After 1945, industrial policy was focused on Small and Medium-sized Enterprises (SMEs) especially in Great Britain. The British government was keen to develop industrial districts, dense networks of SMEs that would supply both the national and global markets (Andreoni & Lazonick, 2020). The British experience showed that SMEs derived several benefits from industrial policies, including increased competitiveness, better adaptation to specific sector conditions and increased exports.

It should be noted that, in industrialized countries, transformation of the agricultural sector was considered an opportunity for industrial development (Andreoni, 2011). The US was one of the first countries to try to increase agricultural productivity through the design of specific economic policies. Up to the end of the nineteenth century, the US was primarily an agrarian economy with agricultural products accounting for almost 75% of total US exports (Ferleger & Lazonick, 1993). The US government was searching for ways to spur a transformation in agriculture, based on giving state land to agricultural colleges and establishing government research institutes. However, improved agricultural productivity depended not just on technological upgrading; it was a function, also, of farmers' organizational and managerial capacities. The US Department of Agriculture advised farmers on increasing seed varieties, seed use, fertilizer use, controlling plant diseases, etc. The provision of these services and the diffusion of technology enabled by networks of public technology intermediaries, were critical for the industrialization of the US economy (Ferleger & Lazonick, 1993). Transformation of the agriculture sector stimulated the development of other industries, such as beverages, and facilitated cross-sector learning (Chang, 2002).

The focus of contemporary industrial policies in developed countries is quite different. Nowadays, the emphasis is entirely on technological and digital policies to increase innovation (Stiglitz, 2017). More specifically, in today's world, customs tariffs have reduced dramatically, promoting the introduction of non-tariff barriers to protect national industries.

The emphasis of industrial policies has changed because the governments of industrial countries now realize that trade measures and protection of new industries are not sufficient to promote productivity growth in manufacturing firms. Also, the governments of industrialized countries are recognizing that manufacturing firms cannot be competitive without the support of specific industrial policies aimed at improving their technological capabilities and human capital skills.

## 3.3 Ongoing Debate on the Role of Industrial Policy in the Economy

Academic debate on the rationale for industrial policies is well developed in the economic development literature. Some theoretical and practical arguments favour the use of industrial policies while others are against their implementation (Chang & Andreoni, 2020). The analysis in this section aims to provide an overview of the pros and cons of industrial policy. We begin by examining how theoretical and practical thinking about industrial policy has evolved.

Naudé (2010) suggests that the development of theoretical thinking on industrial policy falls into three main periods (see Table 3.1). In the first

**Table 3.1** Evolution of ideas of industrial policy

| *Period* | *Key ideas* | *Representative contributors* | *Country examples* |
|---|---|---|---|
| 1940s to late 1960s | • Further industrialization is necessary for development;<br>• Market failures would prevent this from happening automatically;<br>• Market failures are pervasive in developing countries;<br>• Industrial policy is needed, particularly infant industry protection, state ownership and state coordination. | Rosenstein-Rodan P. (1961)<br>Hirschman A. O. (1981)<br>Prebisch R. (1959)<br>Myrdal G. (1957) | South Korea<br>Malaysia<br>Japan<br>Taiwan<br>Singapore |
| 1970s to 1990s | • Practical obstacles to industrial policy are considered significant;<br>• Government failure is worse than market failure. Industrial policy is invitation to waste and rent-seeking;<br>• Trade liberalization (exports), privatization and attracting foreign direct investments together with macroeconomic stability and minimum government interference are the basic requirements for growth and industrialization;<br>• The era of the Washington consensus, especially after the debt crisis of the early 1980s and the ubiquity of structural adjustment programmes. | Baldwin R. E. (1969)<br>Krueger A. O. (1974, 1990)<br>Pack H. (1993, 2000) | Argentina<br>Nigeria |
| 2000s to present day | • Market and government failures are present;<br>• The 'how' rather than 'why' of industrial policy is important;<br>• Institutional setting matters but design difficult. Need to understand political context;<br>• Flexibility in the praxis of industrial policy is important;<br>• Differences exist with respect to the extent to which comparative advantage needs to be defined, not the principle;<br>• Innovation and technological upgrading should be a central objective of industrial policy;<br>• Promoting national innovation systems should be an important objective of industrial policy. | Amsden A. (1989)<br>Cimoli et al. (2009)<br>Rodrik D. (2004, 2008)<br>Chang H-J. (2002, 2003, 2007)<br>Lall S. (2004)<br>Lin J. (2009)<br>Nelson R. R. (1993)<br>Robinson J. A. (2009) | Finland<br>France<br>Latvia |

Source: Adapted from Naudé (2010)

period, 1940s to the late 1960s, theoretical thinking was dominated by the view that economic development required industrialization. The phenomenon of market failure means that economic industrialization is not automatic. The state must intervene to eliminate market failure, which requires industrial policies and, particularly, in the context of developing economies. Industrial policies are required to protect developing economies' infant industries, state ownership and state coordination.

In the second period, 1970 to 1990, theoretical thinking about industrial policies was dominated by a completely different perspective and the belief that industrial policies were more harmful than market failure. In this perspective, implementation of industrial policy led to waste, extortion and rent seeking with institutional support. This was the period of the Washington Consensus and the idea that trade liberalization (exports), privatization and withdrawal of foreign direct investment combined with macroeconomic stability and minimal government intervention were prerequisites for industrialization and economic growth.

The third period started in 2000 and was dominated by the idea that market failure was an essential attribute of contemporary economies. Thus, what mattered was not why or if industrial policies should or should not be implemented, but how and at what level they should be implemented to promote strategic industrial sectors. In this perspective, industrial policies should emphasize innovation and technological improvement, that is, government interventions should be aimed at fostering the national innovation system.

The debate on industrial policies is split between their supporters and their opposers. One of the most frequent and powerful arguments in support of the application of industrial policies is the protection of new industries and the premise that without institutional support, nascent industries will not survive. The high costs of production make it difficult for infant firms to compete with established market players and, especially, foreign firms. Protection and direct or indirect institutional subsidies, based on taxes and low borrowing costs, are seen as crucial. Baldwin (1969) suggested that, in the absence of institutional support, business agents operating in the production sector would have no incentive to invest in learning (due to diffusion), workforce training (due to mobility of work), production of new goods (because of the inability to absorb the benefits) and implementation of new projects (due to costs related to project evaluation).

Hausmann and Rodrik (2003) and Rodrik (2004) emphasize that market failure (information externalities, coordination externalities) is the main rationale for industrial policies. In low-income economies, in particular, the motivation to engage in entrepreneurial activities and to diversify are reduced by both types of market failure. Diversification of the production structure requires the entrepreneur to 'discover' the cost structure related to the new activity, through random experimentation with new products and adaptation of foreign technologies to domestic conditions. It has been argued (Hausmann & Rodrik, 2003) that entrepreneurs are reluctant to invest in experimental activities because competitors might exploit these efforts and, through imitation, reap what Schumpeter (1939) described as 'entrepreneurial profit'. Hausmann and Rodrik (2003) and Rodrik (2004) illustrate their arguments using the cases of Bangladesh and Pakistan. They underline, also, that few developed countries have made the transition from developing to developed economy without some kind of industrial policy to support the process of diversification. It is the ability to diversify, spread and share knowledge that has allowed high levels of economic growth and resulted in prosperous societies. In the case of coordination externalities, the authors' arguments are simple, but significant. It is well known that profitable projects require simultaneous investment of large sums that private agents cannot support and which require institutional support. Since many business projects are interrelated, investment in a single project will not be profitable without similar investment in other of the business entity's projects. This requires coordinated investment and, especially, in industries with economies of scale, in the presence of non-tradable inputs (Rodrik, 1996). These phenomena are typical of low-income economies.

The number of industrial policy advocates is large. Many (Greenwald & Stiglitz, 2014a, 2014b; Stiglitz & Lin, 2014; Stiglitz et al., 2014) argue that the drafting and, especially, the practical implementation of industrial policies allow growth and economic transformation. Some argue that development is related more to the capability to identify and promote business activities and technologies. For example, Mazzucato (2018) suggests that governments should aim for the creation of an 'entrepreneurial state' that seeks constantly for new opportunities for growth. Others are even more specific. For example, Rowden (2011) believes that it is difficult to expect developing countries to cease their dependence on international aid if they do not have the abilities required to design and employ industrial policies to enable transformation of their domestic industries, economic diversification and construction of a solid tax base.

Several contributors to the development literature are sceptical about or against the implementation of industrial policies. They argue that, in general, private agents are better informed than government about market conditions. If this situation is compounded by the fact that those responsible for the design of industrial policies are bureaucratic politicians who often make wrong decisions, this weakens claims related to industrial policy successes.

There is another argument that is founded on the belief that politicians do not always work in the interests of society. They may be more concerned with gaining and maintaining power and implementing industrial policies that benefit their political supporters at the expense of the wider society. The uneven benefits from industrial policy implementation can lead to corruption, extortion, etc. (Nogues, 1990).

There is empirical evidence suggesting that industrial policies have not always generated the intended results; some have been ineffective and, in some cases, political interference has reduced their effectiveness. For example, in Latin America, there is evidence of inefficient allocation of economic resources and problems related to exports, which have worked to exacerbate funding problems (Noland & Pack, 2002). Also, in some East Asian countries, firms and industries that received support fared no better, in terms of productivity growth, than organizations that were not supported (Pack, 2000). Table 3.2 presents some typical arguments for and against industrial policies.

Based on the discussion so far, we can conclude that opinions regarding the utility of industrial policies are divided, although in Rodrik's (2008) view, the theoretical arguments for industrial policy are stronger than those against it. The current industrial policy literature proposes three theoretical arguments for application of industrial policy: the interdependence among economic sectors; the accumulation of productive capabilities; and the risk and uncertainty arising from capital markets.

### *Interdependencies Among Economic Sectors*

This first argument is premised on the idea that economic development in a specific sector depends on the level of economic development in other sectors. This notion has its origins in classical economics and early development economics and builds on the idea of demand complementarities

**Table 3.2** Arguments 'pro and against' industrial policy application

| *Arguments 'pro' industrial policy application* | *Arguments 'against' industrial policy application* |
|---|---|
| • Market and coordination failures as well as symmetric information in developing countries justify interventions in markets;<br>• Trade policy, investment climate reforms and providing public goods do not lead to sustained growth because of fundamental market failures;<br>• Most success stories have been based on smart interventions at the industry level;<br>• Selective and sector-specific public interventions make it possible to tackle several investment climate constraints effectively. | • Government intervention leads to increased corruption and state capture;<br>• Governments do not have the necessary information and capacity to pick winners (sectors who have already have pace or emerging comparative advantages);<br>• Industrial policy distracts from key investment climate and trade policy reforms;<br>• If public support is carried out, government support should be limited to non-selective policies (horizontal policies) such as providing public goods (infrastructure, education, R&D);<br>• Little empirical evidence of working industrial policy. |

Source: Adapted from Benhassine and Raballand (2009)

and increasing returns (to scale) in manufacturing industries (Andreoni & Scazzieri, 2014). This argument exploits Rosenstein-Rodan's (1961) 'big push' and Nurkse's (1959) 'balanced growth' theories, which propose that economic growth is a function of coordinated investment in complementary or interdependent business activities. Subscribers to these theories believe that return on investment is positively related to well-coordinated business investments.

Proponents of big push theory suggest that industry activities generate large economic externalities and require massive investment to enable development of several sectors simultaneously. Similarly, balanced growth theory suggests that economic growth in underdeveloped countries also requires simultaneous investment in a number of industries. Building on these theories, Hirschman (1981) proposed the idea of linkages between industries and suggested that governments should use industrial policies to promote interdependent industries. Interdependent industries include providers of inputs (forward linkages) and consumers (backward linkages), through what Hirschman considers a (upward and downward) chain effect.

Some point to the interdependence among competing business activities. For example, in an oligopolistic industry structure, characterized by irregular investment, simultaneous investment by several competing firms can result in large production capacity increases for some firms, but bankruptcy for others. In other words, if the machinery and skills involved are specialized (which is generally the case in modern industries) and difficult to redeploy, the funding might be wasted. To reduce this risk, some countries, such as Japan and South Korea, have imposed entry restrictions and introduced government-sanctioned investment cartels to ensure that investment occurs at appropriate intervals (Chang, 1994).

Excess investment can lead to overproduction, but temporary disinvestment or structural changes in a specific industrial sector can also cause problems. In some cases, recessionary cartels and negotiated exit mechanisms have been employed to handle periods of economic crisis or promote structural transformation (Dore, 1986). Some governments have implemented protective industrial policies, aimed at supporting specific industrial firms financially and providing them with temporary protection against market forces (Chang, 2003). In general, support for declining sectors can be seen as an attempt to mitigate the risk of bankruptcy for particular firms and promote structural change to increase firm productivity.

The second argument for industrial policies suggests that industrial policies should be aimed at supporting only those firms that invest less and underproduce, through provision of financial and other support for basic R&D and workforce training. The risk, in this case, is that competing firms will reap the benefits and will profit from imitation (Hausmann & Rodrik, 2003; Chang & Andreoni, 2016).

### *Accumulating Productive Capabilities*

Work on the accumulation of productive capabilities to increase competitiveness shows that the time and financial reserves needed vary across industries (Chang, 1994; Andreoni, 2014). Production capabilities comprise individual and collective workforce skills, including the production experience and business knowledge, management practices, etc., embedded in the organization.

In the case of new manufacturing firms, the development of production capabilities is crucial for survival but requires investment of time and money and is a difficult and uncertain process. Governments should implement low tariffs and subsidies for the purchase of digital machinery, R&D, workforce training, etc., alongside policies aimed at attracting foreign investment. Foreign investment is particularly important in the case of developing economies, whose producers may be finding it difficult to catch up with foreign producers.

Governments should implement policies aimed, specifically, at small manufacturing firms and, especially, measures to support the accumulation of skills and machinery. Public universities and private training organizations should provide workforce training, subsidized by government grants. Small producers working as a cooperative could also be granted tax advantages and subsidies for joint activities among firms to enable marketing and export activities, for example.

### *Risk and Uncertainty*

Manufacturing firms are required to manage the risk and uncertainty related to capital markets (Warwick, 2013; Chang & Andreoni, 2016).

Some argue that government is the only actor with the resources required to manage capital market risks. The governments of many developed countries (e.g., the UK and the case of Airbus) have been forced to intervene in the capital market. However, such interventions may not be possible in developing economies. In industries that depend on the most demanding technologies, the risk is incalculable and, thus, analogous situations can turn into great uncertainty. One solution to this problem is the creation of state-owned enterprises to save national strategic industries (Andreoni, 2016); examples include POSCO the South Korean steel producer and the Brazilian aircraft manufacturer EMBRAER. In both these cases, government intervened in the capital market by buying shares to save the at-risk companies from bankruptcy.

In other cases, industrial policies have been implemented to achieve firm or industry restructuring. For instance, in the 1980s, the Japanese government intervened to achieve a restructuring of the shipbuilding industry and US government intervention supported the automobile industry following the 2008 financial crisis. The purchase by government of company shares often results in the government having majority control of the company involved; however, other measures, such as the provision of loan guarantees, public subsidies for severance payments and transitional subsidies, have also been used to support particular firms and sectors.

Structural changes apply, also, to measures related to worker welfare. In the Scandinavian countries, for example, their governments introduced unemployment insurance, employment support, subsidized retraining for unemployed individuals and support for workers who need to physically move their place residence in order to take up a new job. Most workers are unable to support these expenses themselves. Government can also offer preferential rates of interest for loans related to moving house to take up employment (Chang, 1994). Of course, these types of measures cannot be part of industrial policy, but governments can certainly promote the development of its industries through 'soft' structural changes.

## 3.4 The Impact of the Manufacturing Sector on the Economy

Traditionally, industrial policies have been aimed at the manufacturing sector, for several reasons. Some of these were discussed in Chap. 1. Here, we focus on the practical arguments, such as the effect of manufacturing sector development on national economic development.

The economic literature sees the manufacturing sector as the driver of economic productivity and the modern economy (Andreoni & Chang, 2016). In order to remain competitive in the market, manufacturing companies—to a greater extent than companies in other sectors—need to use the latest production technologies, whereas in agriculture or services, for example, this is less important. This is the main reason why, throughout history, the productive sector has been considered the driver of productivity growth (Stiglitz, 2017).

Also, several authors (see, e.g., Chang et al., 2016; Andreoni & Gregory, 2013, etc.) argue that it is the manufacturing—and especially the capital goods—sector that can be considered the learning centre of capitalism. For instance, it enables production of inputs, primarily machinery, which facilitate productivity growth in other economic sectors (agricultural sector growth is heavily dependent on the production of new machinery). New technologies in the field of transport, computing, mechanized warehousing, etc. have enabled productivity growth in services. The application of these devices has particularly influenced the significant increase in the efficiency of logistics applied to the business activities of services enterprises.

Another reason for the importance of the manufacturing sector for national economic development is innovation related to the organization of work. New ways of organizing work tend to originate in the manufacturing sector and spread to other economic sectors (Andreoni & Scazzieri, 2014). For example, changes to work practices in agriculture stem from manufacturing sector innovations (e.g., computerized control of food) (Andreoni & Chang, 2016).

Increased productivity in the manufacturing sector has an influence on productivity in other economically significant sectors (Pisano & Shih, 2012). For example, increased efficiency and effectiveness of work in finance sector, transport and some services companies are the result of increased demand from manufacturing companies. This increased efficiency depends, also, on interactions between providers and customers (Berger, 2013).

Finally, manufactured products tend to be physical and non-perishable goods, which increases their marketability compared to sectors such as agriculture and services (Andreoni & Chang, 2016) where, generally, the service provider and the customer need to be in the same physical space at the same time. For example, hairdressing services require face-to-face contact. An increase in the service sector means, also, that, in order to pay for imports, exports of manufactured goods need to increase (Andreoni & Chang, 2016).

## 3.5 Industrial Policy and Finance

Availability of finance is a vital part of the industrial policy framework. Finance and availability of financial institutions and long-term financing schemes play a significant role in the industrialization process and depend on a range of financial institutions and financial models. Industrial policies in Germany and Japan are based on strong networks of savings banks, credit cooperatives and development banks, operating according to corporate governance regulations and allowing for a long-term perspective.

The German Development Bank (Kreditanstalt für Wiederaufbau—KfW), founded in 1947, played a central role in Germany's industrialization. It was a powerful instrument in post-war reconstruction and implementation of government industrial policies following reconstruction (Naqvi et al., 2018). KfW is owned and financed by the federal government and, since its creation, has offered loans on preferential terms mainly to private agents operating in the manufacturing sector (Mazzucato & Penna, 2016). One of the bank's objectives was to subsidize the local industrial sector through direct loans and provide financial support for competitive German companies' exporting and investment activities. Since 1990, it has subsidized and financed renewable energy industry firms; an estimated 80% of investments in wind power plants and 40% of total renewable energy development. In 2014, three (Nordex, Siemens and Enercon) of the top ten wind turbine manufacturers were German companies, with a combined world market share of 21.5% (Naqvi et al., 2018). KfW's contribution to these economic achievements has been substantial.

The manufacturing industry in Japan is supported by the Japan Development Bank, the Industrial Bank of Japan and the Long-Term Loan Bank of Japan. All of these institutions offer both long-term capital and management consultancy to small firms.

In the US, support for industry tends to take the form of R&D grants, delayed tax payments and tax exemptions. The Small Business Administration, Small Business Investment Company, Small Business Innovation Research programme and the Small Business Technology Transfer programme are particularly successful in supporting small businesses. Over time, the operations and financial capacity of the Small Business Innovation Research programme have extended; its funding has been found to be more effective than tax measures for incentivizing private investment (Mazzucato, 2013; Andreoni, 2016).

## 3.6 Industrial Policies in Emerging Economies

As discussed above, historically, industrial policies have been seen as important tools to promote economic development. Economies in Western Europe, North America and East Asia that once were predominantly agrarian have been transformed into modern and advanced economies, based on government interventions to help individuals and firms overcome coordination and externality problems (Lin, 2017). High-income developed countries continue to design industrial policies aimed at supporting strategically important producers. However, as the economist Justin Lin (2017, p. 4) points out, despite some policies aimed at business, in most developing countries, industrial policies have failed.

After World War II, many ex-socialist and developing countries invested efforts in the building of capital-intensive industries similar to those in the advanced economies (Lin, 2011). These developments tended to be based on a comparative advantage strategy or a comparative advantage defying strategy, in line with the structuralist thinking that dominated economic development thinking during the 1950s and 1960s. The idea behind the comparative advantage defying strategy was that firms should be encouraged to ignore existing economic comparative advantages in their industry/technology entry/choice (Lin 2003, 2009). The governments that favoured this strategy protected those economic enterprises that they considered to be of fundamental importance to their particular country's economic development. These measures included enabling monopolistic market positioning, provision of preferential loans, overvaluation of the local currency and, in some cases, controlling the prices of raw materials. The ultimate goal was to reduce the costs of investment and increase the operational efficiency of enterprises.

According to Lin (2017), government interventions, in the form of industrial policies, have not always been successful and, in some cases, have had negative effects on funding, foreign exchange and availability of raw materials. Some developing and former socialist countries have achieved competitiveness in some sectors, although these efforts have often resulted in less efficient distribution of economic resources, reduced employment incentives, more unequal income distribution, etc.

Despite the failure in many developing countries of industrial policies to promote the economic growth, governments continue to rely on these mechanisms. In some cases, they have reduced the gap between developing and developed or industrialized countries and enabled catch-up. For instance, in the 1950s, Japan experienced around 10% annual growth, through the changes made to the agriculture sector and the creation of sectors related to agriculture. Similar developments occurred in the 1980s in South Korea, Taiwan, Singapore and China.

Since the 1990s, economic growth in China, India and Brazil has increased the importance of these economies (World Bank, 2011) and reduced their levels of poverty. The number of people living in extreme poverty (on $1.25 a day) across the world reduced from 52% in 1981 to 26% in 2005 and in China numbers reduced from 84% in the 1980s to 16% in 2000 (World Bank, 2011). A Growth Commission (2008) report underlines that, although growth factors differ, effective implementation of industrial policy is probably paramount.

Since the 2008 financial crisis, several developed economies, including especially the US and Germany, have recognized the value of industrial policies (Mazzucato, 2013). Also, the development achieved by the Chinese economic model has demonstrated to many developing countries, which, in the 1980s and 1990s, virtually abandoned industrial policies, that such measures are required for economic improvements (Andreoni, 2016). This applies, in particular, to some middle-income countries in Asia and Latin America, which are now recognizing that well-designed and well-implemented industrial policies are effective for escaping the middle-income economy trap (Felipe et al., 2014; Noman & Stiglitz, 2016). In addition, some Gulf region countries consider industrial policy as the most appropriate tool to achieve economic diversification (Cherif & Hasanov, 2014), while several African countries see industrial policy as the means to alleviate or eliminate poverty in their societies (Noman & Stiglitz, 2015; Chang et al., 2016; Kanbur et al., 2019).

## 3.7 A Brief Overview of the Concept of Industrial Policy

There is a lack of agreement on the definition of industrial policy (Chang, 1994: Stiglitz & Lin, 2014; Warwick, 2013; Andreoni, 2016), with different authors proposing different interpretations. Most of the definitions in the industrial policy literature refer to government actions to support industrial development, especially in the manufacturing sector. These actions are linked to a range of areas, such as infrastructure, technology, education, innovation, taxes, etc. (Andreoni, 2016; Noman & Stiglitz, 2016). In what follows, we present some of the most frequent definitions in the industrial policy literature.

In their analysis of European industrial policies, Foreman-Peck and Federico (1999, p. 3) define them as 'any form of state intervention that affects industry as a separate part of the economy'. Chang (1994, p. 66) defines industrial policy as government measures 'targeting particular industries (and their constituent firms) to achieve outcomes perceived by the state as efficient for the economy as a whole', whereas Soete (2007), for instance, proposes a more precise definition. Soete (2007, p. 273) considers industrial policy as reflecting government's strategic objectives and defines it as a set of 'structural policies designed to strengthen the efficiency, scale and international competitiveness of domestic industrial sectors, usually containing an element of national champions, self-reliant to bring about growth and development'.

Others argue that industrial policies are designed and implemented mainly to promote the manufacturing sector and manufacturing firms (Chang, 2002; Reinert, 2007; Cimoli et al., 2009; Noman & Stiglitz, 2016; Best, 2018; Andreoni & Lazonick, 2020). To understand which industrial policies are likely to be effective requires an understanding of the production system and the feasible policy alternatives (Marengo & Scazzieri, 2014). In what follows, we discuss the theoretical and practical justifications for industrial policies.

The most comprehensive definition of industrial policy was proposed by Warwick (2013, pp. 16–17), who defines it as 'any type of government intervention that tends to improve the business environment or change the structure of economic activity towards sectors…which are expected to offer better prospects for economic growth and social welfare than would occur in the absence of such intervention'. Table 3.3 presents some definitions and their sources.

The industrial policy literature also emphasizes policy content, in terms of whether it is more general (horizontal) or is specific (vertical). Most discussion of industrial policies refers to horizontal, vertical or selective policies. While the first refers to policies with a broad dimension, vertical and selective policies are more specific and aimed at improving business performance in a specific sector or among a specific set of firms. However, all sectors and firms require a good transport infrastructure and measures aimed at infrastructure improvements will benefit all firms. Both horizontal and vertical policies are aimed at improving firm productivity. Individual firm performance has a major impact on the national economic competitiveness and participation in the global market. Since manufacturing production is more tradable internationally and growth in manufacturing tends to be at higher rates than in other sectors, most industrial policies are aimed at supporting manufacturing. Table 3.4 presents some typical horizontal and vertical policies.

Table 3.4 shows that the policy instruments used by governments vary considerably. Horizontal measures may be aimed at improving the overall business environment, whereas vertical measures may be aimed at improving the conditions for doing business in a particular sector, perhaps through targeted subsidies. These measures and instruments are discussed in the development literature and reflect a particular industrial policy rationale (Warwick, 2013).

**Table 3.3** Concepts of industrial policy

| |
|---|
| Industrial policies are concerned with promoting industrial growth and efficiency. (OECD, 1975) |
| Industrial policy may be generally defined as any government measure, or set of measures, to promote or prevent structural change. (Curzon-Price, 1981) |
| ...the term industrial policy indicates the relationship between business and government on a microeconomic level... (Wachter & Wachter, 1981) |
| ...everything which is useful to improve growth and competitive performance. (Adams & Klein, 1983) |
| Industrial policy...means government policy aimed at or motivated by problems within specific sectors. (Tyson & Zysman, 1983) |
| Industrial policy means the initiation and co-ordination of governmental initiatives to leverage upward the productivity and competitiveness of the whole economy and of particular industries in it. (Johnson, 1984) |
| Industrial policies refer to those policies intended to affect in some ways manufacturing or service industries. (Graham, 1986) |
| ...a wide-ranging, ill-assorted collection of micro-based supply initiatives which are designed to improve market performance in a variety of occasionally mutually inconsistent ways. (Geroski, 1989) |
| Industrial policy is an attempt by a government to encourage resources to move into particular sectors that the government views as important to future economic growth. (Krugman & Obstfeld, 2009) |
| Industrial policy is one 'aimed at particular industries (and firms as their components) to achieve the outcomes that are perceived by the state to be efficient for the economy as a whole'. (Chang, 1994) |
| Industrial policy 'can be defined as any policy affecting the allocation of resources to industry and in this sense embraces both macroeconomic policy...as well as the more traditional areas of microeconomic policy'. (Sharp, 1998) |
| Industrial policy is 'every form of state intervention that affects industry as a distinct part of the economy'. (Foreman-Peck & Federico, 1999) |
| Narrow view: 'Restrict attention to policies that target particular firms and industrial sectors'.<br>Broad view: any policy that shapes or influences the competitiveness of a country's firms and industries. (Beath, 2002) |
| ...restructuring policies in favour of more dynamic activities generally, regardless of whether those are located within industry or manufacturing per se. (Rodrik, 2004) |
| Industrial policy is 'the activity which creates a favourable environment for European business in general, the manufacturing sector and its industries in specific'. (Aiginger & Sieber, 2005) |
| Industrial policy refers to a set of measures taken by a government and aiming at influencing a country's performance towards a desired objective. (Pitelis, 2006) |

Source: Adapted from Aiginger (2007) and White (2008)

**Table 3.4** A typology of industrial policy instruments by policy domain

| *Domain* | *Horizontal policies* | *Selective policies* |
|---|---|---|
| Product markets | Competition and anti-trust<br>Indirect tax<br>Product market regulation<br>Exchange rate policy | National Champions<br>Nationalization/privatization<br>Output subsidies/state aids<br>Export promotion<br>Price regulation (e.g., pharma)<br>Public procurement<br>Trade policy<br>Car scrappage |
| Labour and skills | Skills and education policies<br>Training subsidies<br>Wage subsidies<br>Income and employment tax<br>Management advisory services<br>Labour market regulation | Targeted skills policies<br>Apprenticeship policies<br>Sector-specific advisory services |
| Capital markets | Loan guarantees<br>Corporate tax/capital allowances<br>Macro/financial stability<br>Financial market regulation | Strategic Investment Fund<br>Emergency Loans<br>State Investment Bank<br>Inward investment promotion |
| Land | Planning regulation<br>Land use planning | Enterprise zones<br>Place-based clusters policy<br>Infrastructure |
| Technology | R&D tax credit<br>Science Budget<br>IPR regime | Green technology<br>Lead Markets<br>Public procurement for innovation<br>Patent Box<br>Selective technology funding<br>Centres of expertise |
| Systems/Institutions | Entrepreneurship policy<br>Scenario planning<br>Distribution of information<br>Overall competitiveness strategy | Indicative planning<br>Foresight initiatives<br>Identifying strategic sectors<br>Sectoral competitiveness strategy<br>Cluster policy |

Source: Adapted from Warwick (2013)

Table 3.4 shows, also, that government policies can provide direct or indirect support for specific sectors and firms. For example, horizontal product market policies might be aimed at promoting competition among firms, refining product market regulation or influencing prices via imposition of indirect taxes and exchange rates. On the other hand, selective policies can be aimed at promoting competition in specific markets or changing prices through indirect tax changes. Selective policies might be employed to promote the export of a specific product. In the case of capital markets, horizontal policies could take the form of credit guarantees for SMEs, capital allowances and general corporate taxation, and macroeconomic and financial stability measures including capital market regulations. Vertical or selective policies could be related to the types of loans available from a state investment bank or a strategic investment fund, promotion of domestic investment through awareness raising, tax relief, subsidies, etc.

Economic development is related to workers' skills and abilities, which, in turn, are related to the national education system. Vertical government policies can provide grants for workforce training, internships, etc. Horizontal policies provide support for entrepreneurship, information flows, strategizing, establishment of systems and institutions to facilitate communication between government and the business community to allow the identification of areas where industrial policies are likely to be the most effective, etc. Selective policies could include indicative planning, identification of sectors that might have strategic importance for the country's economy, etc. Policies related to the use of land are very important. In this area, policy measures might be related to regulation and plans related to designation of industrial zones, infrastructure improvements, etc.

## 3.8 Conclusions

The focus in this chapter was on the historical development of industrial policy thinking and contemporary industrial policy. Since the emergence of industrial policies at the end of the eighteenth century, interest in them has increased continuously. Industrial policy developments cover three phases: 1940s–1960s; 1970s–1990s; 2000 to the present. Contemporary interest in industrial policy is the result, in particular, of shocks (e.g., COVID-19), climate change, international trade tensions, digital transformation, etc.

We discussed the role and importance of industrial policy for national economic development. The arguments provide a strong case for use of industrial policy. Current debate on the role of industrial policy tends to focus more on its implementation and less on whether it should be a government responsibility.

There is still no consensus on the definition of industrial policy; most definitions in the literature refer to horizontal or vertical interventions.

The review in this chapter suggests that industrialization, promotion of the manufacturing sector, innovation activity and a supporting infrastructure are required for economic development. Many countries once considered agrarian economies have industrialized based on industrial policies to promote sustainable economic development.

Our review highlights the importance of financial resources alongside industrial policies. Industrialization and economic growth require financial systems to support national innovation and export capacity in the manufacturing sector. Industrial policies should be accompanied by financial programmes to reduce risk and uncertainty and support the development of new markets. Traditionally, institutional financial support has been aimed at allowing manufacturing firms time to learn how to produce, that is, to develop and accumulate production capabilities. Modern industrial policies are aimed at increasing national innovation system capacity.

This chapter demonstrates the essential role of industrial policies in the industrialization and economic growth processes. Evidence derived from recent theoretical and practical industrial policy developments suggests theoretical and practical justifications for the implementation of industrial policies. The arguments against industrial policies include the considerable practical difficulties related to their implementation, risks of corruption and rent seeking, possible use of industrial policies for protectionist purposes, the drafting of industrial policies for political speculative purposes, etc. These issues need to be addressed. Arguments for industrial policies are more numerous and better grounded. However, industrial policy success depends largely on economic sector prioritization. It is also related directly to how well and successfully the policies are implemented in practice and the creation of adequate monitoring and evaluation systems. Several studies highlight the need for more systematic industrial policy evaluation and, especially, in a developing economy context.

## References

Adams, F. G., & Klein, L. R. (1983). *Industrial policies for growth and competitiveness*. Lexington Books.

Aiginger, K. (2007). Industrial policy: A dying breed or a re-emerging phoenix? *Journal of Industry Competition and Trade, 7*, 297–323.

Aiginger, K., & Sieber, S. (2005). *Towards a renewed industrial policy in Europe, Background Report of the Competitiveness of European Manufacturing, Prepared as Chapter 1 for the Background Report of the Competitiveness of European Manufacturing*. European Commission, DG Enterprise.

Amsden, A. (1989). *Asia's next giant: South Korea's late industrialization*. Oxford University Press.

Andreoni, A. (2011) Manufacturing Agrarian change: Agricultural production, inter-sectoral learning and technological capabilities, DRUID Working paper series No. 11/2013.

Andreoni, A. (2014). Structural learning: embedding discoveries and the dynamics of production. *Structural Change and Economic Dynamics, 29*, 58–74.

Andreoni, A. (2016). Varieties of industrial policy: Models, packages and transformation cycles. In A. Noman & J. Stiglitz (Eds.), *Efficiency, finance and varieties of industrial policy* (pp. 245–305). Columbia University Press.

Andreoni, A., & Chang, H. J. (2016). Industrial policy and the future of manufacturing. *Economia e Politica Industriale, 43*(4), 491–502.

Andreoni, A., & Gregory, M. (2013). Why and how does manufacturing still matter: Old rationales, new realities. *Revue d'Economie Industrielle, 144*(4), 17–54.

Andreoni, A., & Lazonick, W. (2020). Local ecosystems and social conditions of innovative enterprise. In J. Lin & A. Oqubay (Eds.), *The Oxford handbook of industrial hubs and economic development*. Oxford University Press.

Andreoni, A., & Scazzieri, R. (2014). Triggers of change: Structural trajectories and production dynamics. *Cambridge Journal of Economics, 38*(6), 1391–1408.

Baldwin, R. (1969). The case against infant industry protection. *Journal of Political Economy, 77*(3), 295–305.

Beath, J. (2002). UK industrial policy: Old tunes on new instruments? *Oxford Review of Economic Policy, 18*(2), 221–239.

Benhassine, N., & Raballand, G. (2009). Beyond ideological cleavages: A unifying framework for industrial policies and other public interventions. *Economic Systems, 16*, 293–309, Elsevier, ScienceDirect.

Berger, S. (2013). *Making in America*. MIT Press.

Best, M. (2018). *How growth really happens. The making of economic miracles through production, governance, and skills*. Princeton University Press.

Chang, H. J. (1994). *The political economy of industrial policy*. Macmillan.

Chang, H. J. (2002). *Kicking away the ladder—Development strategy in historical perspective*. Anthem Press.
Chang H. J. (2003). Kicking away the ladder: Infant industry promotion in historical perspective. *Oxford Development Studies, 31*(1), 21, Academic Search Complete, EBSCOhost.
Chang, H. J. (2007). Policy space in historical perspective—With special reference to trade and industrial policies. In A. Deshpande (Ed.), *Globalization and development—A handbook of new perspectives*. Oxford University Press.
Chang, H. J., & Andreoni, A. (2020). Industrial policy in the 21st century. *Development and Change, 51*(2), 324–351.
Chang, H. J., Hauge, J., & Irfan, M. (2016). *Transformative industrial policy for Africa*. United Nations Economic Commission for Africa.
Cherif, R., & Hasanov, F. (2014). Soaring of the gulf falcons: Diversification in the GCC oil exporters in seven propositions, IMF Working Papers 2014/177, International Monetary Fund.
Cimoli, M., Dosi, G., & Stiglitz, J. (2009). *The political economy of capabilities accumulation: The past and future of policies for industrial development*. Oxford University Press.
Criscuolo, C., Gonnei, N., Kitazawai, K., & Lalanneiet, G. (2022). Are industrial policy instruments effective?: A review of the evidence in OECD countries, OECD Science, Technology and Industry Policy Papers, No. 128, OECD Publishing, Paris. https://doi.org/10.1787/57b3dae2-en.
Curzon-Price, V. (1981). *Industrial policies in the European community*. Macmillan.
Dore, R. (1986). *Flexible rigidities: Industrial policy and structural adjustment in the Japanese economy 1970–80*. The Athlone Press.
Felipe, J., Kumar, U., & Galope, R. (2014). Middle-income transitions: Trap or myth? *ADB Economics Working Paper Series*, No. 421.
Ferleger, L., & Lazonick, W. (1993). The managerial revolution and the developmental state: The case of US agriculture. *Business and Economic History, 22*(2), 67–98.
Foreman-Peck, J., & Federico, G. (1999). *European industrial policy: The twentieth century experience*. Oxford University Press.
Geroski, P. A. (1989). European industrial policy and industrial policy in Europe. *Oxford Review of Economic Policy, 5*, 20–36.
Gerschenkron, A. (1962). *Economic backwardness in historical perspective*. Harvard University Press.
Graham, H. (1986). *European industrial policy*. Croom Helm.
Greenwald, B., & Stiglitz, J. E. (2014a). Industrial policies, the creation of a learning society, and economic development. In J. E. Stiglitz, J. Y. Lin, & E. Patel (Eds.), *The industrial policy revolution, vol. 1: The role of government beyond ideology*. Palgrave Macmillan.

Greenwald, B., & Stiglitz, J. E. (2014b). Learning and industrial policy: Implications for Africa. In J. E. Stiglitz, J. Y. Lin, & E. Patel (Eds.), *The industrial policy revolution, vol. 2: Africa in the 21st century*. Palgrave Macmillan.

Growth Commission. (2008). The growth report: Strategies for sustained growth and inclusive development. Washington, DC.

Hausmann, R., & Rodrik, D. (2003). Economic development as self discovery. *Journal of Development Economics, 72*(2), 603–633.

Hirschman, A. O. (1981). A generalized linkage approach to development, with special reference to staples. In *Essays in trespassing: Economics to politics and beyond* (pp. 59–97). Cambridge University Press.

Johnson, C. (1984). The idea of industrial policy. In C. Johnson (Ed.), *The industrial policy debate*. Institute for Contemporary Studies.

Juhász, R., Lane, N. J., & Rodrik, D. (2023). The new economics of industrial policy. National Bureau of Economic Research. http://www.nber.org/papers/w31538.pdf

Kanbur, R., Noman, A., & Stiglitz, J. (2019). *Quality of growth in Africa*. Columbia University Press.

Krueger, A. O. (1974). The political economy of the rent-seeking society. *American Economic Review, 64*(3), 291, Business Source Complete, EBSCOhost.

Krueger, A. O. (1990). Government failures in development. *Journal of Economic Perspectives, 4*(3), 9–23, Business Source Complete, EBSCOhost.

Krugman, P., & Obstfeld, M. (2009). *International economics: Theory and policy* (7th ed.). Pearson-Addison Wesley.

Lall, S. (2004). Reinventing industrial strategy: The role of government policy in building industrial competitiveness, G-24 discussion papers 28, UNCTAD, Geneva.

Lin, J. Y. (2003). Development strategy, viability and economic convergence. *Economic Development and Cultural Change, 53*, 277–308.

Lin, J. Y. (2009). *Economic development and transition*. Cambridge University Press.

Lin, J. Y. (2011). New structural economics: A framework for rethinking development. *The World Bank Economic Research Observer, 26*(2), 193–221.

Lin, J. Y. (2017). Industrial policy revisited: A new structural economics perspective. In A. Noman & J. E. Stiglitz (Eds.), *Efficiency, finance, and varieties of industrial policy: Guiding resources, learning, and technology for sustained growth* (pp. 225–244). Columbia University Press. http://www.jstor.org/stable/10.7312/noma18050.10

Marengo, L., & Scazzieri, R. (2014). Embedding production, special issue. *Structural Change and Economic Dynamics, 29*, 1–88.

Mazzucato, M. (2013). *The entrepreneurial state: Debunking public vs. private sector myths*. Anthem Press.

Mazzucato, M. (2018). Mission-oriented innovation policies: Challenges and opportunities. *Industrial and Corporate Change, 27*(5), 803–815.

Mazzucato, M., & Penna, C. (2016). Beyond market failures: The market creating and shaping roles of state investment banks. *Journal of Economic Policy Reforms, 19*(4), 305–326.

Myrdal, G. (1957). *Economic theory and under-developed regions.* London.

Naqvi, N., Henow, A., & Chang, H.-J. (2018). Kicking away the financial ladder? German development banking under economic globalisation. *Review of International Political Economy, 25*(5), 672–698.

Naudé, W. (2010). Industrial policy: Old and new issues, Working Paper No. 2010/106, United Nations University, World Institute for Development Economics Research, September 2010.

Nelson, R. R. (1993). *National innovation systems. A comparative analysis.* Oxford University Press.

Nogues, J. (1990). The experience of Latin America with export subsidies. *Weltwirtschaftliches Archiv, 126*(1), 97–115.

Noland, M., & Pack, H. (2002). *Industrial policies and growth: Lessons from international experience. Working Paper 169.* Central Bank of Chile.

Noman, A., & Stiglitz, J. (2015). *Industrial policy and economic transformation in Africa.* Columbia University Press.

Noman, A., & Stiglitz, J. (2016). *Efficiency, finance and varieties of industrial policy.* Columbia University Press.

Nurkse, R. (1959). Notes on unbalanced growth. *Oxford Economic Papers N.S., 11*(3), 295–297.

OECD. (1975). *Objectives and instruments of industrial policy: A comparative study.* OECD.

Ohno, K. (2013). *Learning to industrialize. From given growth to policy-aided value creation.* Routledge.

Pack H. (1993). Productivity and industrial development in sub-saharan Africa. *World Development, 21*(1), 1–16, Elsevier, ScienceDirect.

Pack, H. (2000). Industrial policy: Growth elixir or poison? *World Bank Research Observer, 15*(1), 47–67. Washington, DC: World Bank.

Pisano, G. P., & Shih, W. C. (2012). *Producing prosperity. Why America needs a manufacturing renaissance.* Harvard Business Review Press.

Pitelis, C. N. (2006). Industrial policy: Perspectives, experience, issues. In P. Bianchi & S. Labory (Eds.), *International handbook on industrial policy.* Edward Elgar.

Prebisch, R. (1959). Commercial policy in the underdeveloped countries. *American Economic Review, 49*(2), 251, Business Source Complete, EBSCOhost.

Reinert, E. S. (2007). *How rich countries got rich—and why poor countries stay poor.* Carroll & Graf.

Robinson, J. (2009). Industrial policy and development: A political economy perspective. [Online] Available at: http://scholar.harvard.edu/files/jr_wb_industry_policy20-20Robinson_0.pdf

Rodrik, D. (1996). Coordination failures and government policy: A model with applications to East Asia and Eastern Europe. *Journal of International Economics, 40*(1), 1–22.

Rodrik, D. (2004). Industrial policy for the twenty-first century. KSG Faculty Research Working Paper RWP04–047. Kennedy School of Government, Harvard University.

Rodrik, D. (2008). Normalizing industrial policy. Commission on Growth and Development Working Paper; No. 3. World Bank, Washington, DC. © World Bank. https://openknowledge.worldbank.org/handle/10986/28009 License: CC BY 3.0 IGO

Rosenstein-Rodan, P. N. (1961). Notes on the theory of the big push, in Ellis, editor, Economic Development for Latin America.

Rowden, R. (2011, January 10). Poverty reduction is not development, The UK Guardian Global Development/Poverty Matters Blog.

Schumpeter, J. A. (1939). *Business cycles: A theoretical, historical, and statistical analysis of the capitalist process.* McGraw-Hill.

Sharp, M. (1998). What is industrial policy and why is it necessary? paper prepared for TSER project on Science, Technology and Broad Industrial Policy, May 1998.

Soete, L. (2007). From industrial to innovation policy. *Journal of Industry, Competition and Trade, 7*, 273–284.

Stiglitz, J. E. (1999). More instruments and broader goals: Moving toward the post-Washington consensus. In G. Kochendorfer-Lucius & B. Pleskovic (Eds.), *Development issues in the 21st century.* German Foundation for International Development.

Stiglitz, J. E. (2017). Industrial policy, learning and development. In J. Page & F. Tarp (Eds.), *The practice of industrial policy: Government-business coordination in Africa and East Asia* (WIDER studies in development economics). Oxford University Press.

Stiglitz, J. E., & Lin, J. Y. (2014). *The industrial policy revolution, vol. 1: The role of government beyond ideology.* Palgrave Macmillan.

Stiglitz, J. E., Lin, J. Y., & Patel, E. (2014). *The industrial policy revolution, vol. 2: Africa in the 21st century.* Palgrave Macmillan.

Tyson, L., & Zysman, J. (Eds.). (1983). *American industry in international competition: Government policies and corporate strategies.* Cornell University Press.

Wachter, M. L., & Wachter, S. M. (1981). Introduction. In M. L. Wachter & S. M. Wachter (Eds.), *Toward a new industrial policy?* University of Pennsylvania Press.

Warwick, K. (2013). Beyond industrial policy: Emerging issues and new trends, OECD Science, Technology and Industry Policy Papers, No. 2, OECD Publishing, Paris. https://doi.org/10.1787/5k4869clw0xp-en

White, L. J. (2008). Antitrust policy and industrial policy: A view from the US. Paper presented at the Second Lisbon Conference on Competition Law and Economics, Lisbon, Portugal, November 15–16, 2007. Revised January 2008.

World Bank. (2011). *Global development horizons: Multipolarity: The new global economy*. World Bank.

CHAPTER 4

# Industrial Policy Practice in Three Western Balkan Economies and Slovenia

## 4.1 Introduction

Since 2000, the production landscape in the Western Balkan (WB) countries has undergone profound structural change. These structural dynamics have been driven mostly by the systemic changes that occurred in the 1990s, a period marked by dramatic deindustrialization in these economies. Deindustrialization (i.e., loss of strategic manufacturing industries), in parallel with increased trade imbalances and much reduced technological dynamism, has been a major concern for policy makers in the WBs. The model of economic growth based primarily on extraction of natural resources has been questioned and the policymaking focus has shifted to measures aimed specifically at promoting the production sector.

This chapter examines the industrial policies designed and implemented in Albania, North Macedonia and Kosovo. It analyses and contrasts the different industrial policies implemented in these countries with Slovenia's industrial policies, which, historically, have been used as a learning benchmark by the other WB economies.

The three economies examined in this chapter have similar historical and economic specificities. The WB economies have achieved much since the 1990s. The conflicts and national wars that beset this region for so many years have decreased. Economic governance in these countries has become more prudent and there are emerging signs of 'productive



F. Sahiti, *Industrial Policies for Technological Upgrading in Western Balkan Countries*, https://doi.org/10.1007/978-3-031-51429-6_4

entrepreneurship'. These positive changes are reflected in the region's social and economic indicators.

Industrial policy similarities and differences are driven by contextual—institutional and structural—and political economic factors and the different policy spaces and rationales for government action in these countries. Based on the theoretical discussion in Chap. 3, on the role of industrial policy, this chapter reveals and contrasts emerging patterns and trends in industrial policy practices, based on official documentation. These patterns and trends in the three WB countries and Slovenia are reviewed in the context of the different types of their policy instruments, the funds supporting them and their institutional implementation. This chapter focuses, in particular, on the policy packages adopted in different transformation cycles.

Policy instruments can be tailored to provide support to different factors of the national production system, such as technologies, funding and improvements, and to operate at different levels—macroeconomic, entire production sector, sub-sector or specific firm level. The analysis shows that the composition and, especially, the management of industrial packages can be a source of economic advantage and that the success of an industrial policy package depends heavily on the interconnection and interaction among different instruments. This interdependence is determined by several factors including the size of the instrument, its complementarity with other measures and the time horizon or time span of the policy.

Timing is important since, depending on the objective and the specific challenges being addressed, policy measures tend to operate over different time horizons. The industrial policy literature emphasizes that industry policy success depends on how well government is able to manage the policy time frame and how well policy measures are synchronized across subsequent transformation cycles (Chang et al., 2013; Stiglitz, 2017; Andreoni, 2016; Chang & Andreoni, 2020). In some cases, government must guarantee long-term support, whereas in others, government should cancel counterproductive policies. To ensure continuity, it is essential that political groups agree about the policy measures being implemented regardless of which party is in power.

Section 4.2 discusses the importance of industrial policy package alignment and Sect. 4.3 describes the framework applied to examine industrial policy. Sections 4.4, 4.5, 4.6 and 4.7 provide analyses of the industrial policies in the three WB economies and the reference economy, Slovenia. The objective is to identify emerging trends, common themes and industrial policy practices. Section 4.8 concludes the chapter.

## 4.2 The Importance of Industrial Policy Package Alignment

Industry policy success depends largely on the strategic alignment between the policy instruments and institutions. Stiglitz (1996) suggests that, in fact, governance of industrial policy involves governance of a package of industrial policies. To understand industrialization in any country (e.g., Japan, South Korea, Singapore, Taiwan) requires an analysis and appreciation of the whole package of interactive measures. Since industrial policy packages are time specific, the harmonization of measures policies within a coherent policy package is a complex and dynamic process (Stiglitz, 1996). New industrial policies and measures must be integrated with the existing institutions and policies, which highlights the importance of ensuring that new policies will interact positively with the existing policy and institutional framework.

Ha-Joon Chang (2011) points to the importance of combining different policies and shows that even opposing policy instruments can be used strategically to achieve industrial policy objectives. He supports his argument with the example of East Asia and states that in:

> East Asia, free trade, export promotion (which is, of course, not free trade), and infant industry protection were organically integrated, both in cross-sectional terms (so some industries are always subject to each category of policy, sometimes more than one at the same time) and over time (so the same industry may be subject to more than one of the three over time). (Chang, 2011, p. 100)

Andreoni (2016) insists that the harmonization of industrial policies is essential for at least three reasons. First, to achieve policy objectives requires good harmonization and alignment among industrial policies to reduce risk of policy failure. It has been shown that industrial policy failure is related more to inconsistency with existing policies and institutions than to poor policy design (Lee, 2019). Inconsistencies are more likely if policies are copied from other countries with no prior feasibility study.

Second, the complementarity between new policy design and existing policies and institutions matters. For instance, in the case of technology and skills development policies, government should provide funding to allow investment in product and process innovations, technological services related to commercialization and a specialized workforce. These are essential aspects; the absence of a qualified workforce and/or technological services will mean that additional funding will not increase production of the innovation.

Third, industry policy harmonization ensures good coordination among government ministries and agencies involved in formulating policy measures. Poor coordination during policy formulation and implementation is likely to have major negative consequences.

In the comparative analysis in this chapter, we examine industrial policy package alignment in the three WB economies and Slovenia. In Chap. 2, we emphasized some significant differences among these countries that suggest that the industrial policy packages in the three WB economies will differ substantially from those in the reference country, Slovenia. Since we are interested in emerging trends, common themes and industrial policy practices, our analysis focuses on the most recent transformation cycles. In Sect. 4.3, we present our conceptual framework and the policy measures, and the financial funds and government agencies involved (see Fig. 4.1).

## 4.3 Our Conceptual Industrial Policy Framework

National industrial policies vary depending on the context and economic goals, which results in a range of different policy frameworks. In the framework proposed by Klein Woolthuis et al. (2005), rules (i.e., system failures) are contrasted with actors (i.e., missing actors). Dodgson et al. (2011) compare national trajectories, based on market mix and coordination logics, while O'Sullivan et al. (2013) suggest a framework aimed at investigating industrial policies in a selection of Organisation for Economic Cooperation and Development countries. O'Sullivan et al.'s matrix allows for an industrial policy design with different levels of policy intervention and different factor inputs in the national production system. However, in the comparative analysis conducted in this chapter, we use the framework developed by Andreoni (2016).

The policy matrix proposed by Andreoni (2016) is a diagnostic conceptual framework that addresses the problems faced by policy makers in relation to alignment of interoperable policy packages for different industries and economic sectors, their harmonized implementation and their alignment with other policies implemented by different government agents.

This conceptual framework enables the design of policy measures for each country i, where i = 1, 2, ..., n, along two main dimensions: the industrial policy domain, that is, clusters of supply- and demand-side

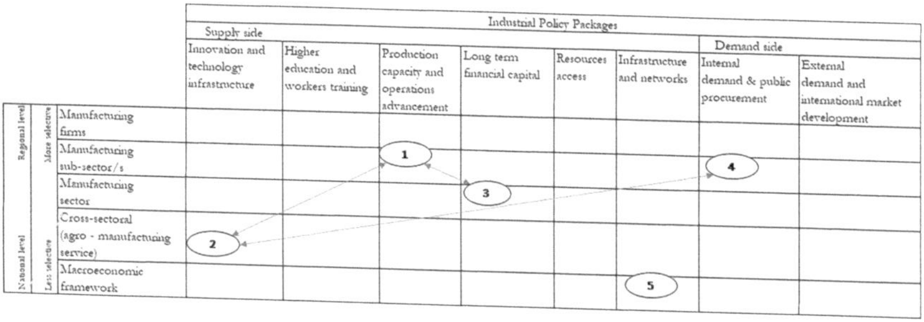


**Fig. 4.1** Policy package matrix and industrial policy measures. Note: Each number (1), (2), (3) … refers to a policy instrument. The matrix depicts five policy instruments used by governments in their industrial policy packages. For example, policy instrument (1) is a supply-side cluster mechanism focused on enhancing production capacity and advanced manufacturing operations in the focal sector. Policy instrument (2) refers to research grants for new software and targets all firms and sectors and supports their innovation and technological efforts. Policy instrument (4) is a demand-side cluster public procurement scheme targeting a specific manufacturing sub-sector and focused on creating internal demand for a specific product. The arrows are the linkages between two policy instruments (1), (2), etc. The direction of the arrow indicates the policy pair and signals their complementarity. The thicker the arrow the stronger the degree of alignment between two complementary policy instruments. Source: Adapted from UNIDO (2020) and Andreoni (2016)

policy instruments; and the level of policy action, that is, degree of policy selectivity. Both these dimensions are time-based or transformation cycle dimensions. Figure 4.1 depicts these dimensions and the issues related to the design of industrial policy.

Note that the design and implementation of industrial policies can be a central or regional/local government responsibility. Governments can design industrial policies based on a core strategy or to respond to different regional and local needs. Core strategies involve top-down policymaking, with national government responsible for policy formulation, implementation and enforcement. Regional and local strategies involve bottom-up policymaking by regional authorities or by national government and regional governments working together.

There are pros and cons to both approaches. For example, although a bottom-up (regional) approach allows for more selective interventions and a degree of flexibility, in countries with weak institutions and poor policymaking capabilities, this model may not be effective (Andreoni, 2016). A decentralized bottom-up approach may also lack coherence; objectives and lines of action may be multi-layered and implementation is likely to be problematic. In a top-down approach, policy objectives and goals are aligned with national plans and strategies but may overlook regional needs and interests. For national policy to be effective, regional specificities and their connection to the broader policy strategy must be taken into account.

The first dimension includes supply-related and demand-related industry policy measures. Supply-related measures include specific input factor policies, such as policies to improve the innovation and technology infrastructure (including pre-commercial procurement), measures to promote higher education and training of workers (education policies) and measures to increase manufacturing capacity (e.g., conditional subsidies and incentives, matching grants, etc.). Supply-related policies also include access to capital for example improved banking and finance regulations, funding for Small and Medium-sized Enterprises (SMEs), development banks, macro interest rate policies, access to resources (energy and technology policies), and infrastructure and network improvements (infrastructure and standardization policies). Demand-side measures include forms of (strategically oriented) public procurement, access to foreign markets and development of new markets.

The second dimension, related to degree of policy selectivity, refers to the fact that some policy measures may target specific manufacturing subsector parameters or specific firms (SMEs) within those sub-sectors. In some cases, policies may be focused on the whole manufacturing sector, for example, measures to promote exports or development of technological platforms and intelligent automation. Some measures and instruments may have cross-cutting objectives, such as those aimed at integration between the agricultural and manufacturing sectors or the linking of manufacturing to the business services sector. Some policies are macroeconomic in scope, such as interest rate or exchange rate interventions. Although macroeconomic policies might appear to be comprehensive rather than selective, they are likely to affect different economic sectors in different ways.

Figure 4.1 shows that the instruments included in industrial packages are linked. For example, measure (1) refers to a grant scheme aimed at auto parts manufacturers and more scale-efficient investment. Measure (1) is linked to measure (2), which is a research grant fund to support cross-sectoral investments in the sensors and software integrated in a range of goods, including cars. Measure (4) is related to government procurement. This measure is aligned with technology policy (2), which means that there is a connection of a component of pre-commercial public procurement that supports emerging technologies. Measure (5) is related to infrastructure measures that appear not to be consistent with other policies (absence of an arrow among these measures). This indicates absence of specific infrastructural measures to increase policy effectiveness.

We analyse national and regional industrial policy approaches at the sub-sector or individual manufacturing firm level, the manufacturing system level and the industry system level. The huge changes that have occurred in the global manufacturing system are requiring industrial policy analyses that focus on specific firms in highly concentrated sectors and macroeconomic policies (Tassey, 2007; Andreoni & Gregory, 2013). We need to identify policy measures appropriate for the overall manufacturing system and individual sectors such as construction, energy and agro-industry.

The policies included in a package may be implemented by different ministries and state agencies, at the national or local level. The findings related to specific industrial policies are provided in Tables 4.1, 4.2, 4.3 and 4.4, which provide information on the funding allocated to policy implementation and the government agency responsible for monitoring implementation. The analysis aims to identify the various measures and their effectiveness in practice as well as the allocated funds and the agencies responsible for the implementation of the policy.

Our choice of conceptual framework is based on three arguments. First, that it provides an understanding of the relationship between two or more policy measures; to be effective, policies must be combined. Effectiveness is measured in the context of other policies and how they are linked in firms, sectors and specific institutions in the production system. This means that policy effectiveness can be changed by the introduction of complementary measures. The literature shows that horizontal measures can have unintended vertical effects (Aiginger & Sieber, 2006; Chang, 2010). Therefore, although the intervention might be at the firm, sector or system level, it might be more or less selective based on its effect on different production sub-sectors or different value chains (Okimoto, 1989, p. 9). The design of policy measures must consider the degree of their complementarity within an overall industry policy package (Andreoni, 2016).

**Table 4.1** Policy measures, model, governance, transformation cycle and budgets in Albania

| *No:* | *Name* | *Transformation cycle* | *Agency/ministry name* | *Budget EUR millions* |
|---|---|---|---|---|
| 1 | Business Development and Investment Strategy | 2021–2027 | Ministry of Economy and Finance, Albanian Investment Development Agency (AIDA) | NA |
| 2 | Smart Specialisation Strategy | 2017–continued | The National Agency for Scientific Research | NA |
| 3 | Albania's Digital Agenda | 2015–2022 | Albanian Investment Development Agency (AIDA) | NA |

Source: Author's elaboration based on Andreoni (2016)

Second, the effect of implementing individual policy measures will differ from the effect of policies implemented in combination, such as policies related to innovation and technology combined with education policies and procurement policies. Changes to the incentive system allow government to change firm behaviour and the distribution of rents, by combining what might appear to be contradictory policies.

Industrial policy measures are designed to address problems at a particular moment in time. This means that they are constructed to respond to that time period and the accompanying level of economic development. Andreoni (2016) proposed the concept of a transformation or T cycle. The T cycle is defined based on the set of policy measures in place at a certain time, which constitute a comprehensive policy package. Over time, government might decide to make changes to these measures, but Andreoni (2016, p. 18) points out that it can be difficult to synchronize policies across cycles. Successful transition from one T cycle to another (i.e., from one coherent policy package to another) will support a continuous process of industrialization.

As already mentioned, policy harmonization is also a dynamic process, which means that to maintain institutional complementarity and policy alignment, both the specific policies and the entire industrial policy package must be updated periodically. Industrial policy success requires some element of experimentation alongside continuous implementation.

**Table 4.2** Policy measures, model, governance, transformation cycle and budgets in North Macedonia

| *No:* | *Name* | *Transformation cycle* | *Agency/ministry name* | *Budget EUR millions* |
|---|---|---|---|---|
| 1 | Macedonian Industrial Policy | 2009–2020 | Ministry of Economy | NA |
| 2 | Revised Macedonian Industrial Policy | 2018–continued | Ministry of Economy | NA |
| 3 | Technological Industrial Development Zones | 2007–continued | Ministry of Economy | NA |
| 4 | SME Strategy | 2018–2023 | Ministry of Economy | NA |
| 5 | Programme for Entrepreneurship Support, Competitiveness, and Innovation of SMEs 2020 | 2020–continued | Agency for Promotion of Entrepreneurship of the Republic of North Macedonia | NA |
| 6 | Innovation Strategy | 2012–2020 | Government of North Macedonia | NA |
| 7 | Strategy for Export Promotion | 2022–continued | Ministry of Economy | NA |
| 8 | Law on Public Procurement | 2019–continued | Government of North Macedonia | NA |
| 9 | Fund for Innovation and Technological Development | 2013–continued | Ministry of Economy | NA |
| 10 | Development Bank of North Macedonia AD Skopje | 1998–continued | Government of North Macedonia | € 100,000,000.00 |
| 11 | The Financial Support of Investments | 2021–continued | Ministry of Economy | 1,000,000 Eur |

Source: Author's elaboration based on Andreoni (2016)

## 4.4 Industrial Policy Package Alignment in Albania

The data suggest that policy makers in Albania are not focused on promoting the manufacturing sector. Chapter 2 shows that the contribution of the manufacturing sector to Gross Domestic Product (GDP) in the WB countries is limited (7%), compared to other sectors and, especially, agriculture (around 20%). However, manufacturing sector potential is good

**Table 4.3** Policy measures, model, governance, transformation cycle and budgets in Kosovo

| *No:* | *Name* | *Transformation cycle* | *Agency/ministry name* | *Budget EUR millions* |
|---|---|---|---|---|
| 1 | Private Sector Development Strategy 2018–2022 | 2018–2022 | Ministry of Industry, Entrepreneurship and Trade | NA |
| 2 | Strategy for Industrial Development and Business Support | 2023–continued | Ministry of Industry, Entrepreneurship and Trade | NA |
| 3 | Digital Empowerment Initiative | 2021–continued | Ministry of Industry, Entrepreneurship and Trade | NA |
| 4 | The Matching Grants Programme | 2021–continued | Ministry of Industry, Entrepreneurship and Trade | € 14.30 |
| 5 | National Strategy for Innovation and Entrepreneurship | 2019–2023 | Ministry of Industry, Entrepreneurship and Trade & Ministry of Education, Science, Technology and Innovation | NA |
| 6 | The Kosovo Credit Guarantee Fund | 2021–continued | Ministry of Economy | NA |

Source: Author's elaboration based on Andreoni (2016)

and, especially, if linked to the potential of the agricultural sector. Albania does not have any government policies directly promoting the agro-industry sector. The largest share of total agricultural production comes from horticulture and livestock. However, there seems to be gap in the alignment of the agriculture sector and the agro-processing industry. Inadequate compliance with international quality and safety standards is particularly evident in the agro-industry sector, especially in markets for higher-value processed goods (see IFC, 2022), but in other sectors, lack of compliance with international quality and safety standards limits the export potential for agro-industrial products.

Foreign investment in the production of vehicle parts in Albania has increased due to the country's relative economic stability, improving investment climate and provision of fiscal incentives. This vehicle parts industry is relatively small (six foreign companies specializing in components such as exhaust systems, rubber parts and wiring) and is part of the European Peripheral Regional Value Chain (IFC, 2022). Although the

**Table 4.4** Policy measures, model, governance, transformation cycle and budgets in Slovenia

| | *Name* | *Transformation cycle* | *Agency/ministry name* | *Budget EUR millions* |
|---|---|---|---|---|
| 1 | Slovenian Industrial Policy | 2014–2020 | Ministry of Economic Development and Technology | NA |
| 2 | Strategy of Smart Specialisation of Slovenia | 2014–2020 | Ministry of Economic Development and Technology | NA |
| 3 | Slovenian Industrial Strategy 2021–2030 | 2021–continued | Ministry of Economic Development and Technology | NA |
| 4 | Recovery and Resilience Plan | 2013–continued | Ministry of Economic Development and Technology | EUR 45 million |
| 5 | Action Plan for Increasing the Competitiveness of the Forest-Wood Chain in Slovenia by 2020 | 2014–continued | Ministry of Economic Development and Technology | NA |
| 6 | Programme for Investment Promotion and Internationalisation of the Slovenian Economy | 2021–continued | Ministry of Economic Development and Technology | NA |
| 7 | SID Bank | | Government of the Republic of Slovenia is the sole shareholder | NA |

Source: Author's elaboration based on Andreoni (2016)

sector contributes only 1% to total exports, its potential is good. However, there are no policies in place to promote this sector. Absence of industrial policy and a strategy to promote investment including a systematic incentive framework is keeping the competitiveness of Albanian manufacturers of automotive parts lower than in other countries in the region, such as in North Macedonia and Serbia (IFC, 2022).

The Albanian economy lacks a specific strategy or policy that would directly promote the production sector. However, Albania's policy makers have tried to address production sector needs in the Government of Albania New Strategy for Business and Investment Development (2021–2027). This document discusses the problems related to changing the economic structure in Albania and emphasizes the need for government measures to increase industry sector exports and productivity. The strategy is aimed, also, at provision of public and private support services for SMEs and coordination of activities to allow knowledge specialization and increase production skills in different industries. It includes policies related to transfer and absorption of knowledge and promotion of public and private innovation activity. The aim is to increase the number of start-ups from 88 per million inhabitants in 2021 to 132 per million inhabitants in 2027 (Government of Albania, 2021).

However, this strategy is quite general and does not focus directly on particular economic sectors including manufacturing. Figure 4.2 defines this strategy as not selective, that is, as a horizontal policy.

There is a lack of statistical data on national innovation system progress; the available information shows continuing low innovative capacity in Albania. Government has taken some steps to strengthen the innovation policy framework, but, in Albania, as in the other WB countries, policy implementation is poor due, mainly, to lack of funds. Our analysis shows that efforts to create an innovation ecosystem are focused mainly on start-ups. It appears that collaboration between academia and industry and key policy objectives, such as establishment of technology transfer offices, is almost non-existent (OECD, 2022).

Our analysis shows that, in addition to lack of funds dedicated to development of research and innovation activities, development of innovative capacities is hampered by lack of coordination in the design of specific and targeted innovation policies and monitoring of their implementation in

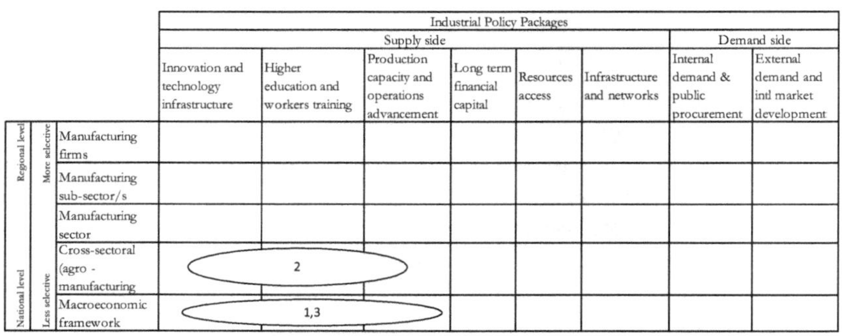


**Fig. 4.2** The policy package matrix in Albania. Source: Author's elaboration based on Andreoni (2016)

practice. OECD (2021) states that it is the Albanian Ministry of Innovation and Investment and Development, the National Agency for Scientific Research and Innovation and The National Agency of the Information Society that are responsible for the implementation of policies related to innovation. This has led to the distribution of responsibilities and competencies, lack of ownership, overlaps, ineffective budget allocations and other weaknesses (OECD, 2022). Albania is part of the Smart Specialization Strategy platform, a Joint Research Centre of the European Commission (EC) initiative. However, as Chap. 2 shows, the benefits derived by Albania are small compared to the potential of this programme.

In Albania, exports are promoted by the Business and Investment Development Strategy (2021–2027) (Government of Albania, 2021). These policies are aimed at improving the conditions and infrastructure for exporting goods produced by local manufacturers and increasing digital business activities. The government agency responsible for drafting policies aimed at stimulating digitization of the economy is the Ministry of Finance and Economy, with the Ministry for Innovation and Investment and Development responsible for their implementation. Although Albania has made considerable progress in harmonizing the legal framework for digital trade and has included provisions for digitization in its main strategic documents, we have no empirical evidence on the application of these measures (World Bank, 2020).

It would seem that, apart from some general strategic programmes, there is no industry policy package in Albania to directly promote manufacturing firms. Policy makers in Albania have designed measures to improve the national innovation system, but these measures lack financial plans and budget and responsibility for their implementation. Albania has no policies or institutional financial instruments providing direct support to manufacturing firms and no public procurement policies or measures to increase domestic demand for innovative products and technologies or exports of agro-industrial products.

## 4.5 Industrial Policy Package Alignment in North Macedonia

Since the changes that occurred to the socio-economic system at the beginning of the 1990s, North Macedonia has experienced three main industrial development phases and accompanying policy instruments. In the first period, after the dissolution of Yugoslavia, the economy of North Macedonia went through a process of privatization of state- and socially owned enterprises. This lasted until 2009 and was characterized by significant deindustrialization and a reduction in the contribution of the manufacturing sector to GDP from 28% in 1992 to 8% in 2004.

In 2009 (2nd period), Macedonia approved its first industrial policy (2009–2020) to promote the manufacturing industry. It included five areas of intervention: international cooperation and support for Foreign Direct Investment (FDI); applied R&D and innovation; development of eco-friendly products and services; growth of SMEs and development of entrepreneurship; and cooperation among companies in clusters and networks.

The third period, is linked to the new industrial policy programme for 2018–2027. Since 2004, the Macedonian industrial sector has experienced significant developments, with manufacturing sector contribution to GDP increasing by 5% to reach an estimated 13% in 2023. The food and beverages and tobacco goods are products typical of North Macedonia's industry. Brewing companies are involved in transnational supply chains owned by foreign companies; a number of wineries are significant exporters; and dairy products are important in Macedonia's food industry.

Several foreign-owned companies are involved in the generation and supply of electricity and oil production in Macedonia and the iron, steel and other non-ferrous and non-ferrous metallurgical products (nickel, zinc, (semi)precious metals) sectors are important.

The textile industry is less profitable than some other sub-sectors but is an important exporter. Production of clothing and intermediate textile goods in Macedonia involves several foreign textile companies that take advantage of low labour costs in this labour-intensive industry (Invest Macedonia North, 2020). The production of chemicals and pharmaceuticals originated in the former Yugoslav state, while, since 2013, production of spare parts for automobiles has taken off. These companies are well integrated in transnational supply chains for the German automotive manufacturing industry, which increases Macedonia's exports. Production of auto spare parts is an important industry sector and is the result of government policies to attract foreign investors. These policies involve deregulation and provision of subsidies and were formulated in collaboration with foreign companies (Invest Macedonia North, 2020).

It would seem that North Macedonia has now accumulated a relatively solid industrial production base and is experiencing steady growth (MAKStat, 2020, 2022), helped by the industrial policies implemented between 2009 and 2020. Growth has been promoted also by other industrial measures which have contributed to growth in the manufacturing sector through the establishment of special economic zones and incentives for foreign investment, in particular.

To address the problems experienced by the manufacturing sector following the 2008 financial crisis, Macedonia formulated a new industrial policy strategy (2018–2027) aimed at expanding and strengthening its industrial production by strengthening the foundations of production, improving manufacturing firms' productivity, enabling the transfer of innovations and technology, supporting green industries and green production, promoting export-oriented production and building a 'learning production sector'. One of the main objectives was to reduce the amount of state subsidies to manufacturing firms, creating the right conditions for growth through the concentration of economic resources and encouraging healthy competition among manufacturing firms.

The establishment of Technological Industrial Development Zones (TIDZ) or free zones has contributed to manufacturing sector development. The creation of TIDZ was accompanied by several policy measures and other means to attract investors, especially in the area of production. The incentives offered to potential investors related, especially, to manufacturing include long (99-year) leases for land for €0.10 /m2 per year, free connection to the natural gas, water and sewerage systems, exemption from municipal taxes and the waiving of building permit fees.

In addition, potential investors operating in TIDZ for periods of ten years are exempt from corporate and personal income tax, value-added tax on imports and traded goods in free zones and exemption from customs duties on purchases of equipment, machinery and other spare parts. Also, the government supports capital investment with 10% return on investment costs in new machinery and all types of equipment, assistance for costs related to education in the form of specific or general development of the workforce, exemptions from the payment of the land development fees, government participation in the costs of building a business facility, etc. (Government of North Macedonia, 2018). Macedonia's main exporters are located in TIDZ, which generated approximately €3 billion of exports in 2021 or 47% of total North Macedonia exports (TIDZ, n.d.).

In 2012, North Macedonia published a plan aimed at promoting the national innovation network by increasing public-private partnerships for innovation activities in green energy, electronics, information technology, etc. There are no available data on the outcomes of this strategy.

The government's 2021 Law on Financial Support was formulated to provide support for business companies in general and manufacturing firms in particular. This funding was designed to increase economic competition and employment. The financial support provided is equivalent to around €1 million annually and many local companies have accessed this funding which has contributed to economic growth. There is a fairly solid financial infrastructure supporting SME investments, technological innovation activities and export strategies.

There seems to be a good awareness among policy makers in North Macedonia about the importance of manufacturing for national economic development. The design and implementation of special instruments and measures began in 2009 in relation to two main transformation cycles. In both periods, policies focused on the problems in the manufacturing sector after the financial crisis. However, their translation into specific programmes and measures is difficult to assess (Fig. 4.3).

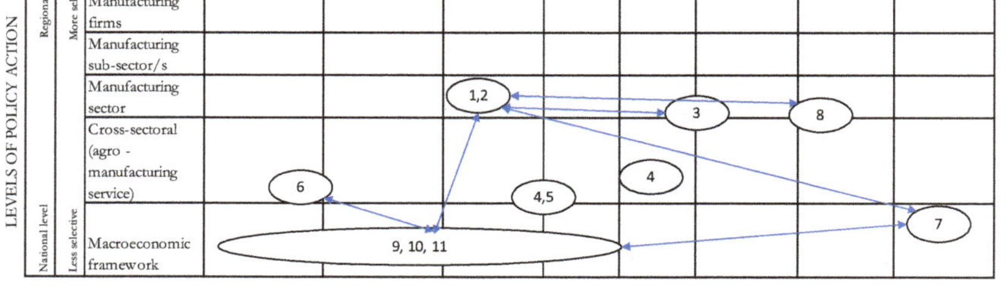


**Fig. 4.3** The policy package matrix in North Macedonia. Source: Author's elaboration based on Andreoni (2016)

## 4.6 Industrial Policy Package Alignment in Kosovo

Up to 2023, Kosovo had no plans in place aimed at structuring the manufacturing sector. In 2023, the Ministry of Industry, Entrepreneurship and Trade of Kosovo (MIETK) published its first industrial policy strategy. It is not clear whether the interested parties, especially the community of manufacturers in Kosovo, were involved in its drafting. However, the Strategy for Industrial Development and Business Support 2030 refers to industrial policy and is the first attempt to address the problems in the manufacturing sector.

Its objective is to help local manufacturers to be more competitive both domestically and in foreign markets. The goal is to increase value added per employee from €541 to at least €809.22 by 2030 or increase the share of manufacturing value added to GDP from 13.6% in 2020 to 16.5% in 2023. This will require interventions related to digitization, investment in scientific research and innovation, access to finance, investment in workforce training, infrastructure improvements, etc. (MIETK, 2023).

The Strategy for Industrial Development and Business Support emphasizes the importance of digital technologies in the manufacturing sector and includes support for industry digitization and automation, promotion of cooperation among entrepreneurs and increasing awareness of the positive impact of digitalization.

Table 4.3 presents some of policy measures aimed at helping the business sector and includes the comprehensive National Development Strategy 2030. This strategy provides support for SMEs engaged in innovation and digitalization and promotes higher levels of productivity. However, there are no strategies in place to encourage entrepreneurship. Entrepreneurship is included in Kosovo's Research, Development, Innovation and Entrepreneurship Strategy, prepared jointly by the Ministry of Education and Research and the Ministry of Economic Affairs and Communications. This policy is aimed at promoting skills and innovation, through workforce training, business advisory services, R&D grants, innovation vouchers and development and launch of new and innovative business models, products and services.

Kosovo is engaged, also, in the design and implementation of programmes to enable linkages between small and large enterprises, based on financial and other support. For example, the Ministry of Industry and Trade and the Kosovo Investment and Enterprise Support Agency

Matching Grants Programme provides grants and co-financing aimed at increasing exports by small firms and the quality of suppliers of local micro enterprises (KIESA, 2021). It provides funding for up to 90% of project activities, to a maximum of €10,000 for micro firms and SMEs. In 2019, the programme was expanded to include standardization, certification and accreditation to match international standards. It was restructured recently to respond better to the needs of small firms following the COVID-19 pandemic shock and includes support for the purchase of manufacturing equipment and machinery and digitalization.

The Government of Kosovo is cooperating with the Austrian Development Cooperation, on ACCESS, a Market Access and Business Digitization Services for Kosovan Companies project, to promote SME internationalization via exports and compliance with international standards. The ACCESS project will support the Kosovo Investment and Enterprise Support Agency's efforts to enrich and further develop export-oriented information and communication technology service providers by facilitating entry to new markets and creating networking opportunities between SMEs in Kosovo and Austria and matching international digital standards.

The Digital Empowerment Initiative provides support for analysis and evaluation of investment needs, digitization of business operations and automation of all firms in the rubber, plastics and furniture manufacturing sub-sectors. This programme is managed by the Kosovo Investment and Enterprise Support Agency. The Ministry of the Economy manages a programme called Kosovo Digital Economy.

In terms of creating an environment to foster the national innovation system and an environment that facilitates cross-border R&D cooperation, Kosovo is in an initial phase. There is evidence that some politicians are making efforts to design programmes and instruments to support innovation activities, but these initiatives seem rather general and lack clear policy priorities and enforcement mechanisms (OECD, 2022). The Strategy for Supporting Innovation and Entrepreneurship (2019–2023), which was approved in 2019, provides general guidelines about how to develop a knowledge-based economy but does not include a specific implementation plan.

One of the main limitations in Kosovo is the absence of a financial infrastructure and funding for the manufacturing sector. The guarantee fund does not include preferential treatment for manufacturing firms and Kosovo industry and business policies lack alignment. The empirical evidence (Andreoni, 2016) suggests that good alignment is key to industry policy success (Fig. 4.4).

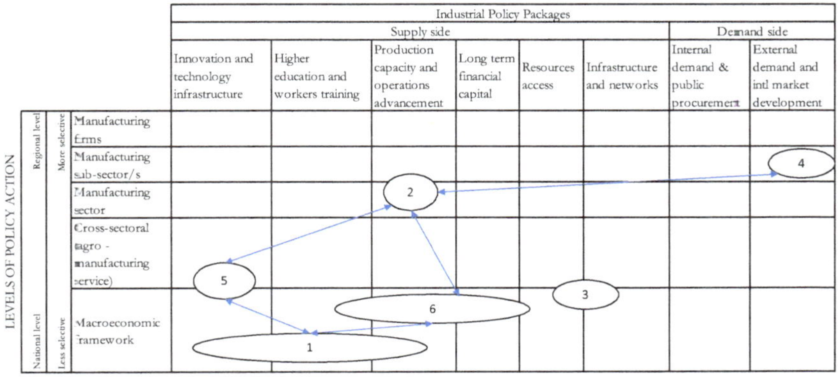


**Fig. 4.4** The policy package matrix in Kosovo. Source: Author's elaboration based on Andreoni (2016)

## 4.7 Industrial Policy Package Alignment in Slovenia

Since 2003, Slovenia has published several policy packages. In 2013, it published an inter-sectoral Slovenian Industrial Policy (SIP), which was approved by representatives of several industries, and other civil society actors such as competence research centres, etc. The aim was to improve productivity and value added per employee from 60% to 80% of the EU-27 average by 2020. It defined four priority areas: adherence to the principles of sustainable development; improving the business environment; strengthening entrepreneurship and innovation; identifying ways to address social challenges, including green economic growth, efficient use of resources and reduced carbon emissions and activities related to long-term development of the industry. The Ministry of Economic Development and Technology was responsible for its implementation with evaluation of achievement of objectives conducted by external experts. The policy was monitored through dialogue among the social partners in the Economic and Social Council.

Slovenia's Smart Specialization Strategy defines a research and innovation plan to stimulate economic growth, achieve regional economic transformation, structural reform and the transition to the new economic development model. It is part of Slovenia's national development strategy and identifies the priority areas of R&D and innovation, start-up activities, growth and development of SMEs and employment, education, training and investment in knowledge and skills. The financial support it provides amounted to 50% of available development expenditure in 2020.

The recovery and resistance plan funding has been used to strengthen the National Contact Points for EU Programmes network and establish project offices in public research organizations and implementing institutions (e.g., Agency for Entrepreneurship, Internationalization, Foreign Investment and Technology), the Slovenian Research and Innovation Agency, etc. It provides funding for collaborations among actors in the research and innovation system and for advice to stakeholders applying for support from EU programmes. In February 2022, the Recovery and Resilience Plan provided €45 million in incentives for business R&D projects and a further €30 million is planned to support demonstration and pilot projects.

The Slovenian government has plans in place to encourage investment and internationalization of the Slovenian economy. They centre on manufacturing companies with export potential and provide support for companies' export-oriented developments from the preparatory phase, through market entry, exporting and diversification into new foreign markets. Maintaining a presence in traditional markets must accompany exploitation of opportunities in foreign markets. Most of these measures are implemented by the Entrepreneurship, Internationalization, Foreign Investment and Technology Agency and the Slovenian Enterprise Fund. Additional export financing is provided by the SID (Slovene Export and Development Bank Inc.), while the Centre for International Cooperation and Development implements part of the bilateral international development cooperation of the Republic of Slovenia. Firms can access information on individual Slovenian suppliers from the Sloexport database, which provides details of demand from Slovenian exporters, links with industry and local authorities and advice on practical matters.

In addition to its sectoral plans and programmes, the Slovenian government has introduced measures to promote certain sub-sectors, for example, the Wood is Beautiful project, aimed at increasing the competitiveness of the forest-wood chain in Slovenia up to 2020. It recognizes the wood processing industry as a strategically important and promising economic sector. The aim was to increase domestic and foreign investment in wood processing factories, promote networks of enterprises, universities and research institutions, increase investments in technological equipment, R&D and innovation in wood processing, harmonize education programmes (secondary education and higher education institutions) aligned to the needs of the woodworking industry and support lifelong education of wood industry workers, expansion into foreign markets, use of wood in building construction, sustainable construction and efficient use of biomass to improve air quality and support energy education and development.

In 2021, the Slovenian government published its Industrial Strategy 2021–2030, which defines goals for Slovenian industry and how to achieve them. The new strategy defines industry development goals and how to achieve them. The purpose of the Industrial Strategy is to move to a circular economy and strengthen innovation in Slovenian firms. Numerous measures to support green, creative and smart developments and help enterprises change their business processes and strengthen their long-term position in the global market will be implemented in the coming years. The aim is to integrate Slovenia's Industry Strategy in the EU's Industrial Strategy, which emphasizes joint commitment of the EU member states and regions, their industries, SMEs and other interested parties in a solid partnership.

The current transformation cycle that began in 2021 with the launch of the New Industrial Strategy 2021–2030 aims to transform the manufacturing industry through the green and digital transition and to increase the strategic autonomy of the entire Slovenian economy. The new multi-instrument industrial policy package emphasizes the importance of research excellence. This package is also focused on the need to capture future markets through a mix of mission-oriented technology. Thus, the systemic and cross-sectoral nature of Slovenian industrial policy shows a healthy alignment among the various industrial policy programmes and instruments. It has smart integration across manufacturing industries and beyond (Fig. 4.5).

## 4.8 Conclusion

This chapter analysed the industrial policy packages in the three WB countries and Slovenia. The analysis reveals increasing adoption of manufacturing system policies and convergence to a multi-layered governance model, similar to the models in advanced economies. The results show that, despite the diversity of industrial policy paths, models and packages, there are several areas where practices coincide. The three WB countries have

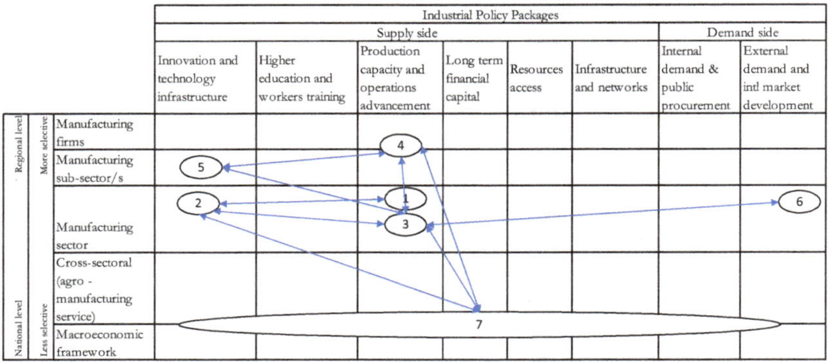


**Fig. 4.5** The policy package matrix in Slovenia. Source: Author's elaboration based on Andreoni (2016)

adopted mixes of less selective sectoral policies and production system policies.

Since early 2000, the WB countries have approved a number of programmes, projects and instruments which are related in some way to industrial policies. Common to the industrial policy packages in all three WB countries is weak alignment between programmes and instruments which is reflected in the lack of vision, frequent duplication, poor management of political economy issues and problems related to coordination of governance in these policies.

The case of Slovenia shows that successful industrialization is not only about the right policy instruments and institutions but also includes learning how to build, use and coordinate them effectively. Essential for industrial policy success are financing measures and monitoring of their implementation. These processes are intertwined and are mutually influencing throughout the industrial policymaking cycle—from design, implementation and enforcement, through monitoring, experimental phases and adaptation. Monitoring policy implementation is a problem in all three WB countries. Governments need to ensure that those manufacturing firms that receive some form of policy support, such as a subsidy, fulfil what they promised in terms of investment to enable higher productivity.

The case of Slovenia shows that, historically, industrialization, manifested by a thriving manufacturing sector driven by innovation and infrastructure support, enables economic development. This stylized fact suggests that the creation of industrial policies to promote development of the manufacturing sector should be considered important for prosperity and economic well-being in developing economies such as the WB economies. These countries need flexible, carefully designed industrial policies adapted to their economic and political contexts.

Industrial policies should focus on promotion of technological capabilities and structural transformation and should include financing schemes—such as those available in Slovenia—and technological services to support the transfer, adoption, adaptation and diffusion of technical solutions and the most advanced management practices. In countries where policy implementation is difficult and funding schemes are vulnerable to exploitation and rent-seeking, intermediary institutions providing technological services may be the best option. Venture finance incentives attract all types of firms—including those interested only in rents—while provision of technology services is more likely to attract only those firms interested in innovation and commercial success.

## References

Aiginger, K., & Sieber, S. (2006). The matrix approach to industrial policy. *International Review of Applied Economics, 20*(5), 573–560.

Andreoni, A. (2016). Varieties of industrial policy: Models, packages and transformation cycles. In A. Noman & J. Stiglitz (Eds.), *Efficiency, finance and varieties of industrial policy* (pp. 245–305). Columbia University Press.

Andreoni, A., & Gregory, M. (2013). Why and how does manufacturing still matter: Old rationales, new realities. *Revue d'Economie Industrielle, 144*(4), 17–54.

Chang, H. J. (2010). Industrial policy: Can we go beyond an unproductive debate? In J. Y. Lin & B. Pleskovic (Eds.), *Lessons from East Asia and the global financial crisis*. ABCDE, Annual World Bank Conference on Development Economics.

Chang, H. J. (2011). Industrial policy: Can we go beyond an unproductive confrontation? In J. Lin & B. Pleskovic (Eds.), *Annual World Bank conference on development economics 2010, global: Lessons East Asia and the global financial crisis*. World Bank..

Chang, H. J., & Andreoni, A. (2020). Industrial policy in the 21st century. *Development and Change, 51*(2), 324–351.

Chang, H. J., Andreoni, A., & Kuan, M. L. (2013). *International industrial policy experiences and the lessons for the UK, in the future of manufacturing, UK Government Office of Science*. BIS.

Dodgson, M., Hughes, A., Foster, J., & Metcalfe, S. (2011). System thinking, market failure, and the development of innovation policy: The case of Australia. *Research Policy, 40*, 1145–1156.
Government of Albania. (2021). Business development and investment strategy 2021–2027. http://qbz.gov.al/eli/vendim/2021/07/30/466
Government of North Macedonia. (2018). Law on technological industrial development zones–consolidated. Text. https://fez.gov.mk/wpcontent/uploads/2018/01/law-in-tidz-eng.pdf
IFC. (2022). Creating markets in Albania: Country private sector diagnostic. https://www.ifc.org/content/dam/ifc/doc/mgrt/cpsd-albania.pdf
Invest North Macedonia. (2020). Textile and clothing. Retrieved August 26, 2022, from https://investnorthmacedonia.gov.mk/invest-textile-and-clothing/
KIESA. (2021). Digital empowerment initiative - Announcement of beneficiary companies. https://kiesa.rks-gov.net/Page.aspx?id=1,5,509
Klein Woolthuis, R., Lankhuizen, M., & Gilsing, V. (2005). A system failure framework for innovation policy design. *Technovation, 25*, 609–619.
Lee, K. (2019). The art of economic catch-up. In *The art of economic catch-up: Barriers, detours and leapfrogging in innovation systems* (p. I). Cambridge University Press.
MAKStat. (2020). MAKStat (database), State Statistical Office, Republic of North Macedonia, Skopje. Retrieved June 11, 2022, from http://makstat.stat.gov.mk/PXWeb/pxweb/en/MakStat/MakStat__NadvoresnaTrgovija__KumulativniPod/125_zemji_kumulativ_ml.px/?rxid=e70e8868-e6a5-4557-87cc-fc8b565e5da3
MIETK. (2023). The Strategy for Industrial Development and Business Support (SIDBS) 2030 ("Industrial Policy"). https://mint.rks-gov.net/desk/inc/media/242E31B4-01F1-461C-A4FA-911B8E66E9BD.pdf
O'Sullivan, E., Andreoni, A., Lopez-Gomez, G., & Gregory, M. (2013). What is new in the new industrial policy? A manufacturing system perspective. *Oxford Review of Economic Policy, 29*(2), 432–462.
OECD. (2021). Multi-dimensional review of the Western Balkans: Assessing opportunities and constraints, OECD Development Pathways, OECD Publishing, Paris. https://doi.org/10.1787/4d5cbc2a-en
OECD. (2022). SME policy index: Western Balkans and Turkey 2022: Assessing the implementation of the small business act for Europe, SME Policy Index, OECD Publishing, Paris. https://doi.org/10.1787/b47d15f0-en
Okimoto, D. I. (1989). *Between MITI and the market: Japanese industrial policy for high technology*. Stanford University Press.
Stiglitz, J. (1996). Some lessons from the East Asian miracle. *World Bank Research Observer, 11*(2), 151–177.

Stiglitz, J. E. (2017). Industrial policy, learning and development. In J. Page & F. Tarp (Eds.), *The practice of industrial policy: Government-business coordination in Africa and East Asia* (WIDER studies in development economics). Oxford University Press.

Tassey, G. (2007). *The technology imperative*. Edward Elgar.

Technological Industrial Development Zones (TIDZ). (n.d.). Republic of North Macedonia. The North Macedonia Free Zones Authority. https://www.mpo.cz/assets/cz/zahranicni-obchod/mezinarodni-obchod-dle-teritorii/vychodni-evropa-zapadni-balkan-a-stredni-asie/2022/4/TIDZ-North-Macedonia-Investment-opportunities.pdf

UNIDO. (2020). Industrialization as the driver of sustained prosperity. https://www.unido.org/sites/default/files/files/2020-04/UNIDO_Industrialization_Book_web4.pdf

World Bank. (2020). Albania e-commerce diagnostic: Leveraging the digital trade opportunity. https://openknowledge.worldbank.org/bitstream/handle/10986/35000/Albania-E-Commerce-Diagnostic-Leveraging-the-Digital-Trade-Opportunity.pdf

CHAPTER 5

# Innovation Capacity and Technology Upgrading Issues in the Three Western Balkan Economies

## 5.1 Introduction

The aspiration of the Western Balkan (WB) states to become members of the European Union (EU) is making these countries' economic and technological transformation particularly urgent. EU accession is expected to have a major impact on their competitive positions, but achieving production standards that match EU country standards will require the adoption of policies focused on technology and industry upgrading.

As discussed in Chap. 2, since the great economic changes that occurred at the end of the twentieth century, industrial activity in the WB countries has been declining. In Kosovo and Albania, the focus has been on heavy industry, mainly mining, and in North Macedonia the emphasis has been on the production of undifferentiated products for local or regional markets. The WB country manufacturing firms use technologies that are produced and tested elsewhere to try to produce goods that meet global quality standards and increase production efficiency. They have almost no engagement in innovation and R&D activities. As a result, their economic structure, firm productivity and the technological models used for their business activities are far behind the standards in most EU and other developed countries.

The findings in Chap. 4 show that the traditional industrial policy approach has not produced the desired results and there is an urgent need


F. Sahiti, *Industrial Policies for Technological Upgrading in Western Balkan Countries*, https://doi.org/10.1007/978-3-031-51429-6_5

to identify a policy method that will promote the economic and technological transformation of the WB economies. Since all countries have their own specifics, an approach that has proven effective in one country cannot be generalized to other economies. Also, since the local and global economic and technological environment is constantly changing, there is no guarantee that an approach that was successful at one point in time will be equally successful at some future time. This underlines the importance of industry policy packages that are coherent with *current* market conditions and requirements and with individual country specifics. Campos et al. (2017) point to the major changes that occurred in the 1990s, which prompted many developing economies to focus on economic change and reforms through the implementation of industrial policies oriented to economic structural reform. However, University College London Chair of Industry and Innovation Studies, Professor Slavo Radosevic, maintains that, since these policies were designed assuming that the improved business environment would lead automatically to economic and technology improvements, they have clear limitations. For instance, they take no account of market and system failures whose management would require a different type of policy and whose successful address would require measures to enable technology accumulation and economic structural changes.

Therefore, a new conceptual industrial policy approach is required—and one that will offer manufacturing firms an alternative that takes account of the good and bad industrial policy structural reform experiences described in Chap. 4 and this chapter.

Before describing the new conceptual approach to industrial policy (presented in Chap. 6), in this chapter, we discuss the issues involved in improving the innovation capacity and technology in the three WB economies. We employ three analytical frameworks to investigate the problems these economies need to overcome to construct an effective innovation system and improve their technologies. These frameworks involve indicators and variables related to the development of firm technological capabilities to achieve an effective economic organization and drive technology upgrading. Firm technological capabilities and market behaviour are shaped by several factors, including the policy and business environment, infrastructure inputs, interactions between the economic and other environments both foreign and domestic, etc. Our analyses focus particularly on education systems, the state of vocational schools, the functioning of public and private research institutes, the Internet and the Information and Communication Technology (ICT) infrastructure and the logistics infrastructure, among many other aspects.

This chapter is organized as follows. Section 5.2 describes our analytical frameworks, which focus on technology upgrading in the three selected WB economies. Section 5.3 presents our findings regarding the indicators included in the conceptual frameworks. In Sect. 5.4, we discuss the economic outcomes and structural features of three WB economies. Section 5.5 provides a more detailed discussion of the levels of entrepreneurship and firm investment in learning and Sect. 5.6 examines innovation and technological capacity outcomes. Section 5.7 concludes the chapter with a presentation of the main findings.

We describe the conceptual frameworks used for our analysis and provide a brief overview of the challenges faced by the WB countries in their efforts to build innovation capacity and achieve technology upgrading.

## 5.2 The Analytical Frameworks Employed

Our analysis is based on three theoretical frameworks. The first was proposed by Kim (1997) and is appropriate for economies in transition, such as the WB economies. In Kim's framework, the technological capabilities related to economic organization are the main driver of technology upgrading, based on both international technology transfer and local sources of extramural knowledge. However, since firm technological capabilities and market behaviour matter, our framework also considers the balance and complementarity between technology imports and domestic technology development activities (see Fig. 5.1).

Why are technological capabilities the main driver of firm growth? According to Bell (2007), technological capabilities enable the creation and implementation of production innovations, which, in turn, allow changes to the firm's current production forms and configurations. At the firm level, it is production and technological capabilities that matter (Bell & Pavitt, 1993, 1995; Bell & Figueiredo, 2012). In transition economies, there are deficiencies related to both these capabilities, but manufacturing firms have opportunities to catch up with global industry leaders based on the technologies used in their manufacturing processes. They can exploit world leading technical and design specifications to achieve frontier performance and similar levels of productivity and goods to those of their global competitors (Radosevic, 2021).

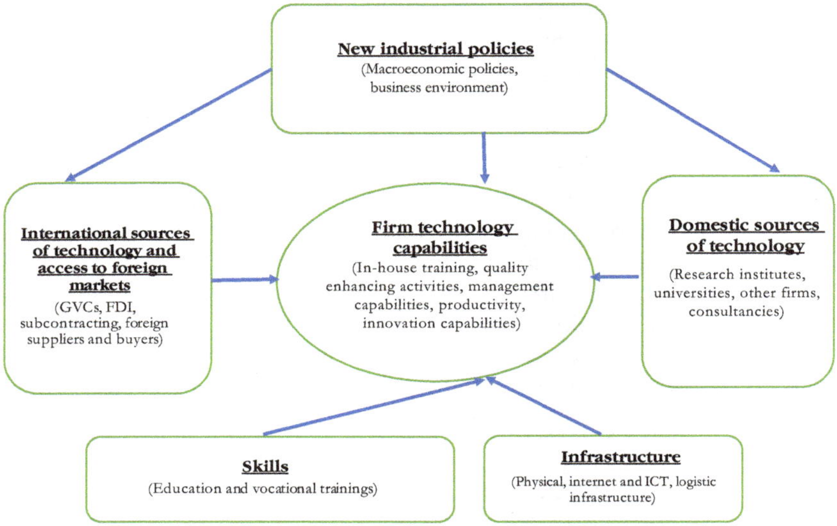


**Fig. 5.1** Catching up economies and sources of technology upgrading. Source: Based on Kim (1997)

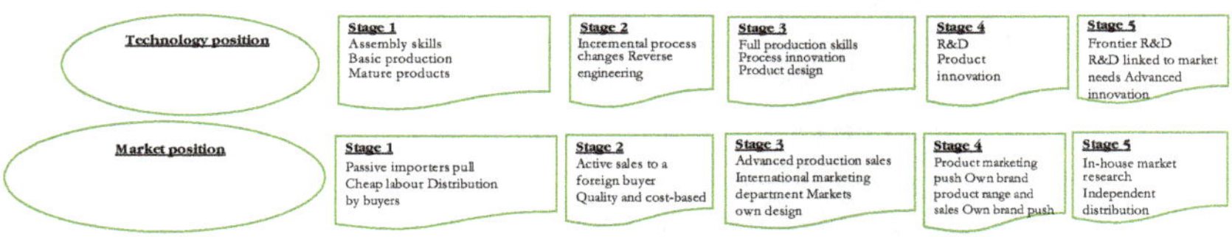


**Fig. 5.2** Technology upgrading path from production to innovation capability. Source: Based on Hobday (1995)

However, developing country firms frequently lack the capacity to innovate and to generate new technology. Weak innovation capacity is a barrier to technology upgrading (see Fig. 5.2). The WB country firms—similar to many other developing economy firms—must make the leap from technology imitators to technology producers and manufacturers of new models. Previous empirical findings suggest that investment in physical assets, on its own, does not guarantee growth; it needs to be accompanied by investments in intangible assets, that is, in the generation of new skills and productivity enhancements. The innovation process requires active acquisition, assimilation, exploration and knowledge upgrading processes. In transition economies, this often means production capabilities and technology capabilities advancements, including R&D capabilities (see Fig. 5.2).

However, it cannot be assumed that investment in R&D activities will promote innovation. Innovation also involves manufacturing, design and engineering capabilities, which are important for manufacturing firm growth in developing economies. Bell (2007, p. 65) believes that design and engineering capabilities are the foundation of and enable development and accumulation of R&D and innovation capabilities.

Figure 5.3 suggests that innovative products are rarely produced directly by R&D laboratories or as the result of commercialization of public research. Innovations are more likely to be achieved by individuals with design and engineering capabilities and good craft and technical training. In the complex and market-driven nature of innovation activity, R&D activity is just one of several necessary activities and capabilities (Brown & Mason, 2014). Firms with a good design and engineering skills base and ability to develop technological capabilities will be able to engage in both R&D and innovation activities (Radosevic, 2021).

Figure 5.1 shows that although local firms are the main actors in the innovation process, they are often dependent on the technological knowledge embedded in their trade, subcontracting and Foreign Direct Investment (FDI) relations, which facilitate technology transfer. Although an open market and presence of FDI are vital, their existence does not

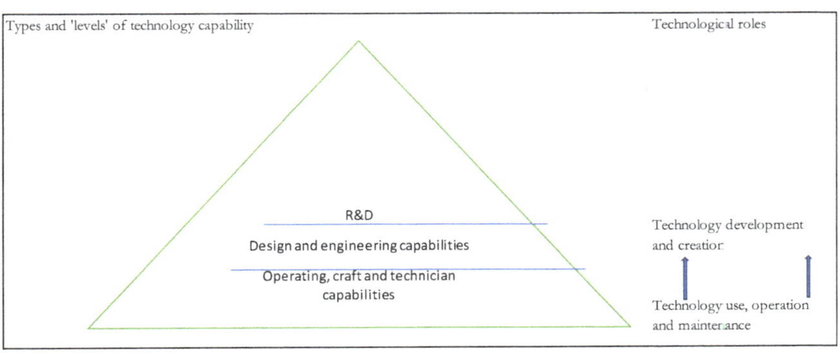


**Fig. 5.3** Technological capabilities and roles. Source: Adopted from Bell (2007)

guarantee successful engagement in innovation activity and the amount of FDI is less important than the learning potential enabled by FDI and trade (Radosevic, 2021). Also, knowledge transfer via trade linkages and FDI is not automatic but requires active efforts to maximize knowledge diffusion (Kim, 1997).

It should be noted that innovation is a systemic activity (see Fig. 5.1) that requires interaction among organizations. Firms that lack the necessary absorptive and organizational skills will find it difficult to integrate and use knowledge from outside the organization. Figure 5.1 shows that the development of extramural R&D and knowledge-intensive services provided by universities and research and technology has an influence on the innovation capacities of firms. An education system that responds to market demands and provides Vocational Education and Training (VET) is vital for enabling developing economies to acquire and absorb knowledge and technology from abroad and promote entrepreneurship.

Finally, the channels of interactions between universities, Public Research Organizations (PROs) and business firms matter for the development of technological capabilities. These channels change with the evolution, over time, of firms' innovation capabilities (Albuquerque et al., 2015). Universities and PROs can provide initial human resources, testing facilities and simple problem-solving services (e.g., consulting and technical assistance) that will allow firms eventually to engage in innovation activities. The R&D conducted in universities and PROs is likely to complement or replace business firm R&D (Radosevic, 2021).

Based on this theoretical framework, in the following section, we focus on and evaluate some 'basic' statistical indicators collected from the three WB economies and our benchmark economy (Slovenia). We are aware that some of these indicators correspond only broadly to the theoretical framework, but these are the only available direct proxies for these indicators (Fig. 5.1). We start with an overview of macro- and microeconomic policies, followed by analysis of statistical data related to the structural features of technology upgrading, entrepreneurship, infrastructure, etc.

## 5.3 Policy and Business Environment Outcomes

Entrepreneurs are often considered the most dynamic agents of change and innovation (Audretsch, 2002). Their business activities occur not in isolation, but rather are time and context specific (Schumpeter 1939; Freeman & Soete, 1997). That is, firms operate in environments composed of a range of socio-economic and institutional conditions that have a strong influence on business outcomes. The development of technological capabilities as the driver of innovation capabilities depends, fundamentally, on external factors, such as human capital quality and the skills acquired via education. In addition, firms interact with both domestic and foreign partners and are reliant on the country's physical infrastructure, including financial, telecommunications, logistics and other services. Policy makers are keen to implement policies to encourage new entrepreneurial activities and the establishment of new firms. Since entrepreneurial firms are considered the most dynamic drivers of change, the expectation is that more entrepreneurial activity will result in more new ideas and technologies being brought to the market.

We examine two types of policies to foster entrepreneurship and innovation: macroeconomic policies (Sect. 5.3.1) and microeconomic policies (Sect. 5.3.2). We conduct a comparative analysis to identify the similarities and differences between our three WB countries and the reference country. The set of macro-level policies includes measures to manage aggregate demand, based on fiscal and monetary plans, and other high-impact public policies such as business regulations, infrastructure plans and business taxation protocols. The micro-policies we examine include those that target entrepreneurs and market failures. We examine five types of more common government interventions, which correspond broadly to the components in Fig. 5.1.

### *Macroeconomic Policies*

Entrepreneurship is often associated with technological innovation. Indeed, entrepreneurship, innovation and technological change, in combination, are at the heart of disruptive business models that transform industries and markets (Schumpeter, 1942; Acs & Audretsch, 2005). Therefore, the creation of favourable macroeconomic conditions is a prerequisite for higher levels of entrepreneurship and innovative activities. In this section, we discuss those policies that have a major impact on entrepreneurship. They are typified by their primary focus not being the entrepreneur, although their impact for entrepreneurs can be substantial. We refer to such policies as macroeconomic policies. They include traditional macroeconomic policies, such as fiscal and monetary policies, business regulations, policies relating to physical infrastructure, institutional and governance indicators, etc.

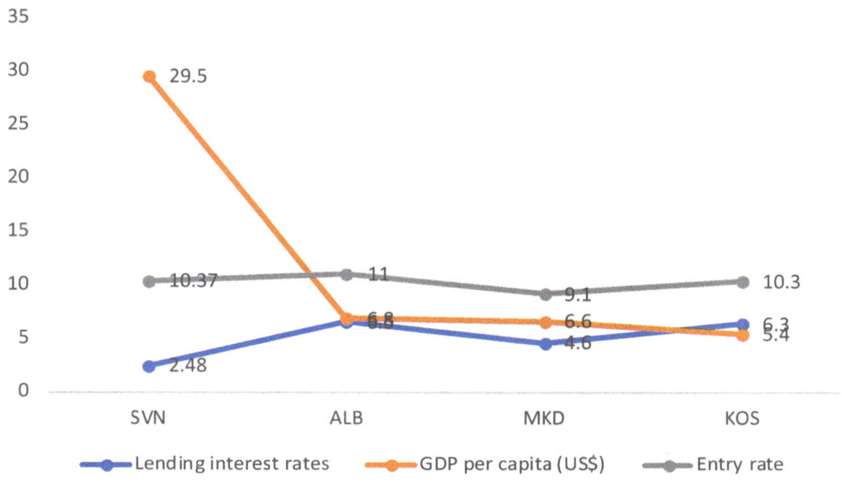


**Fig. 5.4** Macroeconomic indicators and entry rates. Source: Author based on INSTAT, KSA, MAKSTAT, World Bank, EUROSTAT

Previous work (e.g., Shane, 1996) suggests that a more accommodative monetary policy increases the availability of finance and reduces the cost of external finance. More favourable financial conditions can be expected to have a positive effect on entrepreneurial activity. Figure 5.4 suggests that lower interest rates result in higher entrepreneurial-firm entry rates.

Also, since income has an impact on total demand for goods and services, a higher level of national income is also correlated with higher levels of entrepreneurship and increased demand affects the number of new firms (Parker, 1996; Stiglitz, 2000). Figure 5.4 confirms this correlation between income and entrepreneurial activity; countries with higher incomes report significantly higher numbers of new firms compared to economies in transition. Institutional and governance quality are other factors likely to influence the level of entrepreneurial activities. According to the World Bank (n.d.), which measures the quality of institutions and governance on almost all basic indicators, the WB countries perform significantly worse than Slovenia and, especially, in terms of rule of law, political stability and violence and corruption (Fig. 5.5).

Other macroeconomic factors, such as tax policies and business regulations, also have an important impact on levels of entrepreneurial activity.

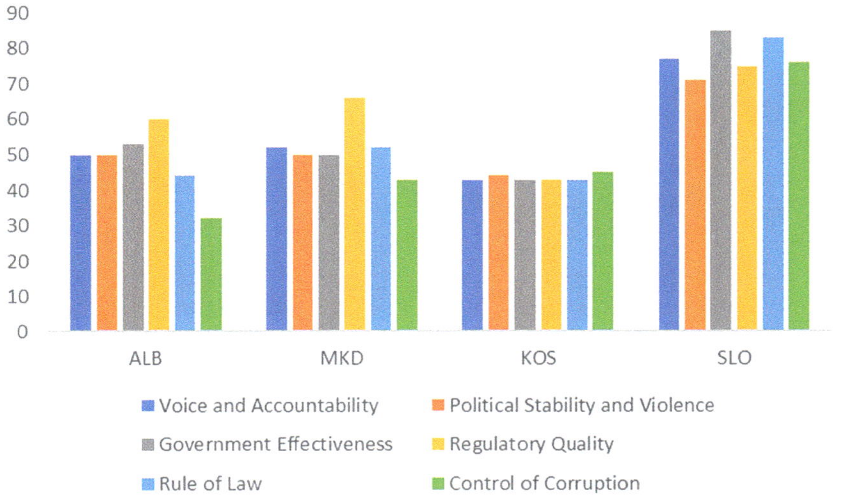


**Fig. 5.5** Institutional and governance indicators (percentile ranking) 2021. Source: World Development Indicators Database

In both cases, the WB countries do not differ much from the developed economies. For example, in the case of business regulations, the WB countries have made significant progress since 2000. This is particularly evident in the procedures related to starting a business but can be seen, also, in other indicators such as lower tax rates. As a result of these improvements, in the 2021 World Bank Doing Business Index, all the WB economies rank quite highly, including North Macedonia which is in 10th position and Kosovo which is in 44th position (World Bank, 2019). However, both of these economies suffer from a range of problems that continue to undermine fair competition, private investment and firm growth more generally. A major problem is enforceability of business contracts, which takes time and is both costly and unreliable. For example, in North Macedonia and Kosova, implementation of a business contract can take up to 330 days, which is significantly longer than the standard in developed economies of 120 days. The fault lies in an ineffective and inefficient judicial system (World Bank, 2020). Contract enforcement is also costly, typically 34.4% of the claim value, which is much higher than the OECD average of 21.5% (OECD, 2021). In the recent BEEPS survey, 43% of firms in North Macedonia and Kosovo identified the courts of law as a

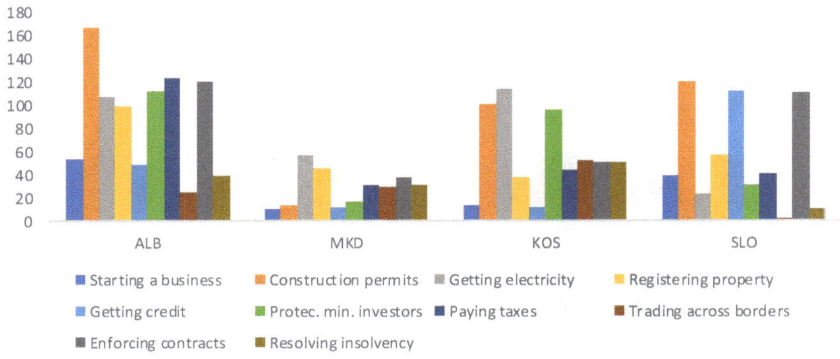


**Fig. 5.6** World Bank doing business indicators 2020. Source: World Bank

major barrier to doing business (World Bank, 2020). Another significant problem is unfair market competition and the size of the informal business market (Fig. 5.6). The World Bank BEEPS reported 63.4% and 54.5% of the managers interviewed in North Macedonia and Kosova considering economic informality as a major obstacle to the growth of their businesses (World Bank, n.d.).

The quality of the road, telecommunication, energy and water infrastructures matters since unreliable or absent services force firms to produce or provide their own energy, transport or communication services, for instance. It has been shown that, despite some progress, the WB countries lack some major infrastructure services (e.g., in Kosovo electricity supplies are unreliable). The EBRD-World Bank BEEPS found that 63% of all firms and 78% of manufacturing firms consider electricity supply a major problem (World Bank, 2020). Despite some improvements, infrastructure deficiencies continue to undermine Kosovo's attractiveness as an investment destination. Rail transport is a particular problem and Kosova is lagging in terms of network size and transported goods, compared to North Macedonia, which has a similar sized output sector (European Commission, 2022; Eurostat, 2018).

The above results show that macroeconomic factors (e.g., interest rates, aggregate demand) have an influence on entrepreneurial activity, which is to be expected since entrepreneurs are particularly sensitive to external uncertainties. These findings suggest, also, that macroeconomic stability has an effect on entrepreneurial activity. Many small firms face real uncertainties about the quality of their country's infrastructure and the ability of government institutions to reduce corruption and criminal activity. At the same time, the quality, continuity and direction of the national political regime have an effect on the investment climate.

In Sect. 5.3.2, we examine the microeconomic factors that have a direct effect on entrepreneurial activity.

### *Microeconomic Policies*

We have shown that although macroeconomic policies may not be aimed primarily at entrepreneurs, their impact on entrepreneurship can be considerable. Here, we discuss microeconomic policies aimed particularly at fostering entrepreneurship. We discuss the rationale for each policy and their impact on entrepreneurship. We examine three main types of interventions implemented in most countries. These policies correspond broadly to the micro-policy elements of the framework in Fig. 5.1: developing an entrepreneurial culture, improving access to and provision of finance and support for technology and innovation activities.

Developing an entrepreneurial culture through education and skills development is crucial for higher levels of entrepreneurship and innovation. The rationale for designing policies to promote an entrepreneurial culture is that the greater the societal awareness of the opportunities that could be exploited, the greater the likelihood that individuals or small groups will consider starting their own businesses (European Commission, 2003). New firm creation potentially benefits the whole of society by increasing employment, market offerings and tax revenue, in particular. We investigate three main institutional mechanisms aimed at building an entrepreneurial mindset in the population: entrepreneurship education as part of the formal educational system, VET and entrepreneurship training.

The most frequent tool adopted by governments to try to develop an entrepreneurial culture in society is inclusion of entrepreneurship education at all formal education levels. Governments around the world are making efforts to provide programmes and materials to encourage entrepreneurial activity (European Commission, 2004; Athayde, 2009).

There are empirical data showing that the three WB economies lag behind the developing countries in terms of providing entrepreneurship training in education programmes at all three levels. According to the OECD (2022), the inclusion of entrepreneurship education in primary and secondary school curricula is significantly lower in the three WB economies than in developed economies: out of a maximum score of 5, Kosovo scored 2.75, Albania 2.65 and North Macedonia 3.11, with the average score for the Balkan countries and Turkey 3.43 (see Table 5.1). At the tertiary education level, entrepreneurship education is crucial for providing potential entrepreneurs with practical skills, including how to write business plans, and providing simulations of real business situations. OECD (2022) reports that, despite the inclusion of entrepreneurship programmes in formal education curricula, the production of future entrepreneurs is insufficient. This report highlights the absence of a coherent policy to promote coordination among different government levels and agencies and, specifically, among municipalities, higher education institutions and the private sector. The three WB countries have not put in place functional mechanisms to monitor the implementation of plans and strategies aimed at the development of an entrepreneurship culture or to measure the impact of these plans in practice. Unlike, Slovenia, where the government SPOT point programme targets user groups, none of the countries in transition offer systematic training for individuals who want to start their own businesses (SBA, 2019). Data from other organizations, such as the EBRD, show that the WB economies are lagging behind the developed countries in other aspects, such as the knowledge economy index. This indicator is a measure of the country's ability to benefit from scientific discoveries and applied research. The WB economies score much lower on this index than the reference country (see Table 5.1).

VET provides entrepreneurial skills. In Albania, Kosovo and North Macedonia, in theory, VET is part of the education system, especially upper secondary education, but is not compulsory (see Table 5.1). Among

**Table 5.1** Entrepreneurship education and training indicators

| | *ALB* | *KOS* | *MKD* | *SLO* |
|---|---|---|---|---|
| Entrepreneurship learning at school (1–5)[a] | 2.1 | 1.8 | 2.06 | 2.07 |
| VET (% of total secondary education enrolment) | N/A | 53 | 60.2 | 70.8 |
| Tertiary education (aged 30–34) (%)[b] | 32.1 | 32.3 | 39.7 | 44.9 |
| Staff training 1–7 (best)[c] | 2.7 | 2.7 | 3.2 | 4.5 |

[a] Source: OECD for WB countries, World Bank for Slovenia
[b] Source: for Kosovo European training foundation, for other countries Eurostat
[c] Source: for Kosovo European training foundation, for other countries WEF

secondary school students, about 53% in Kosovo and 60.2% in North Macedonia (above the EU average of 47.8%) choose vocational education (EUROSTAT, 2018). However, in the three WB countries, there are numerous problems related to VET, for example, a mismatch between the training provided and market needs, poor quality teaching and learning, paucity of practical teaching materials and insufficient opportunities, such as internships, to enable accumulation of practical experience (European Commission, 2022; OECD, 2022). In the developed countries, practical experience is a compulsory component of VET, and in Slovenia, there is a legal requirement for VET students to spend 50% of their time on practical work experience (SBA, 2019). We have no data for Kosovo and North Macedonia on the employability of VET graduates, but in Slovenia it is 84.5%.

Funding is often the main barrier to entrepreneurship. Governments need to provide funding and establish institutional mechanisms to help existing and potential entrepreneurs. We investigate three micro-institutional approaches to this problem: loan guarantee schemes, business grants and provision of equity financing for new firms.

It would seem that for entrepreneurs in developing countries, debt is used to fund business activity. However, it can be difficult for start-ups and small firms to obtain bank loans. Banks tend to require substantial collateral to secure a loan. To try to overcome this obstacle, governments in transition countries offer guarantee schemes that share the responsibility for small loan repayments with the borrower. These loan guarantee schemes are financed by public funds and donor organizations such as USAID, KfW and others. However, according to the OECD (2022), the schemes available are not sufficient to meet the requirements and needs of start-up businesses. In Slovenia, the number and scope of these loan guarantee schemes are significantly higher than in the WB countries (see Table 6.3).

Business grants can support start-ups to invest in equipment, workforce training and consultancy—for both managers and employees. Table 5.2 shows that the amounts of the business grants available to start-ups and young firms in transition economies are small compared to Slovenia, for instance. In most cases, the grants available to firms in the developing economies come from donor organizations and amount to between $US3,000 and $US5,000. In the EU countries, there are several well-established government agencies that provide grants to start-ups and young firms (see Table 5.2).

**Table 5.2** Access to finance indicators

| | *ALB* | *KOS* | *MKD* | *SVN* |
|---|---|---|---|---|
| Loan guarantee schemes | AASF, The Italian-Albanian Programme for the Development of SMEs, The KfW RCGF, European Investment Fund (EIF) | The Kosovo Credit Guarantee Fund | Development Bank of North Macedonia | SEF—Slovene Enterprise Fund |
| Business grants | The Albanian Investment Development Agency (AIDA) | The millenium foundation Kosovo (MFK), USAID, KfW. | Fund of Innovation and Technological Development (FITD) | Slovenian enterprise fund, Employment service of Slovenia, SPIRIT Slovenia |
| Equity financing from business angles | The Albania Reconstruction Equity Fund (AREF), Albanian American Enterprise Fund (AAEF), The American Bank of Investments (ABI) | Gjirafa Lab | IFI-supported Enterprise Innovation Fund (ENIF) | SEF—Slovene Enterprise Fund, Slovenian Regional Development Fund, SID Bank, Business Angles of Slovenia |

Source: National Banks

Equity financing is a particular problem for firms in the transition countries, which lack institutional equity financing mechanisms. There are some venture capital programmes, but they are immature and small in number and magnitude (OECD, 2022). Table 5.2 shows that, in the developed economies (including Slovenia), the number of agencies offering equity financing to young entrepreneurs is significantly higher than in the three WB countries. For example, the Slovenian Enterprise Fund works to connect business angels with entrepreneurs.

Entrepreneurship tends to be linked to technology and innovation, which points to the potential benefits of improving the innovation skills of would-be entrepreneurs. One of these benefits derives from spillover effects, as new businesses diffuse their ideas to other businesses and customers. Government can facilitate these spillover effects through interventions, such as provision of business incubators and R&D funding.

WB country policy makers are keen to support innovation and contribute to the building of a knowledge economy. Their greater awareness of the importance of innovation activity for increasing economic productivity has encouraged WB country governments to try to create business environments that support innovation and technology developments. However, these countries continue to lag behind the developed countries due, in part, to poor practical implementation of government strategies (OECD, 2022). For example, in Albania, innovation and technology policies are part of the country's National Strategy for Science, Technology and Innovation (2017–2022) and Business and Investment Development Strategy (2021–2027). These plans include Action Plan 3, which was developed by the Albanian Ministry of Finance and Economy to facilitate implementation of the proposed strategies. Although we lack precise statistical data, it would seem that Albania's innovation capacity is very low (OECD, 2022). Business incubators provide the facilities, conditions and services required by start-ups and innovative firms. Table 5.3 presents the number of incubators operating in Albania, although, as in the other two WB countries, statistical evaluation of their activities is difficult.

Kosovo has a good institutional framework and several business incubators, although they do not have a very stable basis. The two most important incubators, the Innovation Centre Kosova and the Gjirafa Lab, lack stable, long-term funding and are financed mainly by donor grants. In the case of the other incubators in Kosova, their activity seems to have reduced (OECD, 2022) and we have no data allowing any measurement of their productivity in terms of the number of start-ups supported.

**Table 5.3** Business incubators and R&D financing

| | |
|---|---|
| ALB | Elevator Lab, Tirana Inc., Yunus Social Business Balkans' Women Founders Network Albania, Ofiçina, Metropolitan Incubator, Innovation Hub Gjirokaster. |
| MKD | YES Foundation, TechPark which operates within the South East European University, CEED Hub in Skopje, Center for Technology Transfer and Innovation. |
| KOS | Innovation Center Kosovo (ICK), Gjirafa Lab, The Jakova Innovation Center, Innovation and Training Park (ITP). |
| SVN | ABC Accelerator (200 start-ups in 6 years), Reveris, Kovačnica—business incubator Kranj, Hekovnik Startup School, Incubator Sežana, Ljubljana University Incubator, SAŠA Incubator. |

Source: Government agencies for WB economies, and Eurostat for Slovenia

North Macedonia established an innovation policy framework as part of its Innovation Strategy 2012–2020. In 2013, government set up a Fund for Innovation and Technology Development, as an agency aimed at implementing innovation policies. Among the several active incubators in North Macedonia is the YES Foundation business incubator located in Skopje, which provides services, training, mentoring and networking opportunities for ICT firms. In addition, the TechPark business incubator, which is located in the Southeast European University in Tetovo, and the CEED Hub in Skopje co-operate with young entrepreneurs and provide education and mentoring programmes. The Faculty of Electrical Engineering in Skopje hosts the Centre for Technology Transfer and Innovation incubator, which functions mostly as a technology transfer office, but also offers some (limited) space and cooperation services for start-up businesses.

## 5.4 Economic Outcomes and Structural Features of WB Economies

Productivity performance is one of the main drivers of long-term and sustainable economic growth and there is a correlation between productivity performance and per capita income. That is, higher productivity performance produces higher levels of income per capita. Figure 5.7 shows that labour productivity levels (expressed as GDP per employee) in the WB countries are significantly lower than in the reference country, Slovenia. The differences are due, in part, to the structure of the economies of these countries and the efficiency of their firms. For example, the higher productivity in Slovenia is related, in part, to this country's economic structure, which is dominated by productive industries, and in part to the efficiency of the economy.

Figure 5.8 depicts the WB countries' economic structure, which is dominated by natural resources industries whose productivity levels and capital intensity tend to be low. These structural features are especially pronounced in Kosovo and Albania, which have significantly low productivity levels, but large shares of GDP derived from natural resources rents.

Data on industry sector size and manufacturing sector size confirm the large share of natural resources sectors in the WB country economies. Figure 5.6 shows that all three of the WB countries considered have lower shares of GDP from industry than the average middle-income country. Compared to the group of world middle-income countries, WB

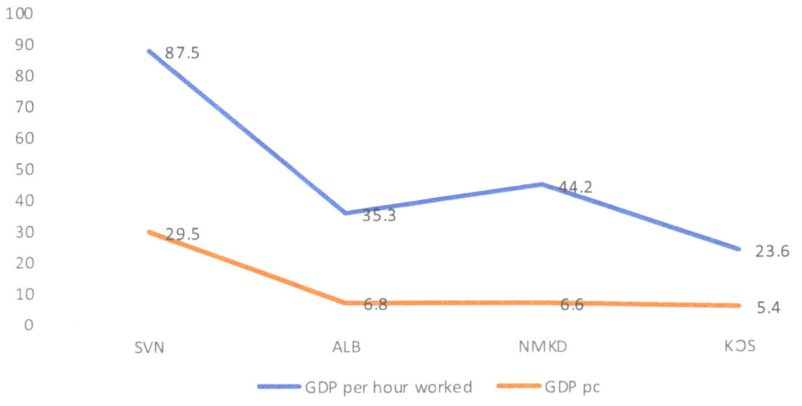


**Fig. 5.7** Income (GDP) per capita and productivity (GDP per employee) 2022. Source: World Development Indicators Database

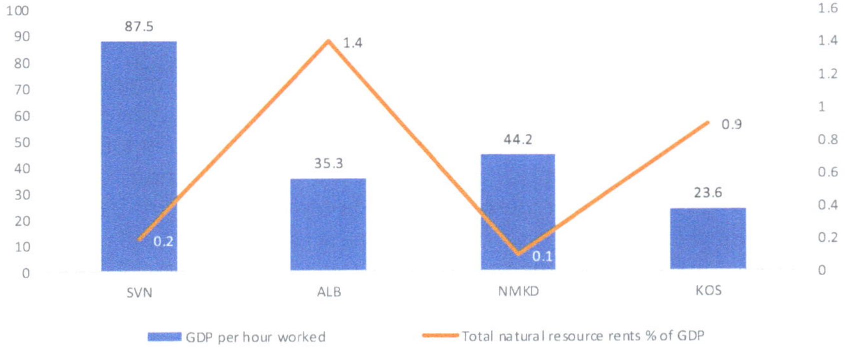


**Fig. 5.8** Productivity (GDP per employee) and total natural resource rents as a percentage of GDP, 2021. Source: World Development Indicators Database

countries could be classed as deindustrialized or 'de-manufacturing'. De-manufacturing of the economy typifies most former socialist countries. Figure 5.6 shows that the average share of manufacturing in middle-income economy GDP is 21% and much lower in all the economies in the WB region.

Among the countries analysed, the share of medium- and high-technology value-added manufacturing is 34% in North Macedonia and

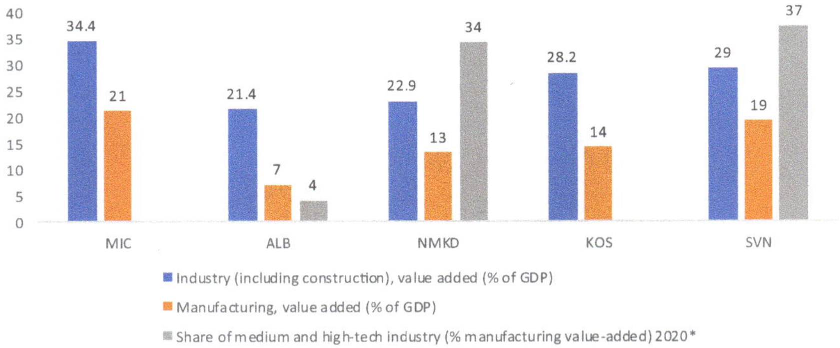


**Fig. 5.9** Shares of industry and manufacturing in GDP 2022. Source: World Development Indicators Database

zero in Albania with no data available for Kosovo. Data for Slovenia show high levels of participation in medium- and high-technology industry in manufacturing value added and higher levels compared to the middle-income countries (Fig. 5.9).

The ICT sector is considered a supporting factor that contributes to the modernization and technology upgrading of many other economic sectors and the degree to which the economy is sustained by knowledge. Figure 5.10 shows that exports of ICT goods are almost non-existent in the WB region, which suggests that these economies are not part of the international electronics and telecommunications production networks. Of more concern is that the share of ICT imports is low compared to the middle-income countries and Slovenia. These data indicate the degree of engagement of these countries in distributing and adopting new technologies in the economy and in society.

Statistical data on the contribution of manufacturing to total exports show a marginal contribution of manufacturing to total exports in the WB economies. This is especially true for Albania and Kosovo; in North Macedonia, export of manufactured products is above the average for this group of countries (see Fig. 5.8). These data are indicative of the problems these countries face in relation to improving their trade balances and achieving technology and industry upgrading. Therefore, manufacturing sector growth, based on existing potential, will be a major industry and innovation policy challenge for the WB countries (Fig. 5.11).

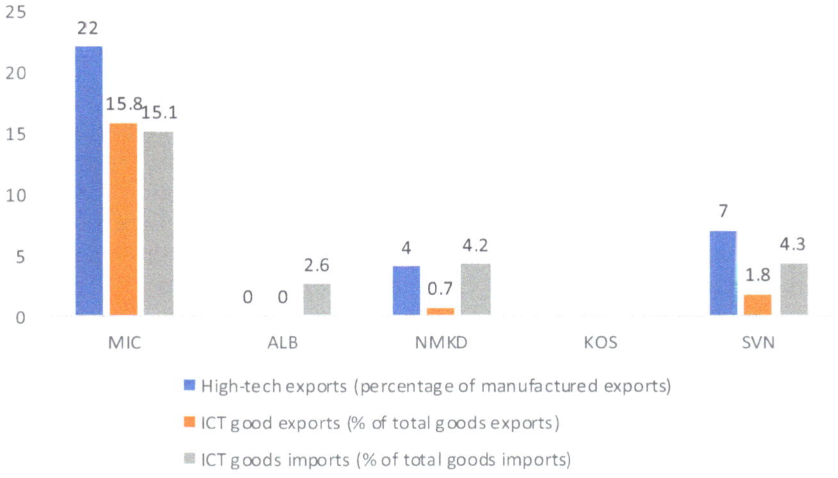


**Fig. 5.10** High tech-export and ICT trade in WB and middle-income countries, 2021. Source: World Development Indicators Database. Note: data for Kosovo are not available

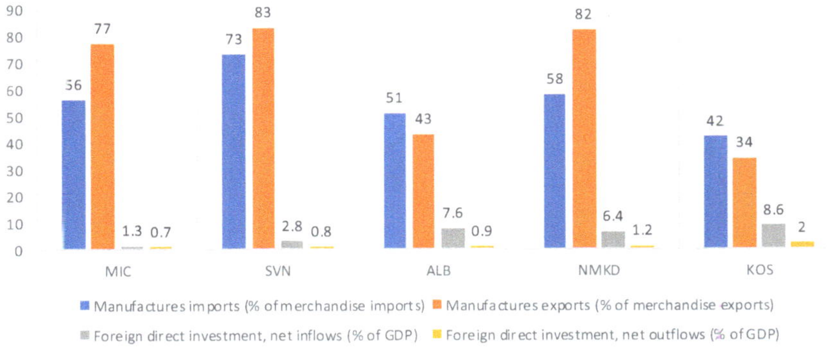


**Fig. 5.11** Trade in manufactures and FDI (2022). Source: World Development Indicators Database. Note: Data for Kosovo were from the EC. Note: Data for Albania refer to 2021

## 5.5 Levels of Entrepreneurship and Firm Investment in Learning

The above data suggest that productivity levels per employee in the three WB economies are significantly lower compared to other WB countries and the reference country, Slovenia. Their low performance productivity is related to their economic structure, particularly in the cases of Albania and Kosovo, where productivity is sustained mainly by the natural resources sectors. Although these countries continue to attract FDI, their manufacturing sectors are fragile and based, mainly, on labour-intensive factors. The absence of both exports and, more importantly (with the exception of North Macedonia), imports of ICT goods should be of great concern to their governments. Before analysing the infrastructure and macro- and microeconomic environments, we examine the main driver of technology and industrial upgrading—entrepreneurship. A good understanding of the dynamics of firm formation and firm learning is essential since, ultimately, technology upgrading occurs at the firm level (Radosevic, 2021).

The new registered business measure is indicative of the dynamics and level of an economy's entrepreneurship. Our data suggest that, among the three WB countries considered, Kosovo and North Macedonia have the highest density of entrepreneurship, compared to the whole group of middle-income countries and Slovenia (see Fig. 5.12). The alternative to establishing a small company is often self-employment and the data

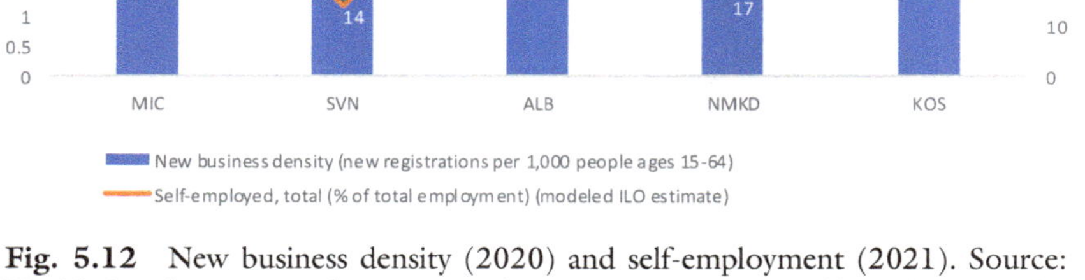


**Fig. 5.12** New business density (2020) and self-employment (2021). Source: World Development Indicators Database. Note: Data on self-employment for Kosovo are from KBRA

suggest that Albania has the highest number of self-employed people among the three countries considered and above the average for the middle-income countries. Figure 5.12 shows that there is some substitution between these indicators in the case of Albania. On average, in Albania, the number of self-employed individuals is inversely proportional to the registration of new enterprises.

Previous studies suggest that the technological capabilities of individual firms depend on their learning efforts, which are crucial, also, for technology upgrading (Kim, 1997). Learning activities among all WB countries are generally comparable with the middle-income countries, although lower in the case of Kosovo and higher in the cases of Albania and North Macedonia.

Analysis of R&D intensity as a share of GDP suggests that R&D is marginal in the three WB economies. Firms in these countries spend significantly less compared to companies in Slovenia, where the proportion of companies investing in R&D is almost 40% whereas in North Macedonia it is 20%, in Kosovo 7% and in Albania 0.15%. Figure 5.13 presents data on gross (domestic) expenditure on research and experimental development activities.

## 5.6 Innovation and Technological Capacity Outcomes

Building on the conceptual framework in Fig. 5.1, we now examine the level of internal technology to measure the technology capacity of WB country institutions, including universities and research and technology organizations. The role of these institutions is to provide knowledge-intensive services to enable development of a knowledge economy, driven by innovation and access to information.[1] We build on an EBRD knowledge economy framework to measure the knowledge economy using the variables: innovation institutions, innovation skills, innovation system and ICT infrastructure.[2]

[1] In this chapter, we adopt the EBRD definition of a knowledge economy which is based on the level of economic development, in which innovation and access to information drive productivity growth (EBRD, 2015).

[2] To allow use of more standardized data and reliable comparative analysis, we use data from the 2019 and 2022 EBRD reports. Note that the 2022 report does not provide any data for Kosovo.

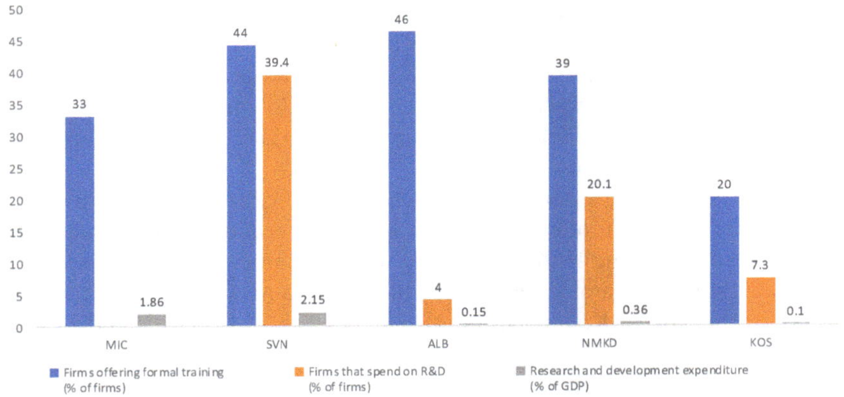


**Fig. 5.13** Share of firms offering formal training and spending on R&D 2020. Source: World Development Indicators Database. Note: data for MIC for firms spending on R&D are not available. Note: R&D expenditure as a percentage of GDP are from the OECD for 2022

Note that the EBRD classifies countries as early, intermediate or advanced knowledge economies. Kosovo is categorized as early, while Albania and North Macedonia are categorized as intermediate. The comparator country, Slovenia, is classed as advanced.

There are several measures for the quality of institutions promoting innovation activity. EBRD (2019) proposes: (i) economies open to trade—labour mobility and investments capture new ideas and technologies (Damijan et al., 2003; Görg & Strobl, 2005; MacGarvie, 2006); (ii) the business environment in terms of rule of law and absence of corruption (Ramalho, 2015) and (iii) governance in terms of political stability and policymaking effectiveness (Barro, 1991). Table 5.4 presents the scores for innovation institutions and shows the large gap between the WB countries and Slovenia. Weak innovation institutions seem to be the main obstacle to the development of a knowledge economy in the WB countries. The biggest gap seems to be related to inefficient public governance and a weak business environment. Government effectiveness, rule of law and perception of corruption seem to be low in the WB countries.

**Table 5.4** Knowledge index performance (2019)

| *Country* | *Total score (out of 10)* | *Institutions for innovations* | *Skills for innovation* | *Innovation systems* | *ICT infrastructure* |
|---|---|---|---|---|---|
| ALB | 4.36 | 5.64 | 4.79 | 2.36 | 4.67 |
| KOS | 3.22 | 4.81 | 2.75 | 3.12 | 2.2 |
| MKD | 4.50 | 5.74 | 3.83 | 3.27 | 5.18 |
| SVN | 6.65 | 7.4 | 7.32 | 5.14 | 6.73 |

Source: EBRD

Previous empirical evidence suggests that an adequately trained workforce that meets the needs of the private sector is important for knowledge transfer, innovation and technology upgrading (Muysken & Nour, 2006; Gennaioli & Tavoni, 2011). In terms of innovation skills, two dimensions stand out: general skills as a prerequisite for any economic activity (i.e., school enrolment and secondary education) and specialized skills (number of technicians), which enable value-adding activities. The innovation skills gap between the WB countries and Slovenia is substantial (see Table 5.4). The differences among Albania, North Macedonia and Slovenia in terms of general skills are less stark, but the difference with Kosovo is sizeable. There is also limited availability of specialized skills in the WB countries and, in Kosovo, for example, few firms offer formal training to their employees, whereas Slovenia shows relatively good performance on this indicator. The number of R&D technicians per million inhabitants is very low in the WB countries.

Innovation system data show a large gap between the WB countries and Slovenia (1.87 vs 2.78 index points—see Fig. 5.4). This reflects the low level of expenditure on R&D in the WB countries. For example, the WB countries invest an average of 0.2% of GDP in R&D, significantly less than Slovenia at 1.86% of GDP. This low level of spending on and small budget devoted to R&D (i.e., low inputs) results in similar low innovation system outputs. Patent application numbers are low in the WB countries; the most recent World Bank data for number of patent applications per 1000 inhabitants are 255 for Slovenia compared to 4 for Albania and 47 for North Macedonia (there are no data for Kosovo). Linkages within the innovation systems in the WB countries are limited by lack of academic-corporate research collaboration, particularly in Albania and Kosovo (OECD, 2022).

Finally, despite significant improvements in their ICT infrastructure, the three WB countries show a significant gap (on average 2.71 index points) with the reference country (see Table 5.4). The empirical data show that the WB countries have persistent problems related to ICT availability and ICT sophistication. OECD (2022) suggests that Albania and North Macedonia have, respectively, only 19.6 and 23.7 fixed broadband subscriptions per 100 inhabitants (compared to 31.7 in Slovenia), although, according to the EBRD (2019), Kosovo has the highest number of fixed broadband subscriptions (38).

The logistics infrastructure is an important indicator of entrepreneurship levels. Entrepreneurial activity requires a good logistics infrastructure, including a good quality trade and transport infrastructure and an efficient customs clearance process. The logistics performance index, which considers all of these aspects, scores North Macedonia at 3.1 not far from the average for Slovenia (3.3). Albania's score is 2.2 and there are no available data for Kosovo (World Bank n.d.).

## 5.7 Conclusions

In this chapter we analysed the challenges of innovation capacity and technology upgrading in the three WB economies. The outcomes showed the range of problems that these economies face in their efforts to build an environment that will promote the development of firm technology capabilities and an innovation system enabling technology upgrading.

The evidence from the three WB economies analysed highlights the limited role of the manufacturing sector, in terms of number of firms and their contribution to employment, added value and exports. Our data suggest that the drivers of growth in the WB economies are correlated with the natural resources-based industries, including agriculture. The weight of the manufacturing sector in GDP and exports is much lower than the average in other middle-income countries and, especially, Slovenia. Manufacturing sector data show that the WB economies are composed of a small percentage of medium- and high-technology industries and a large proportion of low-technology, low R&D-intensive sectors. The available statistics show that, apart from some natural resources-based firms, manufacturing firms generally have no participation in global value chains and have weak innovation systems. Past growth was based on exports of goods and mineral resources but was fragile. These features of the WB economies reflect the state of their innovation and industrial policies. Existing policies related to the development of a dynamic and productive manufacturing sector (with some exceptions) do not seem to be driving structural change or technology upgrading.

Our data also reveal some major manufacturing sector constraints, stemming from unsatisfactory institutional environments and non-competitive markets, and limited sources of financing, innovation activity capacity, etc. Recent evidence (OECD, EBRD, WB, etc.) suggests that the WB countries have made progress in terms of promotion of entrepreneurship and innovation, but there are persistent problems and gaps. Their governments have formulated policy documents and specific measures to support the growth and development of entrepreneurship and innovation, but the implementation of these measures has often been poor due to lack of impact analysis or weak coordination among the various responsible agencies and ministries.

We identified several commonalities among our WB countries. Although we have incomplete data for Albania and Kosova, it seems that the WB economies' manufacturing sectors are dominated by low-tech, low-intensity R&D sectors. In addition, with the slight exception of North Macedonia, export and import of ICT goods are very weak. All three economies show poor innovation performance based on the EBRD knowledge economy index. It would seem that a weak innovation system is one of the main obstacles to the development of a knowledge economy in the three WB economies. The lack of innovation capacity is mostly excluding the manufacturing sectors in the WB economies from participation in global value chains (the exception is some resources-based manufacturing activities). The manufacturing sectors suffer from low levels of production sophistication and poor management, and manufacturing firms in WB economies are characterized by poor product differentiation compared to those in Slovenia. New industrial and innovation policies will be needed to facilitate participation of the manufacturing firms in these economies in global value chains.

In Chap. 6, we extend this discussion to consider the need for a new approach to industrial policymaking in the WB economies.

## References

Acs, Z. J., & Audretsch, D. B. (2005). Entrepreneurship, innovation, and technological change. *Foundations and Trends® in Entrepreneurship, 1*, 149–195. https://doi.org/10.1561/0300000004

Albuquerque, E., Suzigan, W., Kruss, G., & Lee, K. (2015). *Developing national systems of innovation: University–industry interactions in the global south*. Edward Elgar.

Athayde, R. (2009). Measuring enterprise potential in young people. *Entrepreneurship Theory and Practice, 33*(2), 481–500.

Audretsch, D. B. (2002). Entrepreneurship: A survey of the literature for the European Commission, Enterprise Directorate General. http://europa.eu.int/comm/enterprise/library/enterprise-papers/pdf/enterprise_paper_14_2003.pdf

Barro, R. J. (1991). Economic growth in a cross section of countries. *The Quarterly Journal of Economics, 106*(2), 407–443.

Bell, M. (2007). Technological learning and the development of production and innovative capacities in the industry and infrastructure sectors of the least developed countries: What roles for ODA? UNCTAD the least developed countries report 2007 background paper, University of Sussex.

Bell, M., & Figueiredo, P. N. (2012). Innovation capability building and learning mechanisms in latecomer firms: Recent empirical contributions and implications for research. *Canadian Journal of Development Studies/Revue Canadienne D'Etudes du Développement, 33*(1), 14–40. https://doi.org/10.1080/02255189.2012.677168

Bell, M., & Pavitt, K. (1993). Technological accumulation and industrial growth: Contrasts between developed and developing countries. *Industrial and Corporate Change, 2*(2), 157–211.

Bell, M., & Pavitt, K. (1995). The development of technological capabilities. In I. U. Haque (Ed.), *Trade, technology and international competitiveness* (pp. 157–211). The World Bank.

Brown, R., & Mason, C. (2014). Inside the high-tech black box: A critique of technology entrepreneurship policy. *Technovation, 34*(12), 773–784. https://doi.org/10.1016/j.technovation.2014.07.013

Campos, N. F., De Grauwe, P., & Ji, Y. (2017). Structural reforms, growth and inequality: An overview of theory, measurement and evidence, IZA discussion papers, no. 11159, Institute of Labor Economics (IZA), Bonn.

Damijan, J., Knell, M., Majcen, B., & Rojec, M. (2003). The role of FDI, R&D accumulation and trade in transferring technology to transition countries: Evidence from firm panel data for eight transition countries. *Economic Systems, 27*(2), 189–204.

EBRD. (2015). *Transition report 2015—Integration across Borders*. EBRD. https://www.ebrd.com/documents/oce/pdf-transition-report-201516-english.pdf

EBRD. (2019). *Introducing the EBRD knowledge economy index*. EBRD. https://www.ebrd.com/documents/policy/download-the-ebrds-knowledge-economy-index.pdf

European Commission. (2003). *Entrepreneurship in Europe: Green paper*. Enterprise Publications.

European Commission. (2004). *Helping to create an entrepreneurial culture: A guide on good practices in promoting entrepreneurial attitudes and skills through education*. Enterprise Publications.

European Commission. (2022). Commission staff working document, Kosovo 2022 report, Brussels. https://neighbourhood-enlargement.ec.europa.eu/system/files/2022-10/Kosovo%20Report%202022.pdf

Eurostat. (2018). Length of transport networks, 2008, 2013 and 2018 (km). https://ec.europa.eu/eurostat/statisticsexplained/index.php?title=File:Length_of_transport_networks,_2008,_2013_and_2018_(km)_CPC20.png

Freeman, C., & Soete, L. (1997). *The economics of industrial innovation*. Routledge. https://doi.org/10.4324/9780203064474

Gennaioli, C., & Tavoni, T. (2011). Clean or "dirty" energy: Evidence on a renewable energy resource curse, working papers 2011.63, Fondazione Eni Enrico Mattei.

Görg, H., & Strobl, E. (2005). Spillovers from foreign firms through worker mobility: An empirical investigation. *The Scandinavian Journal of Economics, 107*(4), 693–709. http://www.jstor.org/stable/3441021

Hobday, M. (1995). *Innovation in East Asia: The challenge to Japan*. Edward Elgar.

Kim, L. (1997). *Imitation to innovation. The dynamics of Korea's technological learning*. Harvard Business School Press.

MacGarvie, M. (2006). Do firms learn from international trade? *The Review of Economics and Statistics, 88*(1), 46–60. http://www.jstor.org/stable/40042958

Muysken, J., & Nour, S. (2006). Deficiencies in education and poor prospects for economic growth in the Gulf countries: The case of the UAE. *The Journal of Development Studies, 42*(6), 957–980.

OECD. (2021). *Competitiveness in Southeast Europe 2021: A policy outlook, competitiveness and private sector development*. OECD Publishing. https://doi.org/10.1787/dcbc2ea9-en

OECD. (2022). *SME policy index: Western Balkans and Turkey 2022: Assessing the implementation of the small business act for Europe*. SME Policy Index, OECD Publishing. https://doi.org/10.1787/b47d15f0-en

Parker, S. C. (1996). A time series model of self-employment under uncertainty. *Economica, 63*(251), 459–475. https://doi.org/10.2307/2555017

Radosevic, S. (2021). Towards industrial policies to support technology upgrading for sustainable development in Central Asia (SPECA subregion), Report prepared for the UN Economic Commission for Europe., Geneva.

Ramalho, A. (2015). Section 5: Intellectual Property. In F. Amtenbrink, D. Curtin, B. De Witte, P. J. Kuijper, A. Mcdonnell, & S. Van Den Bogaert (Eds.), *Law of the European Union (New Edition Kapteyn/Verloren)*. Kluwer Law International. (2016, Forthcoming). https://ssrn.com/abstract=2723932

SBA. (2019). Enterprise and industry European Commission, Brussels. Retrieved May 7, 2022, from https://ec.europa.eu/docsroom/documents/32581/attachments/26/translations/en/renditions/native

Schumpeter, J. (1942). *Capitalism, socialism and democracy*. Harper and Row.

Schumpeter, J. A. (1939). *Business cycles: A theoretical, historical, and statistical analysis of the capitalist process*. McGraw-Hill.

Shane, S. (1996). Explaining variation in rates of entrepreneurship in the United States: 1899–1988. *Journal of Management, 22*(5), 747–781. https://doi.org/10.1016/S0149-2063(96)90021-5

Stiglitz, J. (2000). Unravelling of the Washington consensus. *Multinational Monitor, 21*(4), 13–17.

World Bank. (2019). *Doing business report*. World Bank. https://www.doingbusiness.org/content/dam/doingBusiness/media/Annual-Reports/English/DB2019-report_web-version.pdf

World Bank. (2020). Enterprise surveys, World Bank. https://www.enterprisesurveys.org/en/data/exploreeconomies/2019/Kosovo

World Bank. (n.d.). Current account balance (% of GDP) - North Macedonia, World Bank DataBank website. https://data.worldbank.org/indicator/BN.CAB.XOKA.GD.ZS?locations=MK

CHAPTER 6

# A Primer on Industrial Policies for Technology Upgrading in Three Western Balkan Economies

## 6.1 Introduction

This chapter explores a new method to promote manufacturing firm growth through the implementation of a new 'industrial policy' approach. The aim is to encourage more intensive technology upgrading as the foundation for sustainable economic growth in Albania, North Macedonia and Kosovo—three Western Balkan (WB) economies. The categorization of these three countries as middle-income countries determines the nature of their business activities and their inclusion in this group has substantial implications for their industrial policies. To become political and economic members of the European Union (EU) will require their economic and technological transformation. It is expected that EU membership would require the firms operating in these three economies to be more competitive in both Europe and the wider world.

This chapter proposes an industrial policy that prioritizes development of innovation capacity and technology upgrading in the WB countries. We understand technology upgrading as 'a shift towards higher value-added products and stages of production through increased specialization' (Gereffi, 1999, pp. 51–52). This rather broad definition includes innovation and R&D and production capabilities along with aspects related to structural change and knowledge interactions with the global economy (Radosevic & Yoruk, 2018).



F. Sahiti, *Industrial Policies for Technological Upgrading in Western Balkan Countries*, https://doi.org/10.1007/978-3-031-51429-6_6

By describing our conceptual approach to industrial policy for technology upgrading in the WB economies as a 'new' industrial policy, we are differentiating from the approach discussed in Chap. 4. It suggests that, in addition to conventional structural reforms and infrastructural projects, developing economies such as the WB economies should focus on designing policies to promote accumulation of technological capabilities to drive technology upgrading.

This chapter is organized as follows. Section 6.2 discusses the scope and rationale for adapting the new industrial policy, Sect. 6.3 provides our new industrial policy framework and Sect. 6.4 examines the financial and institutional constraints of the new policies. In Sect. 6.5, we review the principles and criteria that must be respected in the drafting of new policies; in Sect. 6.6 we analyse the strategic orientation of industrial policies and propose four areas for strategic investment to foster technology upgrading. In Sect. 6.7, we propose priority policy areas, and in Sect. 6.8 we discuss governance capacity required for industry policy success. Section 6.9 concludes this chapter.

## 6.2 The Scope and Rationale of a New Industrial Policy

The data presented in Chap. 5 suggest that, during the major changes that occurred in the 1990s, the focus of policy makers in the WB economies was not on the promotion of nascent industries. After 2000, WB country policy makers began to realize the importance of industrial policy, as the result, mostly, of the continuously emerging structural changes and trends in these economies. However, there was an assumption that the solution was implementation of industrial policy (Rodrik, 2014). On its own, industrial policy cannot revive growth in economies with macroeconomic imbalances or prevent deindustrialization. Rather, industrial policy should be seen as a supporting framework that allows policy makers to establish an institutional setup and a structure that will promote innovation activity. Industrial policy could be considered as a way of thinking that allows policy makers to learn by doing or acting, which highlights the importance of the type and quality of the dialogue between policy makers and the business community.

The decline in manufacturing production capacity in developing countries is a real cause for concern and has spread to other sectors. Pisano and

Shih (2012) suggest that deterioration of production capacity leads to backlash and causes harm to adjacent activities (including innovation and technology-related activities) in the upstream and downstream value chains. Over the long term, weak production sectors in Kosovo, Albania and North Macedonia will cause significant damage to the competitiveness of rivals in the regional market and beyond, which points to the importance of industrial policies to mitigate these negative effects.

Industrial policy is generally seen as a priority. During the socialist economy period, many then socialist countries tried to build capital-intensive industries (Lin, 2017). In Kosovo, industrial policy was focused on the development of heavy industry and ores (Sahiti, 2019) and a strategy of comparative advantage or challenges to comparative advantage. This thinking was the result of the structuralism that dominated economic development reasoning in the 1950s and 1960s. According to Lin (2017), government interventions as part of such strategies were unsuccessful and, in fact, had negative effects on the economy, inducing major shortages of funds, negative foreign exchange, even more inefficient distribution of economic resources, reduced work incentives, worsening of the income distribution, etc.

More recently, in both developed and developing countries, change has been based on Foreign Direct Investment (FDI) and innovation and regional policies (Rodrik, 2007). Industrial policy implementations have shifted from foreign trade and trade protection to the domestic regulatory and support system, but within a relatively open trade and FDI context. According to Baldwin (2012), this structural change was the inevitable result of the spread of Global Value Chains (GVCs), while Radosevic (2021) considers that certain processes and events with global effects revealed the need for design and implementation of industrial policies. The first of these processes was the 2008 global financial crisis, which underlined the need for industrial policies. This shock undermined the confidence of many developed country policy makers, in the 'free market' as the only governance mechanism. The need for industrial policies was triggered, also, by the deindustrialization in many developed and developing economies and regions, caused by China's economic growth. What became known as the 'China factor' prompted many world governments to review their existing industrial policies. At the same time, Radosevic (2021) believes that the fact of climate change has caused many policy makers to realize that technology-led, laissez faire trajectories do not guarantee the emergence of technologies able to mitigate its negative effects.

Alongside the persistent issue of climate change, the negative effects of the COVID-19 pandemic resulted in policy makers around the world, formulating and trying to implement measures to confine and reduce the consequences of the pandemic.

The importance and duration of all these processes are different and required different political philosophies and new political approaches or industrial policies (Radosevic, 2021). We should first define what we mean by 'new' industrial policies and clarify how they differ from 'traditional' or old industrial policies.

Old industrial policies include policies implemented between the 1950s and the 1970s, mainly in the developing economies, and aimed at import substitution (Radosevic, 1999; Ramos, 2000; Crespi et al., 2014). However, in some developed economies, old industrial policies were linked to so-called national champion firms. In the former socialist countries, industrial policies aimed at import substitution were the most frequent and consisted of planning policies and extreme administrative regimes, aimed at improving national trade balances and protecting and promoting domestic industrial products (Lombardozzi, 2020). Between 1990 and 2010, in particular, and accompanied by increased globalization and the emergence of the Washington Consensus, the state's role in the economy became especially important. Policy makers considered the role and influence of the market in the economy to be paramount (Williamson, 1990). For instance, policies based on the idea of the Washington Consensus were promoted widely in most developing countries and, especially, in the transition economies, including the three WB countries which are the subject of our analysis.

Supporters of the Washington Consensus or 'neoliberalists' share the view that free market functioning and reduced state involvement in the economy are crucial for developing country growth. Most former socialist country economic reforms have been based on these principles, which focus, mainly, on how to privatize state and social assets, how to create market-oriented economic incentives and how to create macroeconomic stability. In this perspective, once the 'right' incentives and the 'right' institutions are in place, developing countries will experience automatic economic growth. However, this ignores important factors such as accumulated production capabilities, organizational and innovative capabilities and other significant internal business factors (Radosevic, 2021). Neoliberalists believe that, for an open economy, these factors matter very little and will emerge if private entrepreneurs are offered the 'right incentives', and the influence of the state in economic affairs is reduced significantly. Neoliberals ignore the fact that economic growth derives primarily from firms' capabilities to acquire and use knowledge accumulated from private and public external sources. For neoliberals, the only legitimate policies that can stimulate economic growth are those that focus on correcting market failures; they believe that the 'right' policies do not differentiate among sectors, firms or technologies. For them, the right policy is a horizontal policy, aimed at improving the overall business environment or encouraging and attracting higher levels of FDI. There now is general agreement that the policies offered by the Washington Consensus have failed to deliver on their key promises (World Bank, 2005).

During their social and economic transition processes, most former socialist countries embraced and implemented the policies supported by the Washington Consensus. The results of the transition process have been reported regularly by the European Bank for Reconstruction and Development (EBRD) (see transition reports since 1994). However, the contemporary measurement framework now includes sectoral reform indicators and measures of state institutional quality (Besley et al., 2010). Thus, this framework recognizes the role of the state and its institutions in market developments. Also, in the new framework, there is no clearly defined final transition position, which implies that there can be different versions of capitalism and that it is the historical and institutional contexts of individual countries that define successful transition. Besley et al. (2010, p. 2) favour transition, understood as an intermediate objective and underline that the focus should be on the final goal towards which the transition is oriented.

The reason why (completed) transition process cannot be measured by the achievement of a well-defined goal is because the growth and recovery of economies in transition cannot be explained only by the variables included in the progress-in-transition framework and reflect a broader set of resources-based, technological and institutional factors (World Bank, 2005). Radosevic (2021) points out that the growth of countries in transition, including the WB countries, depends strongly on efficient markets and on effective government, which functions as a complement to and not a substitute for the market. The experience of many countries in transition shows that market opening, in the absence of a coherent industrial policy led by an effective government, is not sufficient (Nayyar, 2019). In addition, the degree of dependence of the transition country on foreign technology, whether through FDI or licensing processes, and the capacity of such countries to generate technology internally depend on their level of economic and social development. What the role of the state should be in these processes depends on the nature of the state, which, in turn, depends on the degree of political development of its society and the state's historical circumstances.

So, what is the role of the state in industrial policy? We draw on evidence provided in the most recent industrial policy literature to try to give a brief answer to this question. The literature seems unambiguous about state involvement in national economic and industrial policies. What is less in agreement is the involvement of the state in market regulation. Radosevic (2021) proposes a taxonomy of the dominant rationales for state intervention in the economy (see Table 6.1). This categorization draws on his previous work (Radosevic, 2021) and that of other authors including Evans (1995), Block (2008), Block et al. (2020) and Mazzucato (2013).

In the case of the regulatory state, seen as a type of 'guardian' or 'market fixing' state (Evans, 1995; Mazzucato, 2013), its role is to formulate policies aimed at correcting market failures. For example, the state can create rules to guard against or correct R&D and innovation market failures, through the imposition of taxes or provision of subsidies. Proponents of a regulatory state believe that the state should intervene only minimally and that any major interventions would have a negative effect on the economy and discriminate against other sectors or firms.

In the developmental state, government plays an active role in the economy by engaging in macro- and microeconomic planning, ostensibly to improve the welfare of the population through the best possible use of economic resources (Johnson, 1982, 1999). Supporters of the developmental state consider the state's role as crucial for economic development, which is government's main objective and is achieved through both policy and direct interventions in the economy (Przeworski, 1985). Direct state

**Table 6.1** State roles in industrial policy

| *Role* | *Rationale* |
|---|---|
| Regulatory state | Market failure |
| Developmental state | Capability failure |
| Developmental network state | Network (system) failure |

Source: Adopted from Radosevic (2021)

interventions range from protecting the domestic manufacturing sector from foreign products, to facilitating imports of machinery, to creation of state financial institutions. An example of a direct intervention is exploitation of the state and its institutions by a domestic company barred from entering a particular industry by the competition or encountering problems related to linking with foreign companies. Examples of states that have intervened in the economy include Germany, Japan and South Korea among many others. In a 1992 paper, Peter Evans refers to two characteristics of the developmental state—bureaucratic capacity and embeddedness, understood as the embeddedness of the public bureaucracy in society and in the business community. For Evans (1995), public bureaucracy in the developing state is a strategic role, but a successful developmental state requires the business community to be pivotal in decision-making. Evans (1995, p. 12) believes that the developmental state can become 'predatory' and, especially, if it 'lacks the ability to prevent individual functionaries from pursuing their goals … or, when personal ties are the only source of cohesion and individual maximization takes precedence over the pursuit of collective goals'.

The idea of a Developmental Network State (DNS) is relatively new and refers to the importance of state intervention in networks or systems, rather than market failures (Block, 2008; Block et al., 2020). Network failures refer to problems related to achieving collective action, which, in the case of innovation activities, is particularly important since such activities often require cooperation among different parties. The description of DNS tends to be reserved to developed countries, especially the US and the EU countries, but should be applied also to developing and growing economies (Radosevic, 2021).

In a DNS approach, failure to create an innovation network stems from endemic coordination failures both among firms and between firms and public institutions. This type of failure can occur despite strong incentives for firms to innovate and can be overcome or mitigated by the creation of mechanisms that allow identification of specific sector or technology issues that can be addressed through joint actions, facilitated or mediated by the state.

Compared to developed economies, the importance of DNS in developing economies is related more to attracting FDI and, especially, to business relations between foreign and domestic firms. It has frequently been claimed that foreign firms' innovation experience is decisive for the creation of innovative capacity in domestic firms and is achieved by encouraging foreign firms to integrate in the domestic economy.

The DNS may be an appropriate new industrial policy analytical framework. However, state involvement in mitigating or eliminating network failures requires institutions with appropriate capacities and a well-developed and organized private sector (Radosevic, 2021). In addition, in order to respond to individual practical and contextual project issues, the form of state institutional intervention must be identified on a case-by-case basis. New industrial policies need to be based not on best practice but should involve plans that respond to specific problems and are in line with the capacities and coordination conditions of both the state and the private sector.

At the time of writing, debate was focused less on whether or not the state should intervene in the economy and more on the types of intervention needed and their design, that is, on the state and its design of industrial policy. The three state roles described above should be considered stylized terms, since, in practice, none of them is regularized. State roles are rarely mutually exclusive and their implementation in practice depends on each country's individual circumstances. In some circumstances, government may be the market regulator, in others, government might assume all three roles in combination, acting as regulator and working on the development of the state and state networks. Thus, the boundaries between the state's roles are often blurred. Its institutions may be responsible for market regulation and, also, provision of financial support for R&D. Both roles may have emerged as the result of market failures, system failures or skills failures. Also, the role of the state changes with the country's social and economic evolution. Take the example of South Korea; Choung and Hwang (2021) show that the role of the Korean state in state development has been relatively successful but now involves more active interventions to promote technology improvements. The change in Korea's circumstances confronted the state with new and qualitatively different challenges compared to the development period.

## 6.3 A New Industrial Policy Framework for Technology Upgrading

According to Radosevic (2021), industrial policy options for developing economies should focus on big thinking and new thinking alongside conventional thinking. Conventional industrial policy refers to government measures aimed at structural reforms and measures to improve the business and regulatory environment. Although the WB economies have made considerable progress in improving their business environments, various reports from international and local organizations (e.g., World Bank, European Commission, Organisation for Economic Cooperation and Development, EBRD, etc.) draw attention to a number of problems related to the business environment.

Thinking big involves strategic measures and projects aimed at improving those areas where countries are most vulnerable. For example, for Kosovo, an improved electricity supply is essential. Thinking big also includes education system reforms to match contemporary trends and satisfy internal and external market demand and the building of basic services to allow expansion of industrial activity.

Thinking new refers to the need for a new industrial policy paradigm. Policy makers need to make efforts to design industrial policies that focus on exploring new (non-traditional) potential export business areas to facilitate participation in the global economy and GVCs. An example is the promotion, in Kosovo, of the beverage industry, which it is hoped could allow entry to the international market. Identifying firms in different industries with export potential would help to achieve this goal.

These three aspects should be considered not in isolation, but as complements, allowing a new, diverse policy mix. For example, structural reforms could be supported by policies aimed at promoting a certain business sector with export potential or creating a basic infrastructure that provides the conditions required for the development of industries that will attract foreign investors.

Industrial policies to achieve technology upgrading will fail unless complemented by other strategies. Technology upgrading and catch-up are complex processes that require a multidimensional approach, although it should not be assumed that a multidimensional industry policy will solve all economic problems. Rodrik (2014) emphasizes that what can be achieved by industrial policy should not be overstated. On the other hand, the success experienced by China, Vietnam and, in the past, Korea and

Japan demonstrates the significance of industrial policy. In Sect. 6.1, we discussed the intellectual and broader ramifications of the new industrial policy approach within this eclectic policy perspective, highlighting those elements relevant to the WB economies.

In this section, we conceptualize industrial policy as a possible alternative, based on the positive and negative experiences of both structural reforms and old industrial policies. This new approach to industrial policy takes account of the innovative and political capacities of the three WB countries. It is based on the idea of technology upgrading, which, as described in the previous section, is defined as a shift to higher value-added products and production stages through increased specialization. This definition includes R&D and innovation capabilities, production capabilities, dimensions of structural change and knowledge interactions with the global economy.

We propose a new conceptualization of industrial policy as a possible alternative, based on the positive and negative experiences of both structural reform and old industrial policies. This concept aims to acquaint the reader with new approaches to industrial policy, taking into account the innovative and political capacities of the three WB countries. It is based on the idea of technology upgrading, which as described in the previous sections is defined as a shift towards higher value-added products and production stages through increased specialization. This is a broad definition that includes not only R&D and innovation capabilities, but also production capabilities, dimensions of structural change and the knowledge interactions with the global economy.

We propose a conceptual framework to explore technology improvement in the three WB economies (see Fig. 6.1). This framework includes four main areas. First, new policies must be based on the focal country's financial and institutional limitations. Second, new industrial policies should respect certain basic principles and criteria. Third, new policies should be focused on strategic areas related to the development of innovative activities and technology upgrading. Fourth, the success of these new industrial policies will depend largely on the country's administrative capabilities and institutions. This conceptualization is aimed at providing a new approach to industrial policy based on technology upgrading in the WB economies.

We discuss the constraints on the implementation of new industrial policies and their main principles, the strategies involved and the administrative capabilities required for successful implementation.

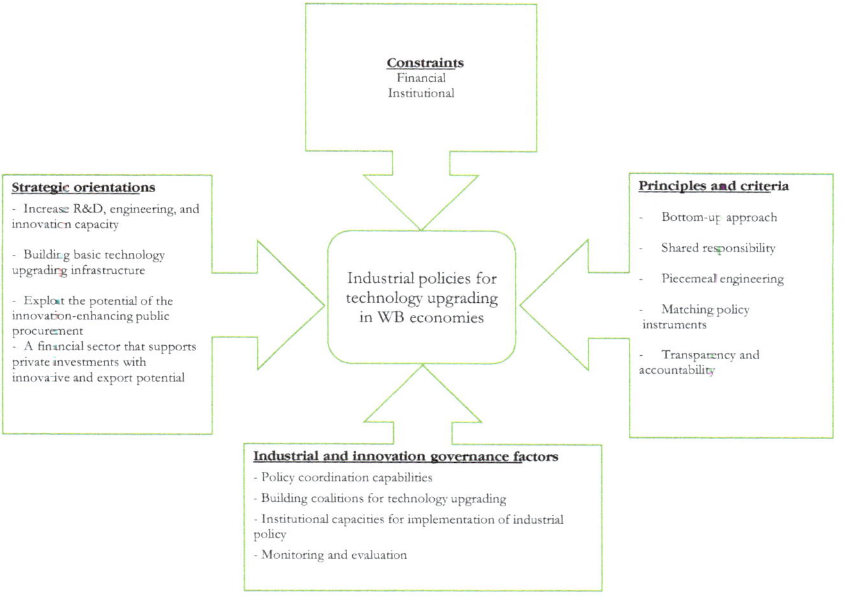


**Fig. 6.1** New industrial policies framework for the WB economies. Source: Author's elaboration based on Radosevic (2021)

## 6.4 The Constraints on Industrial Policies in the Western Balkan Economies

Our discussion of the constraints that define and determine the range of industrial policy approaches available to policy makers in the WB economies should not be considered exhaustive. Below, we discuss the limitations identified by our analysis.

The first limitation is related to the technological capacity of the firms operating in the WB economies. These middle-income economies include mainly technology laggard business firms, whose innovation systems are different from those in developed countries. Developing country innovation systems focus on adoption and assimilation of foreign technology (Radosevic, 2021). R&D in developing economies tends to be extramural, that is, conducted in public R&D organizations rather than firms which generally lack the required managerial capabilities and qualified workforce. Firms in developing economies are more interested in productivity and production and service capability improvements to satisfy export markets, while developed country firms invest in R&D and improved absorptive capacity (Radosevic, 2021). In developing economies, such as the WB economies, the firm's technological position has implications for the role of industrial policy, which tends to focus less on how to improve R&D processes and more on technology upgrading.

The second limitation concerns the weak contribution of the WB economies to GVCs. With the minor exception of some resources-based industries, the WB economies are poorly integrated in the global economy and GVCs and their main challenge is increasing competitiveness through production efficiency and technology enhancements. Firms in developing economies need to find other ways and other approaches to participate in GVCs. International supply chains can be exploited for learning to improve domestic firms, but this requires that the organizational and political boundaries between industrial, innovation, trade and FDI policies can be breached.

The analysis in Chap. 5 suggests that conventional industrial policies follow a mainly top-down approach, aimed at promotion of a particular manufacturing sector, to enable national comparative advantage. Industrial policies generally involve expensive programmes, affordable only by countries with good financial capacity and effective and stable administrative institutions. Our findings suggest that WB economy budgets are limited and the quality and efficiency of their state institutions are weak. This weak policy and administrative capacity of WB governments constitutes another constraint on the pursuit of expensive top-down policy programmes. Poor-quality institutions and implementation capacity suggest a bootstrap approach, that is, industrial policy design compatible with the individual country's financial constraints and administrative capacity. It also requires good communication with the local business community in policy efforts to provide incentives for technology upgrading and conduct performance assessments. In turn, this requires smart industry and innovation governance, which highlights the governance dimension of industrial policy as significant for the success of new industrial policies. In Sect. 6.8, we discuss aspects related to the building of intelligent industry governance.

## 6.5 New Industrial Policies for the Western Balkan Economies: Principles and Criteria

In the context of the limitations described above, new industrial policies for the WB economies should respect two criteria: (i) definition of specific priority technology areas and support instruments and (ii) identification of private and public sector capacity for self-organization to enable achievement of the defined goals and objectives. In this approach, it is assumed that, first, the state lacks the resources required to finance innovation policies and, second, even if funds are available, the state lacks the administrative capacity to implement, manage, monitor and evaluate the policies. Nevertheless, the state remains an important, but not the only actor involved in implementing new industrial policies.

Government's role as mediator and main coordinator of the implementation, monitoring and evaluation of policies requires detailed knowledge about the sectors that require interventions and expertise in the organization of work processes. Thus, the role of the state includes identification of strategic problems and facilitation of coordination among different organizations and actors to find solutions to problems (Radosevic, 2021). These numerous problems include definition quality and performance standards, creating joint processes related to export certificates, etc. It is important also that the state, as the main network coordinator, includes private sector actors. The success of new industrial policies will depend on the creation of forums and effective working between state agencies and the business community.

The basic principles of new industrial policies are numerous. Below, we discuss what Radosevic (2021) identifies as the five most important ones.

First, industrial policymaking aimed at technology improvements must be bottom-up. Top-down, government-led initiatives that do not involve private sector and non-profit sector actors and donors will not achieve the results intended by new industrial policies.

Second, since new industrial policies are about facilitating and moderating self-organized activities undertaken or proposed by government and non-governmental organizations, their implementation must include both government and other actors. Also, identification of strategic sectors that require interventions and responsibility for their implementation and evaluation should be the responsibility of government along with the business community and non-profit organizations.

Third, the strategic problems targeted by new industrial policies are likely to require large investments of financial and human resources. Solving these problems will call for what Popper (1963) describes as 'piecemeal engineering' and a process of learning by experimenting or learning from mistakes. The implementation of new industrial policies should be based on small pilot projects and experimentation. Pilot projects could be implemented in specific sectors, sub-sectors, industries and regions. If successful, they can be replicated at scale, while, since they are necessarily small projects, if they fail they can be more easily corrected or cancelled.

Fourth, limited financial and institutional capacity for implementation will require careful formulation of new industrial policies and particular attention to the instruments used for implementation. The new industrial policies should promote only those actions that are a good match with the aim of the policy and the economy's implementation capacity.

Fifth, transparent and competitive public policy programmes and benefits are essential for new industrial policies. These aspects are particularly important in contexts with corruption at the government and institutional levels. Transparent and institutional mechanisms must include access to credit, accountability over the distribution of state support and a system of controls and fines. Again, implementation of pilot projects allows early identification of risks, diagnostic monitoring and early warning systems.

## 6.6 Industrial Policy Strategic Orientations

Based on the new industrial policy principles presented above, this section discusses some strategic orientations relevant to the WB economies. We are not suggesting they will be the complete solution to the many problems faced by the WB countries. Rather, we try to identify some solutions that are based on the realities that policy makers need to consider in trying to address their respective countries' economic problems. The strategic orientations proposed could act as a framework for the formulation of new industrial policies. Moreover, the strategic solutions proposed respond to continually changing issues in today's world, which make skills, flexibility, openness and receptivity to technological change crucial for prosperity and economic growth.

Our proposed solutions could become the sources of growth for the WB economies. Recall, first, that the primary goal of new industrial policies is promotion of innovation and technological capacities in business organizations to drive economic development. We suggest that the four broad strategic areas listed below should be prioritized.

1. Innovation system upgrading, by increasing gross expenditure on R&D and engineering and innovative capabilities.
2. Creation of an essential infrastructure for technology upgrading.
3. Exploitation of innovation-enhancing public procurement.
4. Creation of a financial sector to allow investment in innovation and export projects.

We examine each of these in more detail below.

### *Upgrading the Innovative System by Increasing R&D and Engineering and Innovation Capabilities*

An effective and efficient innovation system is vital for technology upgrading. Existing evidence and EBRD data in particular show that the innovation systems in the WB economies suffer from multiple problems. Some of these are due to their economic structure, which is dominated by natural resources-based industries and a small share of medium- and high-technology sectors, but are due, also, to the inadequate funding provided for innovation and R&D activities. These characteristics make structural changes to enable technological improvement almost impossible.

To remedy this situation, the three WB economies should make efforts to increase their R&D spending to at least the levels achieved by the other middle-income economies (1.86) by 2028. Increased public funding of R&D would allow business organizations to exploit foreign technology and knowledge, based on improved absorptive capacity and, in turn, this would allow these countries to develop their R&D activities. Internationalization of their R&D systems would increase the WB countries' access to knowledge via cooperation with local research institutes, universities and academies of sciences and development of joint innovation activities with sister organizations in other countries. These activities should include adaptation of imported technologies to local conditions, changes related to daily work activities such as work procedures, cultural norms and customs, etc. (OECD, 2009). New industrial policies should also provide support for engineering and innovation management at the enterprise level to improve production quality and allow application for

ISO certification, including ISO9001, ISO14000 and other industry-specific standards.

Both economic theory and the empirical evidence show that, ultimately, what matters is human capital and its critical contribution to economic and social developments. Improving the quality of human capital could bring huge benefits. Several indicators show that the quality of the education systems in the WB economies is very low compared to the reference country, Slovenia, especially in relation to inclusion of entrepreneurship training in school curricula (OECD, 2009), VET and tertiary education (30- to 34-year age group) (see Chap. 5 Table 5.1). Raising education standards (e.g., to match levels in Slovenia) could set the WB economies on a growth path. It is essential that new industrial policies prioritize improvements to school standards.

There are many reasons why the education systems in the WB countries are inadequate and our recommendations are not exhaustive. However, an immediate failure related to WB education systems is the mismatch between market needs and the curricula offered. Policy should focus on education system reforms in order to produce human capital that will satisfy the demands of local and international markets. This will require:

a. an education system that develops entrepreneurship and innovation skills and secondary- and tertiary-level education that responds to industry needs;
b. rigorous and independent evaluation of schools' and educators' performance: a better salary and promotion system would incentivize better quality teaching. Policies should be implemented to facilitate improved professional development and exclusion of underperforming teachers, including publication of information on teaching performance and teacher quality;
c. higher education should attract the best students and the best teachers. Current student recruitment policies lack criteria, which has a direct impact on graduate quality. Empirical evidence shows that graduates from WB universities are not equipped with the skills required by labour markets (European Commission, 2022). The emphasis seems to be on award of a degree, rather than the learning and skills involved;
d. poor higher education in the WB countries is related to existing policies, rules and regulations and lack of accountability in teaching and research. The WB countries should increase investment in

scientific research and create standards for the evaluation of scientific achievements, publications and performance of academic staff. Various reports point out that academic staff contracts are based more on teaching hours and not on additional research, scientific and innovation work. According to international reports (see, e.g., individual country reports issued by the European Commission in 2022), research institutes and universities tend to have autonomy related to operational decisions and it is important that this autonomy is maintained. However, these institutions should create clear policy structures related to increasing the accountability of public universities based on the above-mentioned criteria. The WB countries do not measure the performance of education organizations. Consistent and professional performance measurement is crucial to enable allocation of appropriate funding to research that addresses industry needs. Links among research institutes, universities and industry are also important. It is vital that governments establish consistent rules and policies for the allocation of funds to public and private education institutions. The distribution of funds should be via open competition, according to the rules related to innovation projects, to satisfy national economic strategies. The outcomes of funding for innovation should also be evaluated;

e. an education system that provides training to prepare students for the workplace. VET enrolment among high school students is 50.3% in Kosovo and around 60% in North Macedonia (see Chap. 5 Table 5.2). However, VET needs to have a higher component of practical training (OECD, 2009). WB policies should make it compulsory for VET to include a large proportion of practical experience and opportunities for apprenticeships. Vocational courses and apprenticeships will require monitoring and evaluation to ensure that industry apprenticeships are properly managed;
f. teaching of digital skills and a policy framework that promotes and prioritizes digital literacy throughout society. Digital transformation of business activities will require a cross-industry and cross-sectoral approach.

Based on the idea that national economic growth depends on national potential to accumulate scientific, technological and managerial knowledge, the WB economies are seriously lagging, not least in their very limited innovation activity. In addition, the funding allocated to the development of innovation and technological skills is significantly lower than in counterpart countries and, especially, Slovenia. The human capital generated by WB country education systems is not meeting industry demands. We suggest an increase in gross spending on R&D to at least the average for the group of middle-income countries, to allow improvements to the above aspects. Education systems need to be aligned to market needs and need to be part of a national accountability framework. Education systems must prioritize development of practical skills and digital skills.

#### *Creation of the Essential Infrastructure for Technology Upgrading*

Two of the limitations affecting domestic manufacturing firms in WB economies is their disconnect with global market trends and small or no participation in GVCs, which reduce their access to knowledge and markets. New industrial policies need to provide incentives for domestic firms to participate in GVCs. This will involve attraction of FDI, which, in turn, will enable industrial upgrading and lead to joint domestic and foreign firm investment projects. Policy should aim at creating a legal and physical infrastructure to support such projects and promote growth (Radosevic, 2021).

Free economic zones would provide infrastructure support for foreign investment and facilitate access to and absorption of the knowledge and experience of foreign firms. Such efforts will require the support of relevant business services and availability of a skilled workforce.

WB policymakers should ensure that FDI investments are managed through clear contract arrangements and benefit both the foreign and domestic partners. Cost-sharing partnerships with subsidiaries of foreign companies could allow better training in technical skills which would improve the quality of human capital. Initially, this may require provision of subsidies for foreign firms. However, the business activity of these firms could be an effective mechanism for generating the skills required by the WB economies more generally. The business activities of foreign firms increase the need for a skilled workforce, which requires the involvement of local education institutions and could generate spillover effects for local vocational training. FDI policies should include programmes to encourage foreign firms to include local suppliers in their value chains. Such a proactive approach to industrial policymaking would create opportunities to exploit the expertise of foreign companies to improve domestic manufacturing capabilities.

Creating links between domestic and foreign firms to allow domestic suppliers to participate in GVCs will require specific and publicly funded programmes. Participation in GVCs would enable WB country firms to learn from the experience of foreign firms, which would allow them to increase their production capabilities. These programmes would need to be managed by a public agency operating according to good commercial and business principles and independent of politics.

WB country structural reforms should prioritize industry upgrading through attraction of FDI and a focus on areas with medium- and long-term growth prospects. Structural reforms should be supported by sector- or technology-specific innovation policies.

Regulatory reforms should aim at removing the general obstacles to doing business, promoting a competitive market and removing the barriers in those sectors with growth potential, such as information and communication technology, food processing and beverages, and removing training barriers. Policies should be implemented to encourage investment in technology-, sector- and industry-specific human capital and training. The design of these reforms will be crucial to ensure that they do not give unfair advantage to foreign investors. Regulatory reforms should be accompanied by sector- and industry-specific technology upgrading policies. For example, agricultural reforms should aim at simplifying land ownership, improving infrastructures, making markets more accessible, improving storage methods and processing facilities and providing good quality seeds and fertilizers. The level of support will vary across sectors, but care should be taken to ensure that regulatory reforms and innovation policy measures are complementary (Radosevic, 2021).

Quality is an issue for both individual firms and the whole manufacturing sector. For the three WB economies, it is essential to provide infrastructure services that help improve national quality programmes. These services might include programmes to promote investment, programmes related to the expansion of technology, productivity centres, information and communication services, etc. Providing these services would extend access to established technologies to smaller firms. Technology extension programmes could provide resources to enable firms to identify needs and find appropriate technological solutions or seek solutions provided by professionals.

Chapter 3 discussed the dominance of Small and Medium-sized Enterprises (SMEs) in the WB economies. SMEs require technical services, testing services and problem-solving skills, which cannot be satisfied only be research institutes and universities. The SME infrastructure needs a network of technical institutes.

Overall, investment in legal and physical infrastructure is essential for economic growth. This type of investment complements other forms of investment and tends to be large scale and long term and requires good coordination to achieve the maximum benefits. Government's role is vital for the planning, implementation and financing of infrastructure projects. The infrastructural architecture we have proposed would create the preconditions for sustainable development of technological capacity as an economic and social development factor.

#### *Exploitation of Innovation-Enhancing Public Procurement*

This chapter showed that, in the WB economies, demand for research and technology is under-developed and the transfer of this demand to the private sector is not easy and takes time. Public procurement provides the opportunity to combine local demand related to the development of the public sector with local technological capabilities (Stojcic et al., 2020).

Procurement to improve innovation is not straightforward. Public procurement is demanding and carries a risk of failure related to a too large gap between needs and capabilities, ex ante failure of bidders to fulfil the technical aspects of the technology to be purchased due to its innovations and when the product must fulfil essential new operational needs (Edler et al., 2005). Also, procurers may not be sufficiently aware of technical changes and might have unreasonable expectations about the technology. However, the WB economies should consider innovation-enhancing procurements for small technology-based firms, similar to those involved in the US Small Business Innovation Research programme. This could stimulate technological innovation by providing government agencies with new, cost-effective, technical and scientific solutions to their problems (Radosevic, 2021). However, procurement criteria would need to be carefully defined, include the goals of the procurement contract and be transparent and fair. Participation should be open to both incumbent and new firms and include some form of grants for innovative firms.

The available evidence suggests that policy makers in the WB economies recognize the potential offered by this instrument. Since proposed e-government reforms will require improved information technology services, public procurement could usefully be implemented in that sector.

### *A Financial Sector That Supports Private Investments with Innovative and Export Potential*

The availability of financial funds is a major component of any industrial policy framework. The creation of institutional financial instruments that support various long-term financing schemes and good commercial conditions is important for achieving the objectives defined in the new industrial policies. Financial support would enable manufacturing firms to invest in new equipment and ideas (technological and managerial) and reorganize production processes in line with international best practice. Greater investment in new equipment and ideas would allow firms to be more competitive in international markets and allow them to anticipate and respond to changing markets and opportunities.

There are several countries, such as Slovenia and Germany, that have used financial instruments to support their industry. This financial support has been aimed at increasing manufacturing firms' competitivity, allowing them time to 'learn to produce', that is, to develop and accumulate sufficient production skills, especially at the beginning of their activity. The industrial policy paradigm has changed to provision of financial support to enable firms to improve their innovation capacity.

The evidence shows that the financial sectors in the WB economies are performing relatively well. However, most WB firms use debt as their main source of financing. Capital markets are weak or, in the case of Kosovo, non-existent. Economic theory and empirical evidence highlight the importance of a supportive investment and innovation environment. Low levels of investment and innovation lead to low labour productivity or low levels of Gross Domestic Product (GDP) per hour. Our data show that in the three WB economies, GDP per hour worked is significantly lower than in Slovenia.

Financial intermediaries in the WB economies tend to take a short-term view when evaluating investment opportunities and this short-termism applies, in particular, to the financing of innovation-related projects, which are considered more risky and more difficult to collateralize. However, innovation should be considered a public good, since it benefits other firms.

New firms with no business history suffer from a 'credit gap'; financial intermediaries find it difficult to differentiate high-risk from low-risk entrepreneurs. However, empirical research suggests that small firms are often more innovative. Since the majority of firms in the WB economies are SMEs, the reluctance of banks to finance innovation projects is having long-term effects on growth.

These problems require different solutions. However, adapting models that have been successful in other countries would result in improvements. For example, competition in the retail banking sector could be encouraged along with liberalization of the licensing conditions for new banks. Increasing competition in the banking sector would encourage banks to search more diligently for profitable lending opportunities and could reduce the cost of loans.

Another improvement would be the creation of a business development bank, along the lines of Slovenia's SID bank. Its capital would be constituted mainly by public finance, which would allow lower costs of capital and credit compared to commercial banks. The development bank's remit would be to support exporting firms, manufacturing firms with innovation capabilities and high-growth firms. In particular, a bank based on sound governance principles would adopt a broader economic perspective on the benefits of investing in specific sectors, including those likely to yield long-term social returns from development of technologies.

The creation of development banks in the WB economies would suffer from particular risks related to political and economic corruption. They would need clearly articulated missions and clearly defined economic objectives and would need to take responsibility for their achievement. An independent board would be needed to oversee operational decisions. The project would need long-term commitment from whichever political party was in power to avoid the banks being abolished, reinvented or rebranded, which are particular risks in the WB countries.

Overall, the limited availability of finance in the WB economies reflects their limited capital market capacity. Economic organizations and, in particular, manufacturing firms rely heavily on banking intermediaries, which provide high-cost loans to growing, dynamic and innovative SMEs. We suggest that WB country policies should aim at increasing retail banking competition and establishing business development banks.

## 6.7 Prioritizing Areas for Intervention and Industrial Policies

In Sect. 6.5 we discussed strategic orientations and policy areas we consider important for the realization of new industrial policies for the WB economies. Both the theory and empirical evidence suggest that industrial policy is about selectivity and spillovers (externalities). This means that the policy makers in these economies should prioritize sectors with competitive advantage and those with potentially strong links to the rest of the economy that are likely to generate a positive impact on the whole production sector.

This suggests an emphasis on specific sectors, technologies or tasks (stages in the value chain) or some combination of all three (Warwick, 2013). Radosevic (2021) suggests that this prioritization of areas has some limitations and is often used as a standard within a portfolio of policy instruments. An example of successful use of area prioritization in the context of new industrial policies is the implementation of the EU's regional smart specialization strategies (Magro & Wilson, 2019). These policy mixes would differ across sectors and would reflect their different market, competition and technological positions. This should allow more effective translation of policy objectives and translation into outputs.

It is important that priority areas be used only as the basis for a series of interventions to be implemented through a policy mix. Mixed policies should be considered at the macro level, but not seen as a portfolio of instruments tailored to each priority area which would require design of mixed policies for each priority area, combined with tailored instruments to address specific features (Magro & Wilson, 2019). Policy mixes will vary depending on the priority area. Also, policy mixes should reflect the different competitive and technological positions of the different priority areas. Such an approach might be more effective for achieving policy objectives and allow states better administrative capacity and better governance of innovation and industrial policies. However, avoiding creation of closer links between policy objectives and their implementation through mixed policies (oriented according to priority areas) would have weak or non-transformative impacts (Radosevic, 2021).

In this perspective, identification of priorities is not the most essential or important part of the industrial policy process. The scholarly industrial policy literature tends to focus more on the institutional context of industrial policy implementation than on the identification of priorities (Stiglitz et al., 2014; Lin, 2017; Chang & Andreoni, 2020). Ultimately, industrial policy success depends on the ability of policy makers to involve both government and other actors such as the business community, academia, research institutions, etc.

However, from an industrial policy perspective, there are four broad industry areas in which WB economies could focus their technology improvement and diversification efforts. These areas also reflect the inherited structure of these economies, which have very different techno-economic requirements and conditions for technology improvement. For instance, mineral resources have traditionally been the drivers of growth in some WB economies and the source of their unstable growth dynamics as in the cases of Kosovo and Albania. As highlighted by OECD (2009), being rich in mineral resources can result in a 'resources curse' situation that offers high rent-seeking opportunities, but no incentives for diversification, due to income inequalities, corruption and weak market competition. However, there may be opportunities for cross-sector diversification, driven by added value and cross-sector-related and unrelated diversification. The four industry areas involved are:

a. resources-based industries such as metals and non-metals and agriculture and food processing;
b. information and communication services;
c. pockets of excellence in the beverages and (in North Macedonia) the textile industries which could be expanded;
d. development of supply chain programmes to facilitate exports and entry to GVCs.

It should be emphasized that one of the main priorities of industrial policies is manufacturing sector diversification. Almost all current high-income economies have strong manufacturing sectors (Pisano & Shih, 2012; Asian Development Bank, 2013; Stiglitz & Greenwald, 2014). However, it is unlikely that the manufacturing sector will be able to absorb all the excess agriculture labour force. However, the creation of a larger information and communication technology sector, which would enable greater dissemination of knowledge and activities with higher added value, might be the solution to this problem.

Priority should be given to the creation of new industrial sectors, sectoral diversification and cross-sectoral technological improvements. This would include encouraging downstream diversification in the resources-based industries (Morris et al., 2012) and spillovers (Bam & De Bruyne, 2019). The WB economies should aim at specialization and diversification in existing and new manufacturing industries with or without comparative advantage.

## 6.8 Governance Capacity in the Context of New Industrial Policies

Successful industrial policy requires specific institutional capabilities and levels of engagement among the actors discussed above. Institutional capabilities are required to ensure continuity and are accumulated based on historical aspects and business and national economic developments. Our findings suggest that the WB countries have failed to create enabling environments in a number of areas important for innovation and growth. The problems involved are persistent and include political instability, weak government, high levels of corruption, etc. (see Chap. 5, Sect. 5.2). Sound industry and innovation governance require social institutions with relevant capabilities at different government levels.

First, it requires social institutions able to coordinate with other stakeholders over policy. This includes both administrative capabilities and the willingness and readiness of the state to establish knowledge networks and interact with the private sector. Both economic theory and the empirical evidence suggest that establishment of adequate state-business relations is crucial for innovation and industrial policy outcomes (Evans, 1995). Implementation failures are due to technical, operational and, also, political reasons (Radosevic, 2021). The various stakeholders involved need mutual incentives.

Second, policy makers must have the capabilities required to form coalitions to enable technology upgrading. This may involve information, negotiation, monitoring and financial issues (Doner & Schneider, 2016).

Third, there needs to be institutional capacity for industrial policy implementation. Policy makers need to be well informed about the type of expertise and capacity of state institutions required for successful implementation of industrial policy measures. Industrial policy implementation requires three basic capabilities: (i) technical capabilities to develop business plans and design tax incentives to promote R&D activity; (ii) operational and managerial capabilities to direct and manage the organization efficiently to professional standards and (iii) political capabilities to ensure political support for industrial policies and avoid political capture of state institutions by political groups (Crespi et al., 2014) and ensure continuity of industrial policy implementation.

Fourth, monitoring and evaluation capabilities to check implementation of industrial policies. Although an industrial policy might be well designed, its success depends on its practical implementation. Interventions need to be monitored and evaluated continuously. According to Pritchett et al. (2012), effective monitoring and evaluation are essential to integrate experiential learning in policy. This suggests that monitoring and evaluation are essential attributes of the institutional structure and implementation of industrial policy. Our data suggest that the WB countries have not established platforms to enable effective monitoring and evaluation of systems (OECD, 2009). Kosovo has no monitoring and evaluation hub; the other two countries suffer from shortages of appropriate personnel and finance. The three WB countries need appropriate institutional, technical, operational and political capacities for industrial policy implementation. Ability to coordinate work between the public and private sectors is crucial for industrial policy success. In countries with weak institutional capabilities, such as the WB economies, establishing a monitoring and evaluation system to assess the overall impact of industrial policies must be the priority.

## 6.9 Conclusions

This chapter has outlined a new approach to industrial policies for the WB economies of Albania, North Macedonia and Kosovo, in order to achieve economic and, especially, manufacturing sector growth. Economic growth requires efficient markets, which require state intervention in the creation of markets. This intervention should include effective industrial policy design to address problems related to endemic market and system failures and promote the desired structural change and technology upgrading.

Successful industrial policies depend not on the quality of the policies, but on the capacities of social institutions to implement the measures involved. This highlights the need for evaluation of the institutional capacity of public agencies involved in the practical implementation of these measures. Our data show that social institutional quality is generally weak. The new industrial and innovative policy approach proposed in Chap. 6 requires that measures should be formulated in line with the operational, technical and political capacities of public institutions in order for the measures to be properly implemented. The coordination capabilities in the public and private sectors will determine the types of policy likely to be most successfully implemented. Horizontal policies would seem more appropriate than vertical policies in this context of weak public-private coordination.

This chapter also considered the importance of institutional awareness to avoid high-cost projects and projects requiring a high level of institutional capacity for implementation. In countries with weak financial and institutional capacity, how to design low-cost policy measures (bootstrapping), establish communication with local entrepreneurs and provide incentives for technology and performance improvements are the main issues.

In conclusion, the success of the industrial policy is not the result of the specific area chosen for industrial policy intervention but is due, primarily, to the complex interactions among the economic potential of the area, the actions of interested parties, the portfolio of supporting instruments and the implementation capacity of government and non-governmental agencies. As emphasized above, the selection of each priority area should be accompanied by a mix of policies. Meanwhile, the range of instruments that can be used for intervention in different sectors of the WB economy is wide and spans mandatory technology transfer requirements contained in FDI regulations, preferential treatment of FDI related to priority industries, joint ventures involving domestic enterprises and foreign investors, financing of strategic industrial projects by development banks, etc. It should not be forgotten that these policies, which are essentially vertical in nature, must be complemented by horizontal policies related to R&D, education, transport, energy, the information technology infrastructure, etc.

## References

Asian Development Bank. (2013). Asia's economic transformation: Where to, how, and how fast? Key indicators for Asia and the Pacific 2013: Special chapter. Manilla.

Baldwin, R. (2012). Global supply chains: Why they emerged, why they matter, and where they are going, centre for economic policy research discussion paper no. 9103, CEPR, London.

Bam, W., & De Bruyne, K. (2019). Improving industrial policy intervention: The case of steel in South Africa. *The Journal of Development Studies, 55*(11), 2460–2475. https://doi.org/10.1080/00220388.2018.1528354

Besley, T., Dewatripont, M., & Guriev, S. (2010). Transition and transition impact: A review of the concept and implications for the EBRD, Report for the EBRD's Office of the Chief Economist, LSE. https://www.lse.ac.uk/economics/Assets/Documents/personal-pages/tim-besley/miscelanea/transition-and-transition-impact.pdf

Block, F. (2008). Swimming against the current: The rise of a hidden developmental state in the United States. *Politics and Society, 36*(2), 169–206.

Block, F., Keller, M. R., & Negoita, M. (2020). Network failure and the evolution of the US. Innovation system. *Journal of Industry, Competition and Trade, 20*, 235–247. https://doi.org/10.1007/s10842-019-00324-1

Chang, H. J., & Andreoni, A. (2020). Industrial policy in the 21st century. *Development and Change, 51*(2), 324–351.

Choung, J. Y., & Hwang, R. (2021). Upgrading non-technological capabilities: Evidence from Korean firms. In *The challenges of technology and economic catch-up in emerging economies*. Oxford University Press. https://doi.org/10.1093/oso/9780192896049.003.0009

Crespi, G., Fernandez Arias, G., & Stein, E. (2014). *Rethinking productive development: Sound policies and institutions for economic transformation*. Inter-American Development Bank and Palgrave Macmillan.

Doner, R. F., & Schneider, B. R. (2016, October). The middle-income trap. *More Politics than Economics, World Politics, 68*(4), 608–644.

Edler, J., Ruhland, S., & Hafner, S. (2005). Innovation and public procurement. Review of issues at stake, Study for the European Commission (No ENTR/03/24) Fraunhofer Institute for Systems and Innovation Research.

European Commission. (2022). Commission staff working document, Kosovo 2022 report, Brussels, https://neighbourhood-enlargement.ec.europa.eu/system/files/2022-10/Kosovo%20Report%202022.pdf

Evans, P. (1995). *Embedded autonomy, states and industrial transformation*. Princeton University Press.

Gereffi, G. (1999). International trade and industrial upgrading in the apparel commodity chain. *Journal of International Economics, 48*(1), 37–70.

Johnson, C. (1982). *MITI and the Japanese miracle*. Stanford University Press.

Johnson, C. (1999). The developmental state: Odyssey of a concept, the developmental state (M. Woo-Cumings ed.). Cornell University Press.

Lin, J. Y. (2017). Industrial policy revisited: A new structural economics perspective. In A. Noman & J. E. Stiglitz (Eds.), *Efficiency, finance, and varieties of industrial policy: Guiding resources, learning, and technology for sustained growth* (pp. 225–244). Columbia University Press. http://www.jstor.org/stable/10.7312/noma18050.10

Lombardozzi, L. (2020). Unpacking state-led upgrading: Empirical evidence from Uzbek horticulture value chain governance. *Review of International Political Economy, 28*(4), 947–973. https://doi.org/10.1080/09692290.2020.1737563

Magro, E., & Wilson, J. R. (2019). Policy-mix evaluation: Governance challenges from new place-based innovation policies. *Research Policy, 48*(2019), 103612.

Mazzucato, M., (2013). *The entrepreneurial state: Debunking public vs. private sector myths.* Anthem Press.

Morris, M., Kaplinsky, R., & Kaplan, D. (2012). One thing leads to another—Commodities, linkages and industrial development. *Resources Policy, 37*, 408–416.

Nayyar, D. (2019). *Resurgent Asia: Diversity in development.* Oxford University Press.

OECD. (2009). *Integrating climate change adaptation into development co-operation.* Policy Guidance, OECD.

Pisano, G. P., & Shih, W. C. (2012). *Producing prosperity. Why America needs a manufacturing renaissance.* Harvard Business Review Press.

Popper, K. R. (1963). *The open society and its enemies (4th ed. rev.)* (p. 1). Princeton University Press.

Pritchett, L., Samji, S., & Hammer, J. (2012). It's all about me using structured experiential learning ('e') to crawl the design space, CID Working Paper No. 249. December 2012 Center for International Development at Harvard University.

Przeworski, A. (1985). Marxism and rational choice. *Politics and Society, 14*(4), 379–409. https://doi.org/10.1177/003232928501400401

Radosevic, S. (2021). Towards industrial policies to support technology upgrading for sustainable development in Central Asia (SPECA subregion), Report prepared for the UN Economic Commission for Europe, Geneva.

Radosevic, S., & Yoruk, E. (2018). Technology upgrading of middle-income economies: A new approach and results. *Technological Forecasting and Social Change, 129*, 56–75.

Ramos, J. (2000). Policy directions for the new economic model in Latin America. *World Development, 28*(9), 1703–1717.

Rodrik, D. (2007). Industrial policies for the twenty-first century. In Rodrik, D., *One economics, many recipes: Globalisation, institutions, and economic growth.* Princeton University Press.

Rodrik, D. (2014). Industrial policy and the EU, presentation at institute of advanced studies. https://drodrik.scholar.harvard.edu/files/dani-rodrik/files/industrial_policy_and_the_european_union.pdf

Sahiti, F. (2019). *The growth of firms in less developed countries: Lessons learned from Kosovo.* Palgrave Macmillan.

Stiglitz, J. E., & Greenwald, B. (2014). *Creating a learning society: A new approach to growth, development, and social Progress*. Columbia University Press.

Stiglitz, J. E., Lin, J. Y., & Patel, E. (Eds.). (2014). *The industrial policy revolution, vol. 2: Africa in the 21st century*. Palgrave Macmillan.

Stojcic, N., Srhoj, S., & Coad, A. (2020). Innovation procurement as capability-building: Evaluating innovation policies in eight central and eastern European countries. *European Economic Review, 121*(2020), 103330.

Warwick, K. (2013). Beyond industrial policy: Emerging issues and new trends, OECD science, technology and industry policy papers, no. 2, OECD publishing, Paris, https://doi.org/10.1787/5k4869clw0xp-en.

Williamson, J. (1990). What Washington means by policy reform. In J. Williamson (Ed.), *Latin American adjustment: How much has happened?* (pp. 7–20). Institute for International Economics.

World Bank. (2005). *Economic growth in the 1990s: Learning from a decade of reform*. World Bank.

CHAPTER 7

# Measuring Technological Capabilities in Kosovo's Manufacturing Sector

## 7.1 Introduction

From a Schumpeterian perspective, national economic growth depends on firms with growth capacity, while firms with growth capacity are defined as business entities capable of combining business skills and generating goods with added value. The identification of the capabilities that lead to business growth continues to be a major research topic with several studies highlighting various internal capabilities that enable and/or constrain firm growth. Nevertheless, our understanding of the firm capabilities that lead to firm growth is scant (Sutton & Trefler, 2016). Also, most empirical work examines developed economies. Several studies use an adapted Schumpeterian approach to study the process of building technological capabilities in developed economies (Lall, 1992; Bell & Pavitt, 1993; Kim, 1997; Kumar et al., 1999; Dutrenit, 2000; Lee et al., 2021, etc.). The absence of research on developing economies is particularly evident in the area of technological capabilities.

So why is it important to study and analyse technological capabilities in firms in less developed economies, such as Kosovo? It might be expected that certain factors, such as technological capabilities, are less important for developing economies. There is also an underlying assumption that firm growth in developing countries is based mostly on availability of the 'factors of production' or natural resources (see, e.g., World Economic



F. Sahiti, *Industrial Policies for Technological Upgrading in Western Balkan Countries*, https://doi.org/10.1007/978-3-031-51429-6_7

Forum Competitiveness Reports) and much less on the unique organizational/managerial production capabilities accumulated by these firms.

A framework based on the Resource-Based View (RBV) of the firm is often used to explain why some firms grow more rapidly than others. Proponents of the RBV contend that the source of the fast growth in some business organizations lies in their ability to accumulate innovation capabilities and that different firm performance is due to different development of organizational capabilities (e.g., Teece, 2017; Dosi et al., 2019). Other approaches draw on the management literature and the idea of firm economic growth being based on managerial capabilities (Bloom et al., 2019). It is expected that these effects will be reduced in the context of developing economy firms since, as previously stated, business growth in these firms derives primarily from the availability of resources (inputs).

The conventional microeconomic approach to the growth of business firms focuses on resources or inputs and ignores the firm's organization and assumes that the market is the main mechanism of growth and the main allocator of resources. Empirical research tends to focus on only a few dimensions of firm internal growth. In the context of economies in transition, the focus has for long been on corporate governance and privatization issues. Work on firm growth has focused mainly on developed economies and our understanding of the factors and pathways of firm growth in developing economies is weak. This chapter integrates several different perspectives to investigate the factors that inhibit and/or stimulate firm growth in the context of Kosovo. Our empirical findings suggest that understanding the factors that lead to firm growth requires a multidimensional or systematic approach. Adoption of a multidimensional approach reveals three types of capabilities or stages in the long-term growth of firms in developing economies. These capabilities are capability to purchase equipment and recruit and train a workforce; capability to manage a dynamic business environment and capability to manage organizational processes and to produce.

The analytical approach we adopt is aimed at opening the 'black box' of technological capabilities. We unpack and analyse the specific roles and effects of the elements involved in technological capabilities, which, in addition to long-term assets, such as machinery and equipment, include human capabilities, product design capabilities, production process capabilities, organizational systems, business networking systems, dynamic capabilities, marketing capabilities, etc. While many of these capabilities are measurable, some are difficult to assess and, in these cases, we use proxies. This chapter is aimed at proposing a categorization of the types of technological capabilities required for Kosovo manufacturing firms' technical aspects. We show that technological capabilities are critical for determining the technical efficiency of manufacturing firms.

Our firm sample is split into high-growth and low-growth firms. It is assumed that the differences between these two groups will reveal the determinants of growth. We interpret our cross-sectional evidence longitudinally. We are interested in the dynamics of firm growth and how it is conditioned by the interaction between the internal and external factors specific to developing economies. Data were collected via in-depth semi-structured interviews with Kosovo manufacturing firms based on an interview questionnaire. To extract the maximum information, we asked about a wide range of variables related to firm capabilities. The aim was to identify the differentiating factors originating in the firm, such as resources or inputs in the form of physical equipment, finance and human capital and production (management) capabilities and organizational capabilities such as network, technology and R&D capabilities.

The findings from the analysis in this chapter indicate the changing importance of different types of capabilities for manufacturing firm growth in a developing economy and supports the idea of economic growth as based on available factor inputs. However, it seems that the quality of manufacturing (managerial) capabilities has a substantial impact on manufacturing firm growth and outweighs the effect of other organizational capabilities. Our results are consistent with the notion of sequenced development of firm capabilities and their effect in low-income economies.

Section 7.2 reviews the literature and Sect. 7.3 discusses our choice of theoretical lens. Section 7.4 describes the data and the methodology and Sect. 7.5 presents the empirical results of the analysis. Section 7.7 concludes the chapter.

## 7.2 Factors of Internal Firm Growth: An Overview of the Main Theoretical Perspectives

The factors leading to sustainable economic growth have been examined using different theoretical perspectives and research methods. The findings of these studies can be interpreted in the form of some stylized facts; it should be noted that they apply more to developed than developing economies. The first stylized fact refers to the significant heterogeneity in firm characteristics, behaviour and performance associated with unobserved firm-specific factors that persist over time (Dosi et al., 1997). The second stylized fact refers to that firms that exhibit even modest growth are more likely to survive (Bartelsman et al., 2004, 2013). The third stylized fact refers to the lower frequency of fast-growing firms. The empirical data suggest that, on average, only 5% of the total population of firms achieve rapid growth (Henrekson & Johansson, 2010). The fourth stylized fact refers to the short-lived, episodic and inconsistent nature of firm growth (Coad, 2009; Grover et al., 2019). The fifth stylized fact refers to the fact that new and smaller firms tend to grow faster than large firms (Hart, 2000; Lotti et al., 2009).

Different approaches draw on different firm theories. Neoclassical theory suggests that differences among firms are due to differences in their fixed capital, for example, plant and machinery and labour inputs. However, even after controlling for numerous observable factors, a large exogenous Total Factor Productivity (TFP) residual persists. Therefore, this theory predicts that firm improvements are due to increases in factor inputs (capital and labour) and TFP and assumes that these factors are fully separable. Some research shows the unreliability of TFP measures and, especially, estimates of revenue-based measures of TFP, which mix physical efficiencies with prices and market power effects (see Grover et al., 2019). The firm is similar to a black box, in which the transformation of resources (their organization and management) occurs (Demsetz, 1997), which recent research on firms suggests that in a definitional sense are central to understanding firm growth.

Some consider the firm to be the locus of capabilities and firm growth to be a function of the firm's ability to accumulate internal capabilities. This idea is rooted in the RBV of the firm (Penrose, 1959), which conceptualizes firms as administrative units that organize bundles of resources. The RBV originally focused on firm differences but provided no explanation of their causes or how firms developed capabilities (Barney, 1991). Teece (2017) proposed the dynamic capabilities view, which assumes that successful firms develop dynamic capabilities which are higher order capabilities and allow the firm to reconfigure its conventional capabilities and adapt them to the constantly changing market environment. Both conventional and dynamic capabilities involve routines; however, dynamic capabilities are related to meta-routines and changes to conventional routines (Helfat & Peteraf, 2003). In both cases, the firm is responsibility for these changes, which allows us to investigate the differences among firms in terms of ability to accumulate capabilities that are not rooted in individuals or included in an aggregate production function (Aistleitner et al., 2021).

There is a strand of work that argues that business performance differences are driven by managerial capabilities/practices. That is, firms with more sophisticated and more structured management capabilities and practices are more likely to achieve higher levels of productivity and higher profits and are likely to record higher rates of innovation and survival (Halac & Prat, 2016). This literature suggests that between a quarter and a third of cross-country and within-country TFP gaps are related to management capabilities (Bloom et al., 2014). It suggests, also, that some basic management capabilities and practices can be considered equivalent to a new technology and/or advanced machinery applied by business organizations (Bloom et al., 2014, 2019). It has been pointed out that there are compelling theoretical reasons to expect that managerial capabilities and practices have a significant impact on the heterogeneity of firm performance (Gibbons & Henderson, 2013; Brynjolfsson & Milgrom, 2013). In general, the management capabilities literature, while informative, is underdeveloped in terms of theoretical explanations. The empirical results are in line with the RBV literature, but this link is mostly ignored. In our context of Kosovo, it is near impossible to separate production from management capabilities. The latter are more extensive and include management of all the processes related to production capabilities alongside other business processes. However, the literature does not make connections between these streams of research.

Some empirical neo-Schumpeterian-based research explores technology upgrading paths in firms in developing economies and proposes technological capabilities and firm upgrading path taxonomies (Bell & Pavitt, 1993; Dutrenit, 2000; Bell & Figueiredo, 2012). These studies are marked by the hierarchy of firm and production capabilities. Manufacturing capabilities are related to the firm's ability to produce using a given level of technology, at world efficiency and productivity levels (see Radosevic & Yoruk, 2016). The ability to produce world class goods requires good operational efficiency, a skilled technical workforce and a supporting blue-collar workforce. This ability is particularly important for developing economies since firms operating mainly behind the technology frontier are more likely to grow based on production rather than technological capabilities or R&D activities. In developed economies, growth is more often based on R&D activities. The evidence suggests that technological and production capabilities in firms are intertwined (Bell & Pavitt, 1993). However, the proposed taxonomies suggest that production and technology capabilities are distinct. Technology capabilities refer to capabilities for change, that is, they are dynamic capabilities; production capabilities are more static. Also, management practices are not about strategic innovation (Bloom et al., 2014). Management practices and production capabilities are strongly correlated to R&D capabilities (Bloom et al., 2019).

The dynamic capabilities literature complements the literature on technology capabilities since, by definition, innovation requires changes to established routines (Tidd & Bessant, 2021). For example, Zahra et al. (2006) argue that change requires firms to manage unforeseen and complex situations, which requires dynamic capabilities. These capabilities help the firm to 'reconfigure the business resources and routines in the manner envisioned and deemed appropriate for decision-making' (Zahra et al., 2006, p. 918). Thus, to cope with change and remain competitive requires development of dynamic capabilities, improvisation and trial and error.

Business networking is also important for business growth. Firms need to have good links to partners, customers, suppliers, creditors, etc., which allows increased efficiency and reduced costs related to securing resources, access to customer information, access to better quality and cheaper raw materials, financing, etc. (Cao & Zhang, 2011). Firms enjoying agglomeration and networking benefits are able to exploit learning and specialization opportunities (Grover et al., 2019).

Different theories and approaches rely on different indicators to explain the origins of business growth. The literature distinguishes between static and dynamic firm capabilities. Dynamic capabilities conceptually correspond well to progression by firms in developing economies which advance from production to technological capabilities exemplified by technology upgrading (Radosevic & Yoruk, 2016, 2018). Firm growth is both an intra-firm phenomenon and an element that is affected by a range of external factors including the firm's business networks.

## 7.3 The Main Themes of the Chapter

It cannot be expected that developing economies, such as Kosovo, will achieve the levels of technological innovation seen in the developed economies (Lall, 1992). Technological innovators are advanced economies whose activities affect the technology frontier. Developing economies rely on equipment and machinery manufactured elsewhere, which means that they are not focused on innovation related to products or business processes. Their aim is to produce world quality products and increase production process efficiency.

Assuming firms can afford to import modern technologies, their focus, then, is on their efficient and effective use. The acquisition and absorption of production technology differs from acquisition and absorption of other physical products. Imported technologies are complex and developing economies tend to lack the capabilities required to exploit them. This capability requires investment in information and the skills required to use the technology efficiently. This makes absorption of imported technologies as complicated and costly as generating new technologies (Lall, 1992). Efficient use of imported technology requires the capabilities to observe the best market practice in terms of response to customer demands and the activities of competitors, building of efficient business networks (supply chain, recruitment of qualified workforce, exploration of opportunities, etc.) and access to finance to allow the purchase of new technologies.

In the Kosovan context, technological capabilities are not related to the firm's innovation abilities, but to its efforts to absorb and develop production process know-how. Know-how includes information, knowledge, experience, etc., which can be purchased in the domestic and foreign market, but also can be developed in-house. The choice made will depend on the technology, the market conditions and the firm's strategy.

In developing economies, acquisition of technology does not ensure business success; purchase of the equipment and receipt of operating instructions do not guarantee efficient use of the technology, which, often requires tacit knowledge and particular work routines. Technology mastery is neither an automatic nor a passive activity. It takes time and knowledge to achieve technical efficiency. Firms need technology 'receptors', that is, qualified technical personnel who will likely require on-the-job training.

Figure 7.1 depicts the range of technological capabilities embodied in a typical manufacturing firm. A successful manufacturing process requires all these tasks to be performed within or outside the firm. These tasks fall into three broad categories.

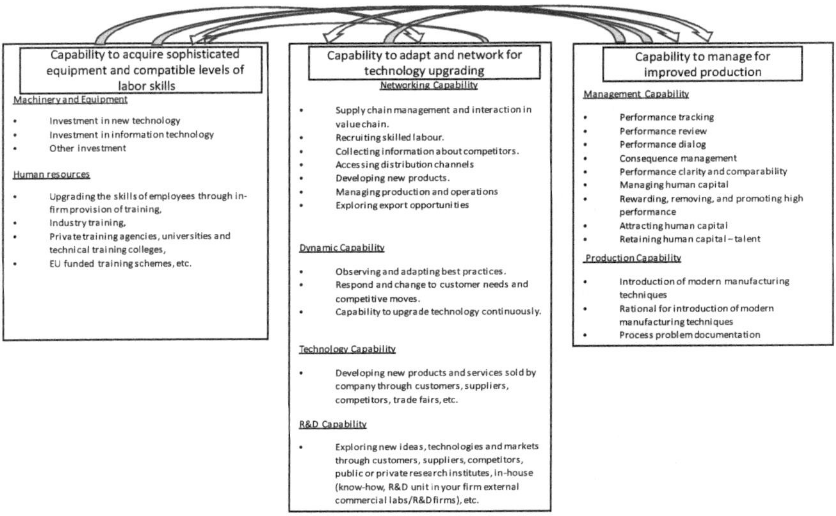


**Fig. 7.1** Firm capability dimensions. Source: Author

### *Capability to Acquire Sophisticated Equipment and Compatible Labour Skill Levels*

These capabilities include manufacturing knowledge and information, from identification of appropriate technology, negotiation and purchase, to post-purchase. The engineering skills involved in commissioning plant are also important, but in developing country contexts may be scarce. Most interviewees said that they used subcontractors from specialized companies outside the region to negotiate their technological investments. The post-purchase period can be particularly complicated due to lack of qualified technical staff which requires recruitment and training in the purchased technologies. Use of subcontractors increases the capital costs of the technology project.

Experience in other countries suggest that improving the above capabilities would reduce costs and allow more efficient use of the equipment (Enos & Park, 1987; Kumar et al., 1999; Minbaeva et al., 2003). Policy measures are needed to improve investment capabilities in both manufacturing firms and nationally, including entrepreneurs.

### *Capability to Absorb, Adapt and Network for Technology Upgrading*

As firms develop and mature, their technological capabilities base increases. The cumulative and evolutionary nature of learning means that firm development depends on their initial positioning, entrepreneurial strategy and external stimuli (Lall, 1993). Firms obtain information from the market and adapt to market changes. Firms need to learn by building routines and institutional systems that allow them to absorb and process information and build capabilities (Lall, 1998) and make better use of external information. This can be enabled by networking with different partners, including suppliers, technology institutions and organizations, and consultants to improve internal learning.

Establishing lasting business networks involves time and effort (Lall, 1993). Networks allow the transfer of technology and skills, which require ability to receive and transmit information. In developing countries, which have undeveloped supply networks and institutions, these activities are very demanding.

### *Capability to Manage for Improved Production*

Manufacturing capabilities include the knowledge needed to operate and improve the manufacturing process. Figure 7.1 depicts these capabilities as ranging from routine functions to intensive and innovative efforts to adapt and improve technology. Acquiring basic managerial capabilities to track and review performance and perform product quality control and production equipment maintenance to achieve efficient production levels is time and effort consuming. We have pointed out that the goal of manufacturing firms in developing countries is increasing production efficiency and product quality to world standards. The more sophisticated the manufacturing, customization and development capabilities needed, the more time and investment will be required. This is especially true in the case of imported rather than in-house developed technologies.

## 7.4 The Conceptual Model Used to Measure Technological Capabilities

The conceptual model in Fig. 7.1 draws on the above-mentioned theories and empirical approaches. However, our measurement framework is novel in its combination of individual components in conceptually new and empirically testable ways to propose a capabilities building framework that includes issues related to growth and capability upgrading in lower income economies.

Using our conceptual model, we investigate the factors that lead to firm growth, based on continuous and reciprocal interactions among resources (inputs), managerial and production capabilities and dynamic organizational capabilities.

Resources includes physical capital (equipment and machinery) and human capital. Management and production capabilities, dynamic and networking capabilities and R&D and technological capabilities depend on the ability of the firm to learn, to improve and to evaluate risks and opportunities. We assume that the level of human capital required to operate the physical capital in lower income economies is relatively less complex and does not necessarily require ability to generate change or innovations. All the other factors require a certain level of skills and education.

The firm's organizational capabilities are the main source of business growth. They can be split into the sometimes-overlapping categories of static and dynamic organizational capabilities, which include the capabilities to manage and improve production and the capabilities to adapt and network to improve technology.

Management practices and production capabilities are considered static organizational capabilities in the sense that they are related to the accumulation of knowledge about production and management practices, which, potentially, can lead to world class productivity. However, management practices and production capabilities are not related to innovation capabilities or technology improvements that require dynamic organizational capabilities. Management practices might seem to overlap production capabilities, but they are different; they go beyond production processes and cannot be reduced to knowledge about the production process. Management practices constitute a large proportion organizational capability, but organizational capabilities are more encompassing and include capabilities to constantly reconfigure their internal work organization and allow adaptation to a changing market environment.

Dynamic, networking, technological and R&D capabilities are the third pillar of our model and the main factors generating change and innovation in the firm.

Networking capabilities are essential for firm growth; firms depend heavily on suppliers and feedback from sophisticated buyers. Networking skills contribute to firms active shaping of their business and innovation ecosystem dynamics with positive effects on growth. Each change-generating capability (R&D, technological capability, networking) is important on its own and improvements to these capabilities can result in periods of high growth.

However, successful companies are distinguished by their dynamic capabilities, that is, their ability to develop change-generating routines in all dimensions of the firm's capabilities. Firms are faced with successive waves of new technologies and new markets and the capacity to develop meta-routines is the ultimate driver of long-term firm growth. The innovation studies and strategic management literatures propose the notion of a technology perspective (Radosevic & Yoruk, 2016, 2018). Dynamic capabilities enable the firm to constantly reconfigure its internal work activities and adapt to the changing market environment. Dynamic capabilities are considered higher level organizational capabilities and are embedded in meta-routines or routines to change routines. Several authors, such as Helfat and Peteraf (2003), have pointed out that changes to conventional firm capabilities do not require dynamic capabilities. Dynamic capabilities are seen more as collections of routines embedded in individuals rather than the firm (Nelson & Winter, 1982). This approach differs from the neoclassical approach in that it allows the heterogeneity of firms to be examined at the accumulated dynamic capabilities level.

R&D requires technological capabilities to enable deployment of technology, along with a range of other activities, such as exploration, process and product engineering and incremental improvements. In our perspective, technological capabilities include ability to design and develop new processes and products, accumulate knowledge about the physical environment and acquire skills to transform this knowledge into instructions and designs to achieve efficient performance (Radosevic & Yoruk, 2016).

Finally, R&D capability is essential for the development of absorptive capabilities and manufacturing capability and the generation of new knowledge. R&D can enable productivity improvements either directly through flows of applied knowledge or indirectly through the adoption of imported technologies and exploitation of the R&D embodied in imported machinery and equipment. For countries behind the technology frontier, such as Kosovo, this ability is the main source of productivity improvements. The role of R&D in countries behind the technology frontier is related to absorptive capacity rather than innovation capabilities. In lower income economies, R&D and technological capabilities are drivers not of growth, but of productive capabilities (for central and eastern Europe, see Majcen et al., 2009; Kravtsova & Radosevic, 2011). Nevertheless, R&D is important for firm growth, but, in lower income economies, its effect derives from applied knowledge or adoption of imported technologies or R&D embodied in imported machinery and equipment. The latter source is the main source of productivity improvements in countries which are behind the technology frontier, and the role of R&D is more as driver of absorptive, not innovation, capability.

The concept of high-growth firms employed in this study is taken from the Eurostat/OECD (2008, p. 61) manual, which defines high-growth firms as firms 'with average annual growth greater than 20% per year, for a three-year period...where growth is measured by the number of employees, or through turnover and sales'.

We expect the potential for business growth in lower income countries, to be a function of their firms' resources (inputs), management and production capabilities and dynamic organizational capabilities. This process starts with development of capacity to use resources and inputs embodied in imported machinery and equipment and to use human resources effectively. As firms improve through purchase of more sophisticated technology and employment of more skilled labour, their quality and productivity also improve. Here, developed management and production capabilities can be decisive. In the next growth stage, the firm develops the adaptation and networking capabilities that allow technology upgrading. This requires mastery of range of change-related capabilities: R&D, technology capability and networking and dynamic capabilities that lead to more acquisition of more sophisticated equipment and better labour skills. The aim is to achieve world-level production efficiency and requires excellent production capabilities and management practices. In this stage, firms are actively engaged in change-generating activities that rely on absorption of external knowledge and contribute to the local innovation ecosystem. Dynamic capabilities are required to manage continuous technological change. It is expected that resources (inputs), labour skills, management/production capabilities and dynamic organizational capabilities will be at different levels depending on their stage of development.

## 7.5 Data Sources and Methodology

The data were collected from a survey administered between 2020 and 2021. The sample includes 101 manufacturing firms from different sectors in Kosovo. The questionnaire included two sections. The first was based on the AEGIS project questionnaire and asked about organizational and dynamic inputs and capabilities; the second was based on the questionnaire designed by Bloom and Van Reenen (2010) and asked about managerial practices. The sample selection used two criteria: belonging to the production sector and employment of between 20 and 250 workers.

The questionnaire contains different variables grouped into three categories. It asked about resources/inputs (machinery and equipment and human capital); dynamic organizational capabilities including networking, technology and R&D capabilities; and static organizational capabilities (management and production capabilities).

The descriptive analysis provides a statistical summary of the empirical findings. The second analysis investigates factors that differentiate the two groups of firms identified.

We employed factor analysis to explain the correlations among multiple outcomes due to one or more underlying factors. This statistical technique reduces the complexity in high-dimensional data while preserving main trends and patterns. It transforms the data into a smaller number of dimensions, which act as feature summaries (Field, 2005).

We employed principal component analysis for the full sample after confirming suitability of the data for factor analysis. We extracted components using varimax and the Oblimin rotation (delta = 0) methods. Decisions about which components to retain were made according to Kaiser's criterion (eigenvalues greater than 1), sceptical inspection and Horn's (1965) parallel analysis.

Suitability of the data for factor analysis depends on sample size and strength of the relationship among the variables (or items). There is a lack of agreement on the sample size considered suitable for factor analysis. However, it is generally agreed that larger samples are more suitable. Concerns about sample size were addressed by considering the strength of the correlations between items. Tabachnick and Fidell (2001) suggest that it is important that the correlation matrix provides evidence of coefficients greater than 0.3. If the number of correlations above this level is small, then factor analysis may not be appropriate. Two other statistical measures can be used to evaluate data factorability: Bartlett's test of sphericity

(Bartlett, 1954) and the Kaiser-Meyer-Olkin (KMO) measure of sampling adequacy. The first should show significance ($p < 0.05$) and the KMO measure should range between 0 and 1; a value of 0 is considered a good fit for factor analysis (Tabachnick & Fidell, 2001).

In the data analysis process, we applied two-factor analysis approaches, that is, Principal Component Analysis (PCA) and Confirmatory Factor Analysis (CFA). We used PCA on the full sample, but after first confirming that the data were suitable for factor analysis. We extracted components using the varimax and Oblimin rotation (delta = 0) methods. The decision regarding the components to be retained for the analysis was based on three rules: Kaiser's criterion (eigenvalues greater than 1), sceptical inspection and the use of Horn's (1965) parallel analysis.

To assess the model fit and using maximum likelihood estimation, we applied CFA (Arbuckle, 1999). The model fit can be assessed using chi-square. However, since, in practice, other factors may affect assessment of the model fit, we applied several fit statistics, starting with the goodness of fit index or GFI, the Tucker-Lewis Index or TLI, and the comparative fit index or CFI, which in the case of lack of fit should show values of less than 0.90. Values between 0.90 and 0.95 indicate reasonable fit and values between 0.95 and 1.00 indicate good fit (Tabachnick & Fidell, 2001). Another important indicator of model fit is Root Mean-Square Error of Approximation or RMSEA. According to Byrne (2001), RMSEA is the most important statistic for determining the model fit because it takes account of the number of variables evaluated in the model. A good model fit is indicated by RMSEA values of 0.05 or lower; values between 0.05 and 0.08 suggest a reasonable fit.

## 7.6 Empirical Results

### *Descriptive Statistics*

Scores for the three capability dimensions range from 1 to 5 (Likert scale), with a mean of 3.08 (SD = 1.1086). The results for both groups of firms generally show a normal distribution. We ran a Mann-Whitney test, which is a non-parametric test commonly used to compare two sample means derived from the same population. The aim is to test whether two sample means are equal or not. The results of the Mann-Whitney test show that resources or inputs such as machinery and equipment (new equipment) have no impact on the variability in the business performance of the high-growth and low-growth groups of firms. In response to a question about whether, in the previous three years, the firm had invested in purchase of new machinery and equipment, about 94% of respondents responded positively. Training is relevant and facilitates upgrading and updating of know-how, knowledge and skills. The results of the survey show that most firms conduct training activities: 50.8% of high-growth firms indicated provision of training and 52.2% of low-growth firms indicated that they provided training. Around 77% of beverages and wood sector firms organize in-house training although firms in the polystyrene production sector considered training unimportant and offered no in-house training. None of the firms interviewed had received support from a university or college and the European Union provided training only for food industry firms (6%).

Among the 44 variables considered in relation to capabilities (managerial and production capabilities, dynamic and network capabilities, and R&D and technological capabilities), the Mann-Whitney U test suggests that only 26 variables are statistically significant and help to explain the difference between high-growth and low-growth firms (see Table 7.1). The next analysis considers a smaller number of factors.

Our findings for dynamic capabilities show that the group of fast-growing firms consider them important, in particular, for responses to industry changes and competitors and responses to customer complaints. About 56% of high-growth firms have a formal engineering and technical studies department and almost 56% of their employees share practical experiences and benefit from internal training (see Table 7.1). These organizational capabilities allow identification of market opportunities and awareness of customer needs.

Business networking was considered an important organizational capability. Owners/managers were asked to rate the extent to which their business network(s) had helped them to improve their operations and achieve and maintain competitive advantage. Among the ten items related to these activities, four were ranked quite high (see Table 7.1). The highest score was assigned to selection of suppliers. This is related to the fact that most firms are new manufacturers and good relations with suppliers are crucial. Networking was helpful for managing production and operations, suggesting that good relations with technology manufacturers is essential for keeping abreast of new technology. Networking also helped recruitment of skilled labour and advertising and promotion activities.

**Table 7.1** Descriptive statistics, Mann-Whitney U test results

| | *Significant variables* | *Mean rank* | | *z* | *r* | *p* < 0.10 |
|---|---|---|---|---|---|---|
| | | *High growing* | *Low growing* | | | |
| Resources | Over the past three years, has the firm invested in new plant and equipment | 50.97 | 51.03 | -0.08 | -0.00079 | *0.98* |
| | Provision of training for employees | 50.8 | 51.2 | -0.025 | -0.00025 | *0.936* |
| Management and production capability (MPC) | Applying modern manufacturing technology (PC1) | 58.98 | 42.86 | -6.875 | -0.06807 | 0.002 |
| | Rational for introduction of modern manufacturing techniques PC2 | 56.82 | 45.06 | -2.163 | -0.02142 | 0.031 |
| | Process problem documentation (PC3) | 59.00 | 42.84 | -5.909 | -0.0585 | 0.001 |
| | Performance tracking (MC1) | 60.17 | 41.65 | -6.667 | -0.06601 | 0.001 |
| | Performance review (MC2) | 53.93 | 48.01 | -3.882 | -0.03844 | 0.260 |
| | Consequence management (MP4) | 59.88 | 41.94 | -2.13 | -0.02109 | 0.001 |
| | Performance clarity and comparability (MC5) | 56.07 | 45.83 | -1.982 | -0.01962 | 0.047 |
| | Managing human capital (MC6) | 60.53 | 41.28 | -1.543 | -0.01528 | 0.001 |
| | Rewarding high performance (MC8) | 59.09 | 42.75 | -3.163 | -0.03132 | 0.002 |
| | Promoting high performers (MC9) | 60.08 | 41.74 | -2.409 | -0.02385 | 0.001 |

(*continued*)

**Table 7.1** (continued)

| | *Significant variables* | *Mean rank* | | *z* | *r* | *p* < 0.10 |
|---|---|---|---|---|---|---|
| | | *High growing* | *Low growing* | | | |
| Dynamic and networking capability (DNC) | Actively observing and adopting the best practices in our sector (DC1) | 57.69 | 44.18 | -2.459 | -0.02435 | 0.014 |
| | Responding rapidly to competitive moves DC2 | 58.46 | 43.39 | -2.753 | -0.02726 | 0.006 |
| | Changing our practices based on customer feedback DC2 | 59.39 | 42.44 | -1.904 | -0.01885 | 0.057 |
| | Quickly understanding new opportunities to better serve customers (DC6) | 56.22 | 45.9 | -1.925 | -0.01906 | 0.054 |
| | A formal engineering and technical studies department in our firm (DC7) | 56.61 | 45.28 | -2.24 | -0.02218 | 0.025 |
| | Systematic internal and external personnel training (DC9) | 56.9 | 44.98 | -3.461 | -0.03427 | 0.033 |
| | Employees share practical experiences on a frequent basis (DC10) | 55.2 | 46.72 | -3.14 | -0.03109 | 0.043 |
| | Selecting suppliers (NC1) | 57.19 | 44.69 | -3.325 | -0.03292 | 0.016 |
| | Recruiting skilled labour (NC2) | 60.42 | 41.39 | -3.508 | -0.03473 | 0.001 |
| | Advertising and promotion (NC6) | 59.86 | 41.96 | -3.214 | -0.03182 | 0.001 |
| | Network in managing production and operations (NC8) | 57.34 | 44.53 | -2.344 | -0.02321 | 0.019 |

(*continued*)

**Table 7.1** (continued)

| | *Significant variables* | *Mean rank* | | *z* | *r* | *p* < 0.10 |
|---|---|---|---|---|---|---|
| | | *High growing* | *Low growing* | | | |
| | Exploring new ideas, technologies and markets through clients RDC1 | 62.74 | 39.03 | -4.29 | -0.04248 | 0.001 |
| R&D and technology capability (RDTC) | Exploring new ideas, technologies and markets through in-house know-how unit (RDC4) | 69.99 | 31.63 | -1.126 | -0.01115 | 0.001 |
| | Developing new ideas, technologies and markets through clients (TC1) | 66.84 | 34.84 | -3.548 | -0.03513 | 0.001 |
| | Developing new ideas, technologies and markets through suppliers TC3 | 59.39 | 42.44 | -5.909 | -0.0585 | 0.002 |
| | Developing new ideas, technologies and markets through in-house know-how unit (TC4) | 69.25 | 32.38 | -3.644 | -0.03608 | 0.001 |
| | Developing new ideas trade fairs, conferences and exhibitions (TC5) | 61.31 | 40.48 | -3.663 | -0.03627 | 0.001 |

Source: Author

Firms were asked to rate the importance on a five-point Likert scale of firm-specific sources of knowledge to explore new business opportunities. This identified and assessed the importance of linkages for the innovation process. Table 7.1 shows that customers, suppliers and in-house ideas are the most important sources of knowledge and new product development. More than 60% of respondents in the high-growth group responded that these sources allowed both exploration and development of new ideas. Another source of knowledge considered important are exhibitions.

### *Reliability*

The suitability of our data for factor analysis was based on a KMO of 0.6 or higher and significance of Bartlett's test of sphericity value ($p < 0.05$). In our case, the KMO value was 0.84 and the Bartlett's test was significant ($p = 0.001$); thus, factor analysis was appropriate. The correlation matrix revealed several correlation coefficients of 0.3 or over. To determine the number of components (factors) to be extracted, we employed the Kaiser criterion of an eigenvalue of 1 or higher. Eight of our components have an eigenvalue above 1, explaining a total of 76.13% of the variance. To reduce the number of components, we used screenplot. We decided that components 1, 2 and 3 explained or captured most of the variance (59.5%). The parallel analysis provided the same results that the first three factors exceeded the value of the determining criteria. We therefore obtained a three-factor solution.

### *Principal Component Analysis*

The 15 dynamic and static organizational capabilities items were subjected to PCA. The three-component solution explained a total of 59.5% of the variance, with component 1 (management and production capability) contributing 36.4%, component 2 (dynamic and networking capability) contributing with 12.4% and component 3 (R&D and technological capability) contributing 10.5%.

The management and production capability items have the strongest loadings—for performance review (0.8) and introduction of modern manufacturing techniques (0.7), followed by dynamic capabilities and networking capabilities, and R&D and technological capabilities. Among the four items related to dynamic capabilities and networking capabilities, the strongest are systematic internal and external personnel training (0.88) and supplier selection (0.6). Among R&D and technological capabilities, the strongest loading was for developing ideas based on in-house know-how (0.86) and ability to explore new ideas and the technology through clients (0.82).

The structure matrix suggests relatively good loading for all factors. For management and production capabilities, the lowest factor loading was 0.65 for item 5 (MC4). Among dynamic and networking capabilities and R&D and technological capabilities, the lowest loading was for dynamics and networking items 4 and 5 (respectively, 0.63 and 0.64). For R&D and technological capabilities, the lowest loading, 0.69, was for item 2 (see Tables 7.1 and 7.2).

**Table 7.2** Pattern and structure matrix for PCA with oblimin rotation of three-factor solution

| | *Item* | *Pattern coefficients* | | | *Structure coefficients* | | | *Communalities* |
|---|---|---|---|---|---|---|---|---|
| | | *Comp 1* | *Comp 2* | *Comp 3* | *Comp 1* | *Comp 2* | *Comp 3* | |
| Management and production capability (MPC) | Applying modern manufacturing technology (PC1) | 0.757 | | | 0.79 | | | 0.631 |
| | Process problem documentation (PC3) | 0.765 | | | 0.749 | | | 0.574 |
| | Performance tracking (MC1) | 0.771 | | | 0.795 | | | 0.641 |
| | Performance review (MC2) | 0.879 | | | 0.827 | | | 0.701 |
| | Consequence management (MP4) | 0.526 | | | 0.648 | | | 0.498 |
| | Managing human capital (MC6) | 0.618 | | | 0.731 | | | 0.607 |
| | Promoting high performers (MC9) | 0.701 | | | 0.683 | | | 0.544 |
| Dynamic and networking capability (DNC) | Systematic internal and external personnel training (DC9) | | 0.879 | | | 0.863 | | 0.758 |
| | Employees share practical experiences on a frequent basis (DC10) | | 0.788 | | | 0.796 | | 0.635 |
| | Selecting suppliers (NC1) | | 0.607 | | | 0.641 | | 0.432 |
| | Recruiting skilled labour (NC2) | | 0.584 | | | 0.638 | | 0.426 |
| R&D and technology capability (RDTC) | Exploring new ideas, technologies and markets through in-house know-how unit (RDC4) | | | 0.827 | | | 0.835 | 0.699 |
| | Developing new ideas, technologies and markets through clients (TC1) | | | 0.656 | | | 0.696 | 0.493 |
| | Developing new ideas, technologies and markets through in-house know-how unit (TC4) | | | 0.862 | | | 0.859 | 0.75 |
| | Developing new ideas trade fairs, conferences and exhibitions (TC5) | | | 0.714 | | | 0.718 | 0.532 |

Source: Author

### *Confirmatory Factor Analysis*

We employed CFA to evaluate the model fit. The process was carried out using the same sample used for the PCA analysis, which consists of 3 principal components and of 15 items (see Fig. 7.1). The main indicators of this analysis suggest that factor loadings in this model are statistically significant. That is, the chi-square test is significant (chi-square (66) = 96.56, $p = 0.005$), but other fit indices also indicate desirable fit. Thus, NFI (0.813), TLI (0.946), CFI (0.961) and RMSEA (0.034) statistics all indicate a very good fit.

Following the structure matrix in the PCA analysis, which showed that the components were clearly distinct constructs, the structure matrix for this CFA model shows that the components are different from each other. On the MPC subscale, the lowest loading was for item MC9 (0.58). The only loading that we obtained in CFA analysis which is significantly lower than required was item NC1 (0.46). Therefore, we removed that item from the model and tested a new three-factor model with 14 items. The results suggest a smaller overlap among the factors, which is supported, also, by the weaker correlation among the factors. Fit statistics for the three-factor model for all 14 items shows a stronger fit with the data. However, the results show no significant difference between the models (Fig. 7.2)

## 7.7 Conclusions

The analyses in this chapter provide the following results.

First, high- and low-growth firms are not distinguished in terms of their machinery and equipment inputs. Purchase of machinery and equipment is secondary to how the technology acquired is exploited. This highlights the importance of firm-specific capabilities versus differentiating firm capacities in qualitatively different categories. This is the difference between potential resources, proxied by quantity and quality of physical capacities, and capabilities which are a proxy for how the firm exploits its resources. This underlines the relevance of Penrose's RBV which distinguishes between resources (capacities) and capabilities and explains the differences among firms. Our results highlight the weak explanatory power of neoclassical theory and a production function perspective for understanding firm growth. This is especially significant in the context of low-income economies where it is generally assumed that capital is the

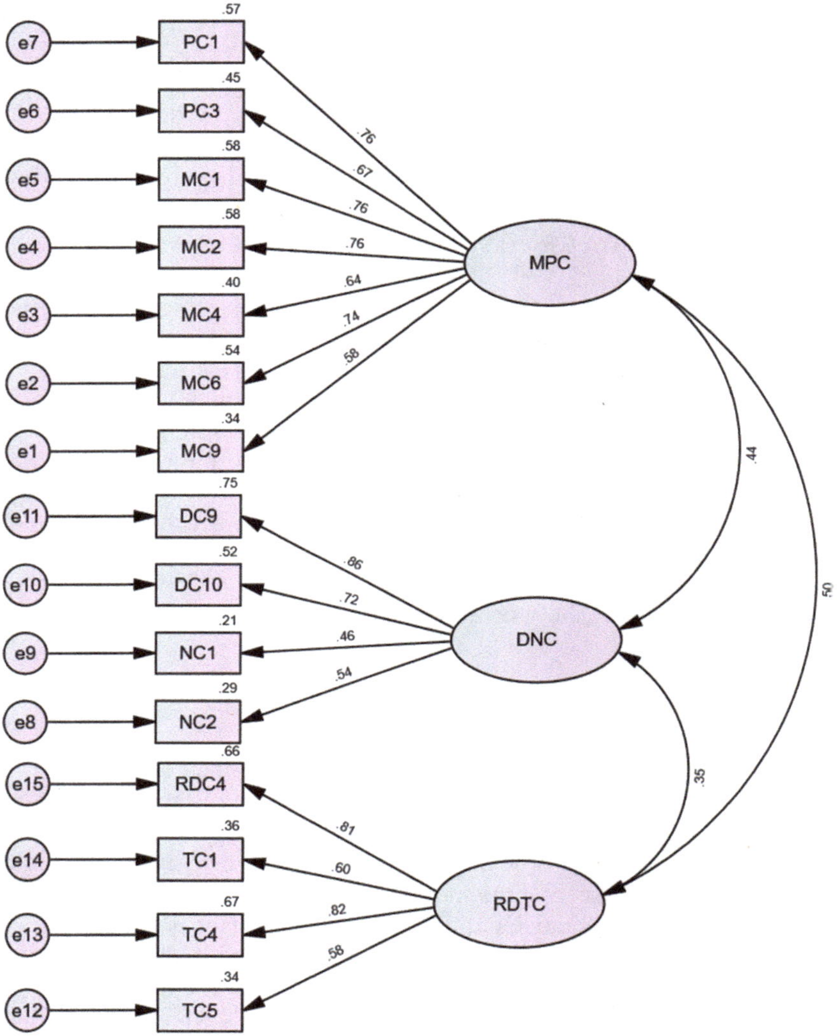


**Fig. 7.2** Three-factor confirmatory factor model with 15 items. Source: Author

main constraint on growth. However, our results suggest that even in low-income economy contexts, the main factor differentiating firms is differences in firm-specific organizational capabilities.

Second, our results show the different importance of different types of capabilities for manufacturing firm growth in lower income economies. The clear majority of the manufacturing firms in our sample invested in and continued to upgrade their broadly defined capabilities. From the three capabilities identified, we found that managerial and production capabilities seem to have the greatest influence on firm growth. This confirms the results of econometric research on the determinants of firm productivity in lower income economies and, particularly, ex-transition economies and suggests also the high relevance of production capabilities as determinants of productivity growth (see Kravtsova & Radosevic, 2011; Feduynina & Radosevic, 2022). It also demonstrates the relevance of managerial capabilities as a specific differentiator of firm performance.

Among the four factors considered, managerial capabilities have the strongest impact on firm performance variability. Among managerial and production capabilities/practices, operations and monitoring capabilities are considered the most important for business growth. Our results suggest, also, that the introduction of modern production techniques and documenting problems based on operations indicators are important for improving business performance.

We found that management competence in monitoring business operations matters and includes performance measurement, performance reviews, rewards for good performance and retraining of staff to allow them to assume more senior positions, all important for business performance. Production and management capabilities are required for world standard productivity and performance for a given level of technology but do not generate capabilities for change. They are related to closing the productivity gap with global best practice.

Our findings show that among the five variables related to dynamic organizational capabilities, business networking and dynamic business capabilities have the greatest impact on firm growth. Previous work shows that business networking activities can stimulate transfers of knowledge and capabilities to enable firm growth (Sims & O'Regan, 2006). In particular, business networking skills have a significant effect on relationships with customers and suppliers (Sims & O'Regan, 2006) and recruitment of qualified personnel. Firms customize their practices based on feedback from customers and provide regular training for employees to update and improve their knowledge and skills. The capability to improve or change organizational capabilities involves both internal and external processes (networking capabilities).

Finally, in our sample, R&D and technology generating capabilities are new to firm and to the country. They are not world frontier activities and, as expected, the differences between high- and low-growth firms in this respect are significant. R&D and technology capabilities upgrading depends on interactions with clients and suppliers.

Finally, we found that the three components of firm capabilities considered are interrelated, but different. Management and production capabilities are needed to close productivity gaps at a given level of technology, and dynamic and networking capabilities and R&D and technological capabilities are required for technology upgrading and are specifically about in-house developments and interactions related to new products or processes.

Dynamic capabilities and networking capabilities refer to changes within firms and their relationships with suppliers and customers, which are related to the broader spectrum of organizational capabilities. Our results show that these capabilities are partly overlapping which questions whether upgrading or growth follows a linear trajectory from management and production capabilities to dynamic and networking capabilities, or R&D and technological capabilities, or some other path. This raises questions about threshold points in this trajectory that could mean some firms remain locked into management and production capabilities while others advance and achieve other capabilities. Our evidence suggests that whatever the path or stage, capacity to acquire embodied technology (machinery and equipment) on its own is not enough to guarantee firm growth even in lower income economies. This finding has implications for strategic management and industrial and innovation policies in these economies which tend to be overly focused on (lack of) financial capital and give less considering to deficiencies in organizational and management and production capabilities. It has implications, also, for development policy where too much focus is given to technology and R&D capabilities with gaps in production capabilities overlooked.

## References


Aistleitner, M., Gräbner, C., & Hornykewycz, A. (2021). Theory and empirics of capability accumulation: Implications for macroeconomic modelling. *Research Policy, Elsevier, 50*(6), 104258. https://doi.org/10.1016/j.respol.2021.104258

Arbuckle, J. L. (1999). *Amos version 4*. Sweet Waters Corporation.

Barney, J. B. (1991). Firm resources and sustained competitive advantage. *Journal of Management, 17*, 99–120.

Bartelsman, E., Haltiwanger, J., & Scarpetta, S. (2004). Microeconomic evidence of creative destruction in industrial and developing countries, discussion paper no. 1374, October 2004, IZA.

Bartelsman, E., Haltiwanger, J., & Scarpetta, S. (2013). Cross-country differences in productivity: The role of allocation and selection. *The American Economic Review, 103*, 305–334.

Bartlett, M. S. (1954). A note on the multiplying factors for various chi square approximations. *Journal of the Royal Statistical Society, 16*, 296–298.

Bell, M., & Figueiredo, P. N. (2012). Innovation capability building and learning mechanisms in latecomer firms: Recent empirical contributions and implications for research. *Canadian Journal of Development Studies / Revue canadienne d'études du développement, 33*(1), 14–40. https://doi.org/10.1080/02255189.2012.677168

Bell, M., & Pavitt, K. (1993). Technological accumulation and industrial growth: Contrasts between developed and developing countries. *Industrial and Corporate Change, 2*(2), 157–210.

Bloom, N., & Van Reenen, J. (2010). Why do management practices differ across firms and countries? *Journal of Economic Perspectives, 24*(1), 203–224.

Bloom, N., Lemos, R., Sadun, R., Scur, D., & Van Reenen, J. (2014). The new empirical economics of management. *Journal of the European Economic Association, 12*(4), 835–876.

Bloom, N., Brynjolfsson, E., Foster, F., Jarmin, J., Patnaik, M., Saporta-Eksten, I., & Van Reenen, J. (2019). What drives differences in management practices? *American Economic Review, 109*(5), 1648–1683. https://doi.org/10.1257/aer.20170491

Brynjolfsson, E., & Milgrom, P. (2013). Complementarity in organizations. In R. Gibbons & J. Roberts (Eds.), *Handbook of organizational economics* (pp. 11–55). Princeton University Press.

Byrne, B. M. (2001). *Structural equation modelling with AMOS: Basic concepts, applications, and programming*. Lawrence Erlbaum.

Cao, M., & Zhang, Q. (2011). Supply chain collaboration: Impact on collaborative advantage and firm performance. *Journal of Operations Management, 29*(3), 163–180.

Coad, A. (2009). *The growth of firms: A survey of theories and empirical evidence*. Edward Elgar.

Demsetz, H. (1997). The firm in economic theory: A quiet revolution. *American Economic Review, 87*(2), 426–429.

Dosi, G., Malerba, F., Marsili, O., & Orsenigo, L. (1997). Industrial structures and dynamics: Evidence, interpretation and puzzles. *Industrial and Corporate Change, 6*(1), 3.

Dosi, G., Pereira, M. C., Roventini, A., & Virgillito, M. E. (2019). What if supply-side policies are not enough? The perverse interaction of flexibility and austerity. *Journal of Economic Behavior & Organization, 162*, 360–388.

Dutrenit, G. (2000). *Learning and knowledge management in the firm: From knowledge accumulation to strategic capabilities*. Edward Elgar.

Enos, J., & Park, W. H. (1987). *The adaptation and diffusion of imported Technologies in the Case of Korea*. Croom Helm.

Eurostat - OECD Manual on Business Demography Statistics. (2008). http://ec.europa.eu/eurostat/ramon/statmanuals/files/KS-RA-07-010-EN.pdf

Fedyunina, A., & Radosevic, S. (2022). The relationship between R&D, innovation and productivity in emerging economies: CDM model and alternatives. *Economic Systems, Elsevier, 46*(3), 100998.

Field, A. (2005). *Discovering statistics using SPSS*. Sage.

Gibbons, R., & Henderson, R. (2013). What do managers do? In R. Gibbons & J. Roberts (Eds.), *Handbook of organizational economics* (pp. 680–731). Princeton University Press.

Grover Goswami, A., Medvedev, D., & Olafsen, E. (2019). *High-growth firms: Facts, fiction, and policy options for emerging economies*. World Bank. http://hdl.handle.net/10986/30800

Halac, M., & Prat, P. (2016). Managerial attention and worker performance. *American Economic Review, 106*(10), 3104–3132.

Hart, P. (2000). Theories of firms' growth and the generation of jobs, review of industrial organization, Springer. *The Industrial Organization Society, 17*(3), 229–248.

Helfat, C., & Peteraf, M. (2003). The dynamic resource-based view: Capability lifecycles. *Strategic Management Journal, 24*(10), 997–1010.

Henrekson, M., & Johansson, D. (2010). Firm growth, institutions and structural transformation. In M. Fritsch (Ed.), *Handbook of research on entrepreneurship and regional development: National and regional perspectives*. Edwar Elgar.

Horn, J. L. (1965). A rationale and test for the number of factors in factor analysis. *Psychometrika, 30*, 179–185.

Kim, L. (1997). *Imitation to innovation: The dynamics of Korea's technological learning*. Harvard Business School Press.

Kravtsova, V., & Radosevic, S. (2011). Are systems of innovation in Eastern Europe efficient? *Economic Systems, 36*(1), 109–126. https://doi.org/10.1016/j.ecosys.2011.04.005

Kumar, V., Kunar, U., & Persaud, A. (1999). Building technological capability through importing technology: The case of Indonesian manufacturing industry. *Journal of Technology Transfer, 24*(1), 81–96. https://doi.org/10.1023/A:1007728921126

Lall, S. (1992). Technological capabilities and industrialization. *World Development, 20*(2), 165–186.

Lall, S. (1993). Policies for building technological capabilities: Lessons from Asian experience. *Asian Development Review, 11*(02), 72–103. https://doi.org/10.1142/S0116110593000090

Lall, S. (1998). Technology and human capital in maturing Asian countries. *Science, Technology and Society, 3*(1), 11–48.

Lee, J., Lee, K., Meissner, D., Radosevic, S., & Vonortas, N. S. (2021). Technology upgrading and economic catch-up: Context, overview, and conclusions. In *The challenges of technology and economic catch-up in emerging economies*. Oxford University Press.

Lotti, F., Santarelli, E., & Vivarelli, M. (2009). Defending Gibrat's law as a long-run regularity. *Small Business Economics, 32*, 31–44.

Majcen, B., Radosevic, S., & Rojec, M. (2009). Nature and determinants of productivity growth of foreign subsidiaries in Central and East European countries. *Economic Systems, 33*(2), 168–184. https://doi.org/10.1016/j.ecosys.2009.03.003

Minbaeva, D., Pedersen, T., Björkman, I., Fey, C. F., & Park, H. J. (2003). MNC knowledge transfer, subsidiary absorptive capacity, and HRM. *Journal of International Business Studies, 34*, 586–599. https://doi.org/10.1057/palgrave.jibs.8400056

Nelson, R. R., & Winter, S. G. (1982). *An evolutionary theory of economic change*. Harvard University Press.

Penrose, E. T. (1959). *The theory of the growth of the firm*. John Wiley.

Radosevic, S., & Yoruk, E. (2018). Technology upgrading of middle-income economies: A new approach and results. *Technological Forecasting and Social Change, 129*, 56–75. https://doi.org/10.1016/j.techfore.2017.12.002

Radosevic, S., & Yoruk, E. (2016). Why do we need theory and metrics of technology upgrading? *Asian Journal of Technology Innovation, 24*(1), 8–32.

Sims, M. A., & O'Regan, N. (2006). In search of gazelles using a research DNA model. *Technovation, 26*(8), 943–954. https://doi.org/10.1016/j.technovation.2005.07.001

Sutton, J., & Trefler, D. (2016). Capabilities, wealth, and trade. *Journal of Political Economy, 124*(3), 826–878.

Tabachnick, B. G., & Fidell, L. S. (2001). *Using multivariate statistics.* Allyn and Bacon.

Teece, D. J. (2017). A capability theory of the firm: An economics and (strategic) management perspective. *New Zealand Econ Pap, 53*, 1–43. https://doi.org/10.1080/00779954.2017.1371208

Tidd, J., & Bessant, J. (2021). *Managing innovation integrating technological, market and organizational change.* Wiley & Sons. ISBN: 978-1-119-71330-2.

Zahra, S. A., Harry, J. S., & Davidsson, P. (2006). Entrepreneurship and dynamic capabilities: A review, model and research agenda. *Journal of Management Studies, 43*(4), 917–955.

CHAPTER 8

# Conclusions: The New Industrial Policy Approach to Technology Upgrading in Three Western Balkan Countries

## 8.1 Introduction

The chapters in this book explored facets of industrial policies aimed at production and technology upgrading in Albania, North Macedonia and Kosovo, three Western Balkan (WB) economies, part of the group of upper-middle-income economies. This characteristic defines the nature of their innovative capacity and industrial activity. It has fundamental implications, also, for the type of industrial policies that can and should be implemented in these economies. Empirical evidence suggests that economic industrialization, based on manufacturing sector growth fuelled by innovation capacity and a supporting physical infrastructure, is at the core of economic development. Thus, a thriving manufacturing sector is considered essential for prosperity and social well-being in the three WB countries considered.

In Chap. 8, we provide a summary of the main findings from this book. Section 8.2 discusses the findings from Chaps. 1, 2, 3, 4, 5. Section 8.3 highlights some features common to innovation capacity and technology upgrading in the WB countries. Section 8.4 sets out the strategic options in our proposed new industrial policy approach and Sect. 8.5 describes potential implementation of these policies. Section 8.6 concludes the book with a discussion of its limitations and directions for future research.



F. Sahiti, *Industrial Policies for Technological Upgrading in Western Balkan Countries*, https://doi.org/10.1007/978-3-031-51429-6_8

## 8.2 The Manufacturing Sectors in Albania, Kosovo and North Macedonia

Chapter 2 showed that, following the political and economic changes that affected the WB at the end of the twentieth century, one of the main pillars of their economies, that is the industry sector, has been eroded. Most WB economies are based on mining sector activities and production of commoditized, mostly undifferentiated goods for sale in their domestic and regional markets. Manufacturing firms in these economies use imported foreign equipment and machinery. Their focus is on increasing production capacity and achieving production efficiency to produce goods that meet international standards. WB firms' technological capabilities are generally weak with the result that their productivity levels and patterns of technology and industrial upgrading are lagging significantly behind the developed economies.

Chapter 2 shows that these economies display some similarities in terms of economic structure, productivity levels and innovative performance. The contribution of their manufacturing sectors to Gross Domestic Product (GDP) is low and almost twice as low as in the benchmark country, Slovenia, and compared to the middle-income country. This low level of productivity is the result of a high degree of informality, weak firm dynamism, negligible innovation activity and their concentration in sub-sectors with low value added, such as food, textiles, clothing and metal production. Our findings underline the importance of firm-level innovation to enable growth in more sophisticated sub-sectors.

The economic profiles of the three WB countries presented in Chap. 2 show that their manufacturing sectors are mostly low-tech and low R&D intensive. These structural characteristics explain the limited capacity of private and public operators to engage in innovation and boost economic growth. The above firm characteristics, especially low level of production sophistication and weak management, generally preclude participation in Global Value Chains (GVCs). Also, manufacturing firms in the three WB countries analysed are characterized by a low level of product differentiation compared to their counterparts in Slovenia. Our data suggest that the WB countries have made some progress towards the construction of a knowledge economy and productivity growth driven by innovation and access to information. The European Bank for Reconstruction and Development (EBRD) knowledge economy index suggests that innovation capacity in these three countries is lacking in some basics that would enable innovation (improved economic openness, improved governance and business environments, innovation capabilities and an efficient Information and Communication Technology—ICT infrastructure).

Macroeconomic policy data suggest that, in recent years, the WB countries have made advances in the areas of regulation and the creation of institutions to promote entrepreneurship and innovation. There is evidence also that factors related to political and economic stability and, especially, institutional quality and governance factors are lagging compared to the benchmark country, Slovenia. Our findings suggest indirectly that the quality, continuity and direction of national public institutions have an influence on entrepreneurial business investment decisions. Entrepreneurial activity and numbers of manufacturing firms in the three WB countries are much lower than in Slovenia. Our findings suggest that although the WB governments have made efforts to include entrepreneurship training in their education systems, many students leave school with low general and specialized skills. Our findings show, also, that policy makers in WB countries understand the importance of promoting innovation and have tried to develop policy frameworks to support the creation of business incubators to support technology and innovation activities. However, the contribution of incubators is limited by available human resources and lack of financial stability.

Several policies have been implemented to promote development of the manufacturing sector, and there are several programmes, projects and instruments that have been implemented in the WB countries to support industry. However, the results in Chap. 4 show that these policies suffer from lack of alignment, which is reflected in their lack of vision, duplication, poor management of political economy issues, poor governance coordination, etc.

## 8.3 Features Common to Innovation Capacity and Technology Upgrading

The findings related to innovation capacity and technology upgrading in the WB economies reveal some common aspects.

First, it would seem that the WB economies have suffered from 'premature deindustrialization' resulting in very low shares of manufacturing in GDP and exports. Compared to the reference country, the three WB economies can be considered relatively industrialized, but de-manufactured economies, with their main exporting sectors based mostly on natural resources (especially in the cases of Albania and Kosovo). This profile indicates the very low level and low intensity of R&D driven by the low share of manufacturing.

Second, although data for Kosovo and Albania are incomplete, it seems that the manufacturing sectors in the three WB economies are dominated by small shares of medium- and high-technology industries and high shares of low-technology low R&D-intensive industries. These structural characteristics help to explain their limited knowledge intensity and fragile business and public sector R&D. With the partial exception of North Macedonia, the WB economies show few similarities with a group of middle-income countries and Slovenia in terms of exports and imports of ICT goods.

Third, the data highlight that innovation capacity in the three WB economies is low. EBRD and other data suggest poor innovation performance, and the 2019 EBRD knowledge economy index shows that the WB countries are lagging behind Slovenia on all the four indicators considered. Weak innovation institutions seem to be the main obstacle to the development of a knowledge economy in the WB region, and this leads to poor performance on knowledge indicators. Innovation skills tend to be weak, due to relatively weak general and, especially, specialized skills. The largest gap between the three WB economies and Slovenia is related to the innovation system and is mainly the result of the small budgets allocated to innovation and R&D activities along with mismanagement and bad governance. The WB economies face persistent problems related to access to ICTs and ICT sophistication.

The data suggest that low levels of innovation in manufacturing exclude the three WB economies from participation in GVCs. There are some resources-based manufacturing activities that are exceptions. The manufacturing sector suffers from low production sophistication and poor management, coupled with poor product differentiation compared to Slovenia, for example. For the manufacturing sectors in the WB economies to enter GVCs will require their governments to coordinate with the business community, to formulate innovation and industrial policies. In Sect. 5.4, we proposed a new approach to industrial policy to foster structural change and technological upgrading in the WB economies.

## 8.4 The Importance of a New Industrial Policy Approach

An appropriate industrial policy approach that would remain efficient and could be applied to all socio-economic contexts is impossible to achieve because the global economic and technological environments are constantly changing. Industrial policies that have been successful in the past are unlikely to show the same results today. Since the socio-economic changes that occurred in the 1990s, the WB economies have tried to change their economic structures through the application of horizontal industrial policies. On the assumption that the right business environment will automatically lead to technology and economic improvements (Campos et al., 2017), the central focus of these policies has been on improving the business environment. The results of the investigation in this book suggest that, despite some progress, the manufacturing firms in the three WB economies are unlikely to participate in GVCs in the near future. It is imperative that these economies learn how to become active players in an open and globalized market based on technological upgrading and industry structural changes (Radosevic, 2021).

In this context, the new approach to the design and implementation of industrial policy can be a possible alternative that draws on the positive and negative experiences of both structural reforms and old industrial policies. One of the main goals of this book is precisely this: to acquaint the reader with a new approach to industrial policy, which draws on the innovative and institutional capacities of the three WB countries considered. This approach is based on the idea of technology upgrading, which Gereffi (1999, pp. 51–52) defines as 'a shift to higher value-added products and production stages through increasing specialization'. As emphasized in the chapters in this book, the approach we propose adopts a broader perspective that includes not only the firm's innovation and R&D capabilities but also other static and dynamic organizational capabilities such as managerial and production capabilities, dynamic capabilities, business networking capabilities, etc.

The need for a new approach to the design and implementation of industrial policies focused on the promotion of technology improvement is discussed below.

First, experience shows that economic progress is the result of efficient markets, based on effective industrial policies that address endemic market and system failures and promote positive structural changes and technology upgrading (Lee, 2019). Our findings show that in the WB countries considered, manufacturing firm growth depends mainly on natural resources. In the countries considered, the share of production in GDP is small and the percentage of high- and medium-tech industries (firms applying R&D) is also small. In addition, the only firms that participate in GVCs are natural resource-based manufacturing firms. In all cases, levels of innovation activity are very low and firm growth-based exports of goods and mineral resources are negligible. These and other production sector characteristics are reflected in the innovation and industry policies implemented by these countries, which are failing to drive structural changes in the economy or technology upgrading.

Second, new industrial policies are quite different from previous industrial policies that were aimed at supporting infant industries. An essential element of the new industrial policies is their proactive philosophy. The overarching aim is to improve innovation systems and technological capabilities at the individual firm, the sectors and the overall economy levels. The new industrial policies are based on a heuristic and piecemeal approach and methodology (see Sect. 8.5), applied to their design and practical implementation. They acknowledge the limits to growth and that the corresponding solutions to various problems cannot be identified ex ante. The basis of these new industrial policies is the idea of comparative advantage and gradual development of exporting activity. The design of the new industrial policies uses data on market failures and economic system failures more generally. They are aimed at private firms, which means that it is imperative that these firms are involved in the design and implementation of industrial policies.

Third, the successful design and especially implementation of new industrial policies in the WB economies is conditional on certain aspects. First, account needs to be taken of manufacturing firms' existing technological capacities. The formulation of industrial policies must be a participatory, bottom-up process. This will enable sustainable growth and improvements to already existing technologies. There must be measures that enable a 'learning to learn' culture and an experimental approach, which highlights the importance of pilot projects. An experimental approach allows unsuccessful projects to be discarded and successful ones to be scaled up and replicated in other contexts. It should be emphasized that the role of state institutions in the development of technological capabilities and the innovation system is crucial. Therefore, new policies should be aligned to the state institutional capacity to oversee their implementation.

Fourth, the four proposed strategic orientations for the new industrial policies could, potentially, be sources of economic growth in the WB countries. The fourth goal of the new industrial policies is promotion of innovation and technological capacities in business organizations which will require particular measures related to strategic areas. These include increasing innovation budgets; improving the technology upgrading infrastructure; the use of public procurement to encourage innovative activities and strengthening of the financial base (through the establishment of development banks) to support investment in innovation and exporting.

Fifth, successful industrial policies must identify and target priorities, in terms of specific production sub-sectors and technologies. Attention should be paid to both potential new sub-sectors and diversification of existing sectors and improvements to cross-sector technology. The priorities identified should be used as additional criteria related to the selection of individual programmes and projects and for the design of policy mixes and interventions for specific areas.

Sixth, the new industrial policies must be accompanied by and aligned to other structural reforms in the production and other economic sectors and to infrastructure projects. Good coordination of these areas will increase the effect on transformation of the economy. During the implementation of industrial policies, the state must act as regulator, developer and network developer. It will be necessary for the focal state institution to intervene in the event of market failures, coordination failures or system failures. This institutional intervention will enable a collective effort to overcome problems that arise and to create links with foreign strategic investors. As already emphasized, state institutions must be in place to evaluate the implementation of all elements of the new industrial policies. In this context, a 'me too' logic is inappropriate. Prior to policy design and drafting, the country's institutional-technical-operational and political capacities must be assessed. Close coordination between the business community and state institutions is required for industrial policy success and, in particular, in the case of horizontal policies, which require alignment with vertical policies. In this context, feedback from representatives of the private business sector is central.

Seventh, the chapters in this book show that the capacities of state institutions in the three WB countries analysed are rather weak, which introduces the risk of formulation of inappropriate policies. The challenge will be how to design policies that respond to the economic reality, which will require good communication between state institutions and private sector firms.

## 8.5 Application of 'Piecemeal Engineering' to Industrial Policies

Developed country experience (e.g., Slovenia) shows that to achieve a flourishing manufacturing sector requires more than implementation of policy instruments and programmes; it requires learning related to how to apply these policies in practice. These processes are intertwined and mutually influencing within the industrial policy-making cycle—from design, implementation and enforcement, monitoring, experimentation and adaptation. Policy interventions must be continuously monitored and evaluated. Even in the case of a well-designed industrial policy, its success depends on its practical implementation. Pritchett et al. (2012) stress that effective monitoring and evaluation are essential to integrate experiential learning into policy, which points to the importance of monitoring and evaluation as essential attributes of the institutional structure. Our data suggest that the three WB countries have no systems in place to enable effective monitoring and evaluation of policies (OECD, 2022).

Countries with limited financial resources and institutional quality problems need to establish adequate monitoring mechanisms, which might be achievable using a 'piecemeal engineering' approach (Popper, 1963). A piecemeal engineering approach to industrial policy is aimed at intervening to resolve urgent problems that arise in national economic sectors and sub-sectors. It involves experimentation and learning from mistakes.

Learning related to industrial policy is part of the policy-making process and has practical implications in terms of improved learning.

First, learning requires creation of mechanisms to monitor progress, which can be a difficult process in the case of unwanted outcomes from industrial policies. It is essential that state monitoring mechanisms allow measurement of achievement of objectives. Determining measurement parameters is particularly important in countries with institutional quality problems and collection of data in some contexts with large informal sectors can be especially difficult. Also, data collection is a costly process, while semi-formal enterprises do not always record information. Finally, there must be government capacity to process and interpret the data.

Second, effective monitoring systems can provide information useful for short policy learning cycles that depend on monthly reporting. This provides information on what works and what does not and why. Monthly reporting should be extended to quarterly and then annual reporting.

Regular monthly, quarterly and annual reports provide an understanding of whether the policies in place are flawed and whether they need significant reformulation. The reasons why policies need reformulation range from lack of selectivity and scope, to an unexpected market response, insufficient support from or collapse of the coalition of interests involved in their formulation and conflicts that undermine their effectiveness which requires design of additional instruments.

The application of piecemeal methods that allow for changes and the ability of state institutions to adapt programmes and policy instruments are critical for policy success. It also requires a governmental not afraid to make mistakes and able to cope with failure, which suggests a trial and error mentality (Popper, 1963). Hirschman (1977, p. 28), a pioneer of industrial policy, emphasized that the design and implementation of industrial policies called for a 'transition mechanism through which decision makers learn to take risks; and the shorter the transition and the quicker the learning, the better'. Lack of government awareness and ducking of responsibility will result in the institutions implementing industrial policies avoiding reporting of failures and ignoring danger signals. A culture that lacks transparency will be damaging in the context of short learning cycles and block learning and policy adaptation.

The governments in the three WB countries should embrace piecemeal engineering and experimental methods related to the design of industrial policies. These methods allow calibration of policy instrument to specific and developing sector dynamics, technologies and markets. Experimentation can lead to demonstration projects which can be scaled up within and across sectors. However, these methods carry certain risks. Not all contexts are suited to experimentation and experimenting with policy instruments can lead to a loss of policy coherence, increased uncertainty among private business agents and hamper a long-term policy vision.

## 8.6 Limitations of the Research and Future Work

This research reported in this book inevitably has some limitations. First, it provides no analysis of the macro aspects of industrial policies and does not deal with macropolitical factors such as those related to the influence of exchange rates on industrial policies. It does not analyse the elements included in the general macroeconomic framework, such as tax systems, which might have an impact on the selection of industrial policies. Second, it does not examine policy capacity or the compatibility between the dominant political interests and industrial policy agendas.

In addition, we would recommend some caveats in relation to the results presented in Chap. 7 where we try to measure the technological capabilities of manufacturing firms in Kosovo. The first caveat is related to the sample and the sample size. Investigating a larger number of cases that included firms from other middle-income economies would further increase generalization of the results. Second, the data used in this book refer only to manufacturing sector firms. Extending the sample to include other economic sectors would provide a more comprehensive overview of the level and quality of organizational and managerial skills in all economic sectors. Third our data collection method was based mainly on the responses to a questionnaire that included closed and semi-open questions. To gain a deeper understanding of the type of organizational capabilities and managerial competencies (configurations) that influence firm growth, and to test and more precisely define the profiles of high-growth firms would require a case study research method to reveal the factors shaping current and future organizational capabilities and managerial practices in manufacturing firms. Finally, our analysis aims to be dynamic, but our data are cross-sectional. Future research should focus on collection of longitudinal data to explore the phenomenon of firm dynamics.

Finally, the analysis and approach in this book are consistent with the wider development of new approaches to industrial policy. Our comparative analysis shows high consistency and complementarity with the general approaches to industrial policy in the industrial policy literature and our application of new industrial policy thinking in the WB regional context.

## References

Campos, N. F., De Grauwe, P., & Ji, Y. (2017). Structural reforms, growth and inequality: An overview of theory, measurement and evidence, IZA discussion papers, No. 11159, Institute of Labor Economics (IZA), Bonn.

Gereffi, G. (1999). International trade and industrial upgrading in the apparel commodity chain. *Journal of International Economics, 48*(1), 37–70.

Hirschman, A. O. (1977). A generalized linkage approach to economic development with special reference to staples. *Economic Development and Cultural Change, 25*, 67–97.

Lee, K. (2019). The art of economic catch-up. In *The art of economic catch-up: Barriers, detours and leapfrogging in innovation systems* (p. I). Cambridge University Press.

OECD. (2022). SME policy index: Western Balkans and Turkey 2022: Assessing the implementation of the small business act for Europe, SME Policy Index, OECD Publishing, Paris. https://doi.org/10.1787/b47d15f0-en.

Popper, K. R. (1963). *The open society and its enemies (4th ed. rev.)* (p. 1). Princeton University Press.

Pritchett, L., Samji, S., & Hammer, J. (2012). It's all about me using structured experiential learning ('e') to crawl the design space, CID Working Paper No. 249, December 2012 Centre for International Development at Harvard University.

Radosevic, S. (2021). Towards industrial policies to support technology upgrading for sustainable development in Central Asia (SPECA subregion), Report prepared for the UN Economic Commission for Europe, Geneva.

# Index[1]



[1] Note: Page numbers followed by 'n' refer to notes.



E. Sahiti, *Industrial Policies for Technological Upgrading in Western Balkan Countries*, https://doi.org/10.1007/978-3-031-51429-6

# GPSR Compliance

*The European Union's (EU) General Product Safety Regulation (GPSR) is a set of rules that requires consumer products to be safe and our obligations to ensure this.*

*If you have any concerns about our products, you can contact us on ProductSafety@springernature.com*

In case Publisher is established outside the EU, the EU authorized representative is:

Springer Nature Customer Service Center GmbH
Europaplatz 3
69115 Heidelberg, Germany

FSC
www.fsc.org
MIX
Papier | Fördert
gute Waldnutzung
FSC® C083411

Kolibri 360 GmbH
Ferdinand-Jühlke-Straße 7
99095 Erfurt, Deutschland
produktsicherheit@kolibri360.de